Teaching Reading Skills in Secondary Schools

Teaching Reading Skills in Secondary Schools

ARTHUR V. OLSON and WILBUR S. AMES

Georgia State University

 INTEXT EDUCATIONAL PUBLISHERS

College Division of Intext

Scranton   San Francisco   Toronto   London

The Intext series in

SECONDARY EDUCATION

Consulting editor

JOHN E. SEARLES
Pennsylvania State University

To GEORGIA STATE UNIVERSITY

and NOAH LANGDALE, JR., President

Preface

This book offers what we believe is a balanced and practical approach to the instruction of secondary school teachers in methods of teaching reading skills. Its aim is to present the approaches and techniques that can be used in any secondary classroom to aid students in getting the most from their reading. The art of teaching reading at the secondary level, in a developmental setting, does not require a mystifying body of information that can be comprehended only after extensive study. The material presented in this text can be readily understood and immediately applied.

All teachers have a responsibility for seeing that their students develop the skills necessary to perform the reading work required of them. Often the skill of reading is the one that is assumed to be known. It is our hope that this book will help teachers to understand the need for questioning their previous assumptions about reading, and to acquire some knowledge about how to help their students, and will encourage them to make a new effort at teaching skills necessary for improved reading achievement.

To facilitate a well-rounded understanding of reading in the secondary school, this book should be used in conjunction with our book of readings: Arthur V. Olson and Wilbur S. Ames, *Teaching Reading Skills in Secondary Schools.: Readings* (Scranton, Pa.: 1970). International Textbook Company.

A. V. O.
W. S. A.

September, 1971
Atlanta, Georgia

Acknowledgments

The authors of this book wish to acknowledge and thank the following for their contributions to this publication: Scott, Foresman and Company, and Harcourt Brace Jovanovich, Inc.; the International Reading Association and the National Council of Teachers of English; Dr. Hazel Simpson of the University of Georgia and Dr. Charles Billiard of Georgia State University, who contributed Chapter 11; and Georgia State University students Linda Owen Dabney and Babs Kalvelage.

Contents

Causes of slow reading. Methods of improving rate. Value of machines in developing reading rate. Flexibility in reading rate. Summary. References.

The content-area teacher's attitude and role. Effective reading in English. Reading in mathematics. Reading in science. Reading in social studies. Reading in other content areas. Summary. References.

Preparation for reading. Directed reading and discussion. Extending skills and abilities. Enrichment and follow-up activities. Sample directed lessons. Extending skills. Summary. References.

Reasons for lack of attention to individual differences. Classroom practices. Oral reading. Attitudes toward reading. Importance of reading. Flexibility in learning. Summary. References.

Adolescent reading interests and tastes. Discovering the reading interests of adolescents. Arousing and developing students' reading interests. Students' reporting on reading done. Censorship of books. Summary. References.

Some basic factors affecting adolescents as readers of literature. Reading interests, reading abilities, and verbal organization of literature as continua. Sequential models of literature for early, middle, and late adolescence.´ The short story. The novel. Reading models built around themes and issues. Poetry. Summary. Selected bibliography of adolescent literature. References.

Contents

The handicapped reader. The slow learner. The school dropout.
The college-bound student. Summary. References.

chapter 1

Development of the Reading Program

Never before in our history has so much attention been given to the need for reading programs at the junior and senior high school levels. Initially, the secondary programs developed were few in number and almost exclusively remedial in nature. In other words, such programs were designed for students who had serious reading problems and were reading significantly below their level of capability.

Clearly there will always be the need for providing remedial reading services at the secondary school level. For a variety of complex reasons, certain students may come to the junior high and senior high level with serious reading deficiencies. This text however, is directed to the need for developmental reading programs at the secondary level.

RATIONALE FOR DEVELOPMENTAL READING PROGRAMS AT THE SECONDARY LEVEL

A basic assumption throughout this book is that if a truly developmental reading program were available for the appropriate students at the secondary level there would be much less need for large, expensive remedial reading programs. Too many school systems still operate a reading program that provides developmental reading instruction through the sixth grade in the elementary school and then discontinues formal reading instruction until such time as the need for a remedial program at the senior high level becomes apparent.

The need for continuous, developmental instruction in reading is now being recognized by a greater number of secondary school personnel. They realize that the programs are needed not because reading has been poorly taught in the elementary grades but because it is a tool for learning that needs reinforcement and refinement as new situations arise. As a student progresses through the secondary school, he is expected to read more complex materials in many different content areas.

It is also increasingly apparent to secondary school teachers that not all reading skills can be taught at the elementary school level. Many skills are not

1

introduced and taught at the elementary level because the students have not developed the necessary prerequisite skills. For example, the development of critical reading skills in elementary schools is at best rudimentary. As other examples, there are relatively few students leaving the elementary school who can understand the comparisons intended by figurative language, the reference of an allusion met within a poem, or the cause-and-effect relationships found in a world history book.

STAGES IN READING DEVELOPMENT

Reading, because it is a developmental process, is closely related to the growth development of the individual. Although the growth in skills is continuous and sequential and often overlapping, it is possible to discuss general levels or stages in reading. It is important for the secondary school teacher of reading to understand these stages, particularly those stages through which a student goes in the elementary grades.

Preschool Level

This period in the child's development extends from birth to the time he enters first grade. It is probably the most important period in his life for determining his adjustment and success in school—a fact disheartening to teachers but nevertheless true. During this period the child is growing rapidly in many of the abilities he will need later for reading. He will learn how to speak distinctly in order to be understood. He will learn to understand others; to understand his native language by using it in all kinds of situations and in a variety of experiences; to control his body; to see likenesses and differences in things; to feel an interest in printed symbols and in books; and to acquire an inquisitive attitude toward the world around him. The environment that stimulates the child to explore, converse, and develop his capabilities to the fullest is the environment that is preparing the child to succeed.

The child brought up in an environment that is limiting intellectually, emotionally, and physically is not likely to find school a pleasant experience. These children will make successful progress only if the school has the time and patience to build the needed background. Unfortunately many of these children are doomed to failure from the beginning because of the inflexibility of our schools.

The Beginning Level

During the beginning stage the student is taught the fundamental skills he will need in order to recognize words. He will be taught that written words represent words he can say; he will learn to recognize the sounds he hears at the beginning of words, to distinguish between look-alike words and the names of these elements (letters), and will be given clues he can use to help recognize words. In short, he will begin to read.

He will put the few words he knows into a sentence, and will learn new words by changing the initial letters in words he already knows. The teacher during this period will strive to maintain a balance of learning skills with interesting materials and good understanding of what is being read.

The Growing Independence Level

This level or state of development would commonly be found at the second-grade level of achievement. The child has learned many of the basic skills for the recognition of words and is beginning to enjoy the discovery that he can read and have fun with his reading. It is during this period that the teacher must be extremely careful that the student is being introduced to the reading skills at a rate appropriate to his learning ability. A student who is pushed too fast or who is not given instruction at the next sequential level when he needs it is in trouble. It is a critical period in the development of skills and in attitude.

The Literacy Level

It is during the third- and fourth-grade levels that functional literacy is established. Making the transition from the skills learned in grades 1 and 2 to this higher level of ability is another critical phase in reading development. During this period the student acquires more speed in his reading and is able to select material from an ever-widening variety. He still needs to be taught the basic skills in a sequential manner, but comprehension skills now receive growing emphasis.

The Intermediate Level

It is during this stage in the development of skills (grades 5 - 6) that speed of silent reading gradually moves beyond the oral reading rate, and the student reaches the peak in the amount of reading he does for enjoyment. He will probably never again do as much recreational reading as now. A whole array of adult reading material is open to him. His use of specialized skills as they apply to content areas is becoming increasingly effective. The dangers of this period are the possibilities of insufficient reading material, rigid teaching techniques, and inadequate teaching that would impede the full development of the skills.

The Advanced Level

Instruction in grades 7 and above should provide for the full maturation of the reading abilities. The student should be asked to apply his reading techniques in a variety of situations so that he can learn to adjust his approach to the material in keeping with his objectives. In other words, a student should develop a flexibility that allows him to perform with a large variety of materials. Such a student likes to read because of the sheer enjoyment and profit of reading.

APPROACHES TO THE TEACHING OF READING

In addition to being aware of the stages of reading development through which students pass, the secondary school teacher of reading should also be aware of the various approaches used to teach reading in the elementary grades. The material that follows describes the interest and controversy concerning various methods. Five different approaches are presented.

Never before has there been such a profusion of materials for the teaching of reading. With the advent of the "space race" and the resulting emphasis upon education, the entire educational system has come under careful scrutiny. The fact that reading skills are the key to knowledge explains the wide public interest in the way reading is taught.

Without the skill of reading, a child cannot make satisfactory progress in school. Not all children learn to read, but the failure of some children is not easily accounted for. It may be because of low intelligence, emotional problems, poor teaching, physical problems, moving from town to town continuously without establishing roots, or poor home environment—one or a combination of these factors. Because of the inability to point to a single factor for reading failure, many approaches and panaceas have been offered within the last few years.

The reading controversy centers on the question of how to teach the reading skills so that more children may succeed in school. Several approaches are in use. The most common is the basal reading approach; second is the basal reading approach used in conjunction with experience charts; third, phonics program; fourth, reading programs based upon the language experience of the child. These four approaches have the greatest frequency of use in our public schools. One other approach, the so-called linguistic approach, is receiving increasing attention and is worth discussing.

The Basal Reading Approach

This approach is the one most commonly used throughout the United States at the present time. Several series of readers are on the market, each of which provides textbook material, workbooks, and supplementary materials for the students, with manuals and guides for the teacher. Usually the basal readers provide instruction from reading readiness up through grade 6, and in many cases through grade 8.

The vocabulary is carefully controlled from book to book, primarily in grades 1 - 3, with careful development of a sequential program of balanced skills. Within the last few years the basal readers have come through many extensive changes. The vocabulary has often been enriched to meet the individual needs and the content has been changed somewhat by the introduction of stories written by well-known children's authors and authors of adult material. Much supplementary material for classroom use has also been included.

The basal readers are used by thousands of teachers throughout the United States with much success. Until a new teacher becomes thoroughly acquainted with the reading program, it is inadvisable for her to try to develop a reading program on her own. The material in the basal reader has been developed through years of study and experience by classroom teachers. Because most of the material has been experimented with in various types of situations, the teacher's guide provides a valuable resource for the teacher in providing interest and productive activities for her class. Even for the teacher who has wide experience and a good grasp of reading skills the basal reader still offers a valuable source of material for devising a skills program. The teacher may want to use the material in a variety of ways—as a part of an enrichment program or an individualized reading program, or to supplement other basal readers. In any case, it should be useful to the teacher as a guide for checking on the skills to be developed.

Occasionally the basal reader has not been used as it was intended. The basal reader is not a total and complete program by itself. It is merely a part of the total program. It is impossible to teach through the basal reader all of the needed skills. Most of the content is story material. Thus, many of the skills that we teach, such as finding main ideas, organization, sequence, study skills, and others, must be taught in the content areas. Although the basal reader does have a number on the outside cover, it is intended to meet the different instructional levels of all the children in every class. Because of the wide range of ability in the classroom it is impossible to take care of all of the instructional needs through one book. A teacher must use other books within the same series for the children below and above the instructional level of the grade, or she may use a cobasal series.

Since reading is a sequential development of skills, there is no such thing as having children cover all pages in a certain reader by the end of the year. The statement has been made by some experts in the field of reading that as many as 30 percent of our children are reading at the frustration level. If this is true teachers are not doing their job.

The teacher's guide was never meant as a detailed prescription to be followed exactly in all aspects for all children. We know that some children are going to need more development in some skills than in others. Some children will not need the drills or some of the skills that are taught.

One of the most important criticisms of the basal reading program is directed against the teacher's use of the workbooks. If workbooks are used indiscriminately with all children, they have little value in developing needed skills. If the teacher fails to check the workbook activities with individual children to see what progress and what errors they are making, the material is being grossly misused. Its value lies in the information it can give the teacher about the application of skills. It has never been intended as a testing situation or as a busy-work acitivity.

In many of the activities involving the basal reader, directions must be given to the children. As this is to be a learning situation, the experience that the child needs for reading must be developed before, and the teacher's guidance through the material is mandatory.

The Basal Reading Approach Used in Conjunction with Experience Charts

Charts based upon the real experiences of children provide available reading material for the beginning stages of reading instruction and for later development. The preparation of the charts involves specific techniques that can be mastered easily by any interested teacher. The charts can usually be divided into two general categories: (1) charts made by the teacher from the dictation of the students, and (2) practice charts made by the children with the aid of the teacher.

The function of the first type of chart is to give the children the experience of seeing their own spoken words converted into printed symbols. The emphasis is not upon reading the chart but upon noticing the fact that words can be written down and the sequence in which we write them—primarily left to right, return sweep to the next line, and left to right again.

Some children who have advanced in reading maturity will probably be able to read a few of the words just from seeing the material written. Some children will even want to learn to read the entire chart by themselves.

The second kind of chart, the practice chart, is prepared primarily to give actual practice in reading and writing. In developing this the teacher will try to guide the children into making simple sentences, with the vocabulary load closely related to those they will find in their reading material. Because the children have a direct and immediate interest in these charts the material will often provide a welcome change from that in their basal reader.

Even as the children progress through the grades, the experience charts will be of value in helping to summarize their ideas of materials they have read in the content areas. It will also afford them the opportunity of having more experiences with the vocabulary they are trying to learn.

The Phonics Approach

Of all the issues in reading instruction, none has received more attention or aroused more discussion and misunderstanding than *phonics* (sounds as they apply to reading). Not only are teachers interested in the role of phonics, but parents have looked upon it as an answer to all reading problems.

The advocates of this approach believe that phonics should be introduced either before a sight vocabulary is established or on a parallel with the beginning basal reader. They reject the "whole-word approach" because they believe the child first sees the word as individual letters and then the larger unit of the word as a whole.

Among the proponents of the "phonics-first approach" there is little consensus of opinion regarding the proper method of teaching. Each approach establishes a step-by-step sequence which its proponents warn must be followed if the child is to read. They emphasize that learning phonics is a memorization process that can be mastered only by repetitive drill. Their material consists of workbooks containing page after page of isolated words and phonic elements.

One phonic system calls for learning the names of all twenty-six letters of the alphabet on the first day of instruction. Another stresses a letter-by-letter approach to reading, with the emphasis upon the sound of each separate letter. Others teach all of the vowel sounds first (long and short), followed by the consonants, while some teach only the long or short vowel sounds first. The teaching of blends, vowels, consonant digraphs, and diphthongs varies to a greater extent even than some of the other elements in the various materials. In some cases only selected elements are taught and others are ignored. In most of the material there is little if any effort to help children evolve or understand phonic principles or to aid them in arriving at useful generalizations.

There is no evidence as to the value of many of the phonics programs now available to our schools beyond the opinions and prejudices of their authors. There is little consensus as to appropriate methods in the phonics approach, and serious doubts should be raised about the use of most phonics materials either in isolation or in conjunction with basal readers.

If the school, for whatever reason, adopts a phonics program, it should be used on a very limited basis rather than schoolwide, and it should be evaluated under the best possible research conditions. Wholesale adoption can result only in confusion, more problems, and no indication as to the worth of the material.

The Language-Experience Approach

The language-experience approach attempts to integrate the communication skills of speaking, writing, reading, and listening. In simplest terms, the approach can be thought of in the following manner. What a child thinks about he can talk about; what he can talk about he can write, or the teacher can write for him. What he writes he can read; he can read what he writes and what others write. What he has to say and write is as important to him as what other people have written for him to read.

From the beginning of the school year the children are encouraged to express themselves through speaking, writing, painting, singing, and playing. The teacher works with individual children and with small groups of children, helping them to write down "talk." Reading skills are taught informally by the teacher's talking to the children about the words, names of letters, beginning sounds, ending sounds, and sounds in between.

The language-experience approach seems to have some merit for beginning reading instruction. It does seem to develop an interest in reading. There is an integration of the language arts and other communications skills. The children understand that reading is an important form of communication, and the approach does encourage creative expression.

Certain aspects of this approach need *careful* consideration. A teacher using this approach has to be aware of the development of reading skills to be sure that the children are getting a balanced and sound program. There would be some danger of continual misspelling, poor expression, and punctuation errors if the teacher, fearing to hamper creativity, failed to correct errors. It is also possible that memorization of written material may be mistaken for reading.

The Linguistic Approach

The science of linguistics has aroused much interest in the last few years as a possible aid in improving reading competencies. Linguistics, because it is a complicated science, has resulted in misunderstanding, confusion, and hastily constructed material when applied to reading. However, its application to reading is evolving.

The contribution of the science of linguistics to reading has come primarily from the descriptive linguists. They believe that in reading the child must be able to respond to the language signals as represented by written symbols (words) in the same way that he responds to the patterns of auditory shapes. The key to an understanding of descriptive linguistics is in the concept of "pattern." It is argued that some of our reading failures are due to the obvious differences between the patterns of speech of children and the patterns we ask them to read. Much of the child's reading material is in a pattern that is unreal to him. It is imperative for a child to have sentence sense—that is, that he should possess a knowledge of word arrangement and corresponding word function.

At the present time there is some confusion regarding where to start beginning readers. Some would have the child begin with the smaller units in structural analysis, such as the *phoneme* (elemental speech sound), *morpheme* (the smallest unit with a meaning), word, and *grapheme* (letter symbol for a phoneme). Others would have us start with the simple sentence first. At the present time the concepts in linguistics, as they apply to the development of reading skills, are not well enough defined or established to arouse more than curiosity and a wait-and-see attitude.

UNDERSTANDING THE READING PROCESS

Some of the many concepts regarding the reading process need to be understood if the teacher is to determine whether what is observed as reading behavior is really adept reading ability or only skills which are superficially adequate. Before one can know how and what he is going to teach one must first understand the reading process, the ways of observing reading behavior, and the art of teaching itself.

Different Viewpoints Regarding Reading Behavior

To some people, the reading process is merely the ability to pronounce the printed word with little or no emphasis on comprehension of the printed symbols. The means by which the learning is accomplished varies but the outcomes are similar. Students who are taught to pronounce the individual sound units in a word and then to combine the individual units into a whole (the word) are usually able to perform the task quite well, yet are often deficient in understanding what they have read. Some students also have difficulty in identifying the words they pronounce as the same words used by others.

Other people believe that the act of reading demands a close association between the spoken language and its written counterpart. This view holds that unless a student makes an immediate association between the symbol he is reading and the spoken language, no reading is taking place.

Reading behavior is, however, generally conceived by most educators as more than pronouncing words correctly or associating meaning with individual words. Reading is seen as requiring thought about what one is reading, reaction to it, and the use of previous experiences to develop new associations and understandings. Effective reading is purposeful and carries the reader beyond where he is and aids him in stretching concepts and imaginations.

This total reading process is stressed throughout the school program from grades 1 through 12. It is a complex process and cannot be summarized as merely the acquisition of skills. Certain stages in skill development can be elaborated upon (Chapter 1) but they do not tell the whole story.

The beginning reader learns to identify the word symbols on the printed page and to associate them or react to them with a group of mental associations. The word becomes known to him by its sound and structure if it is in his listening or speaking vocabularies. It is in these associations that the process begins.

As the reader identifies successive words, they are fused into ideas or thoughts, the reader keeping in mind the beginning of the sentence as he reads. Sometimes as the student reads the first-meaning impressions must be rejected and new concepts developed. Take for example the first part of this sentence: *He walked down the street with a tear* . . . . What is your impression? The rest of the sentence reads: *in his pants*. The mature reader not only has the ability to shift in midstream, but he also is able to retain the ideas in the sentences he has previously read, modifying his total impression as he reads through the paragraph or longer unit. Material will be evaluated, accepted, or rejected, rate of reading will be adjusted according to purpose and difficulty, and reactions will occur.

All of the preceding takes place in the reading act. It does not occur in a piecemeal fashion but in a totality. For the purposes of teaching and discussion, the development of specific skills in a sequential continuum are talked about, but it should be constantly kept in mind that in the act of reading many factors are operating simultaneously. Otherwise the result may be overacceptance of commercially prepared materials for repeated practice on isolated skills.

Reading as a Visual Act

For the student in the junior and senior high school, the visual task of reading is largely related to eye movements and visual perception. Students with serious visual defects certainly should have them diagnosed and corrected by the time they reach secondary school or they will be so retarded in reading as to need immediate evaluation.

The relation of eye movement to reading achievement is usually the area of most interest to the teacher of developmental reading. Although this area has been extensively studied and evaluated, the discussion still continues. Photographic records of eye movements indicate that the eye moves across the page in jerking movements (saccadic); that they move in a series of stops (fixations) and starts.

Sometimes the eyes move backward over the line of print in regression movements. Regression movements do not necessarily mean poor reading. The cause may reflect that the reader has (1) encountered an unfamiliar word; (2) doesn't understand the sentence; (3) needs to change his frame of reference; or (4) has moved too quickly. To this list needs to be added the information that external stimuli can distract the reader and—most important—a thoughtful reader will often stop, reflect, reread, and then continue reading.

With developing age and background of experience, the reader will often develop a smoother pattern of reading on some materials under certain conditions. Students should not be considered to have reading difficulty, however, if their eye movements on specific kinds of materials tend to be more primitive.

Theoretically, a person can see a whole page of print at a single glance. This does not mean that he can comprehend the whole page at the same time, however. A student who is reading material for comprehension and study purposes at the rate of 250 - 300 words per minute is probably reading quite efficiently. Students who read at 800+ words per minute are not reading but skimming. They are skimming to verify what their previous experience tells them is in the particular content they are reading. When they come to new material that must be studied, they too will slow down.

Reading and Cultural Background

The quality and quantity of reading material are directly related to sociological factors. About 10 percent of the population in the United States reads 75 percent of the materials published in the United States. The readers are largely concentrated in the age group 21 - 29 and have been educated beyond the secondary school level. Persons from the upper socioeconomic and educated group form the largest active reader group.

Students in this country's school systems can hardly be considered active readers either in the past, in the present, or indeed in the future. This culture apparently puts little emphasis on intellectual curiosity in relation to reading and provides precious few rewards of any type for sustained intellectual development through reading. Society provides so much early stimulation and organized activity for the young that they never seem to have the time to grow intellectually. So much time is spent teaching them the facts they need for survival that one forgets to educate them. Today's students are probably the best informed and most poorly educated citizens that have ever evolved in any complex civilization.

For the secondary school teacher, an understanding of the socioeconomic class of the students taught is probably the most important single factor in developing reading ability. The poor family's attitude toward reading is often that of disinterest. The parents usually do not give a high priority to expenditures for reading material. They read poorly themselves because of their own parents' attitudes, and leisure-time pursuits are often directed into other channels. A teacher who does not understand socioeconomic factors or consider them in her teaching is perpetuating a system which has proven itself unproductive in the past.

Reading failures are not limited to any particular social class or stratum, although students in the lower strata do have more difficulty in reading. The probable cause of failure by students in lower socioeconomic groups is that the public schools cling to "standards" and teaching practices more closely attuned to the backgrounds and standards of the upper middle class. Another explanation for the failure of the low socioeconomic student to perform well in the school setting is expounded by Arthur R. Jensen (1969), who believes that the differences in measured intellectual functioning reflect not only cultural differences but also genetically determined differences in potential for intellectual development.

Regardless which of the two beliefs is most appealing, the school has done little to adjust its program to meet the needs of the students in low socioeconomic groups. Until teachers are willing to make the instructional program more relevant to the needs and backgrounds of their students it is highly unlikely that any judgments can be made as to the causes of success or failure. Experimentation, modification, and adjustment are the only bases on which progress can be evaluated.

Reading and Intelligence

Reading and intelligence have so much in common that a teacher can be reasonbly sure that good intellectual ability will be highly correlated to reading ability. Correlations of .50 to .80 between intelligence tests and reading measures are frequently reported. The fact that a student has an above-average IQ does not, however, guarantee that he will be a good reader. Intelligence is an important factor in reading, but it is only one of the contributing elements necessary for success. Motivation for success in school, health, attitude toward school, and other factors are of equal importance and in some cases more important than intelligence. The primary factor, for example, in whether a student of limited ability stays in school and graduates or drops out is not so much a factor of ability as the amount of support he gets from his family.

Acceptance of an intelligence test score should be made cautiously by any teacher. Most group intelligence tests require that the student read before he can answer the question. The student with a reading problem cannot help but perform poorly on such a measurement. Students known to have reading problems should be evaluated on an individual test. Even individual tests, however, will not give an accurate picture of the student's ability if the student has been in an environment that has depressed verbal expression as a primary means of communication. Divergent language patterns cannot be compensated for on the group or individual measuring instruments now available.

SUMMARY

If a truly developmental reading program were available to students in junior and senior high school, there would be much less need for large, expensive remedial reading programs.

Reading is a tool for learning that needs reinforcement and refinement as it occurs in developmental stages. Before a student reaches the senior high school he goes through six levels of development: preschool, beginning, growing independent, literacy, intermediate, and advanced. Also he may have been exposed to as many as five methods of teaching reading before he reaches high school. The most common of these are the basal reading approach, and the basal reading approach used in conjunction with experience charts. The phonics approach, which has created much controversy over the past several years, and the language-experience approach are also two popular teaching methods; the linguistic approach is receiving increased attention daily.

It is important to understand the actual reading process in order to grasp what is and what should be happening in schools. Although there are numerous and conflicting viewpoints as to what this process is, we do know that it is a visual act requiring intelligence, and that cultural and psychological factors must be taken into account as contributing factors to the act of reading.

REFERENCE

Jensen, Arthur R. "Intelligence, Learning Ability and Socioeconomic Status," *Journal of Special Education*, Vol. 3, No. 1 (Winter - Spring 1969), pp. 28 - 36.

ADDITIONAL READINGS

Burton, Dwight L. "Heads Out of the Sand: Secondary Schools Face the Challenge of Reading," *Educational Forum*, XXIV (March 1960), pp. 285 - 293.

DeBoer, John. "What Does Research Reveal About Reading and the High School Student," *English Journal* (May 1958), pp. 271 - 281.

Henry, Nelson B. (ed.). *Development in and Through Reading*. Sixtieth Yearbook of the National Society for the Study of Education. Chicago: University of Chicago Press, 1961, Part I, Chaps. V, VI.

Langman, Muriel P. "The Reading Process: A Descriptive Interdisciplinary Approach," *Genetic Psychology Monographs*, LXII (August 1960), pp. 3 - 40.

Umans, Shelley. *New Trends in Reading Instruction*. New York: Teachers College Press, 1963.

REQUIRED READINGS FROM BOOK OF READINGS*

I. Introduction

High School and College Instructors Can't Teach Reading? Nonsense!—Stanley E. Davis.

Reading in the Secondary School: Issues and Innovations—Richard W. Burnett.

The Refinement of High School Reading Skills—J. T. Hunt.

III. The Nature of Reading

Reading and Reading Difficulty: A Conceptual Analysis—Morton Wiener and Ward Cromer.

Learning to Read—Eleanor J. Gibson.

*Arthur V. Olson and Wilbur S. Ames, *Teaching Reading Skills in Secondary Schools: Readings* (Scranton, Pa.: International Textbook Company, 1970). This Book of Readings will be referred to at the end of most chapters.

chapter **2**

Organization and Administration of Secondary School Reading Program

The junior and senior high schools have need for both developmental and remedial programs.

The developmental program reaches every student in the school regardless of ability level. It is based on the premise that no student leaving grade 6 reads well enough to enable him to read advanced material without further instruction. There are some skills for which the student has little use until he reaches secondary school, and most of the skills he has learned in earlier grades must be reinforced and refined.

In order to provide for the development of these skills, systematic reading instruction should be developed up through grade 8. Provision should also be made for all students to receive further instruction upon entering the freshman year in high school. This may be done through the English program or by a specially designed course of specified duration. During the last half of the senior year in high school a more advanced but similar program should be given to help prepare the college-bound student to develop the skills needed for college-level work.

The remedial program should be developed for the students who have serious deficiencies in reading and who require highly skilled help. This type of program should be available to the student as long as he needs help regardless of the grade level.

The developmental and remedial programs are not separate but complementary. A school that hopes to meet the needs of the students must have both.

CHARACTERISTICS OF A GOOD PROGRAM

1. A set of well-defined objectives must be acted upon which will promote the development of the reading skills and which will raise the level of achievement.
2. The program *must* have the coordinating efforts of the entire staff. All

of the teachers must be involved in in-service programs that will help them to achieve the desired outcomes.

3. Careful appraisal of the reading abilities and needs of the students should be made.
4. Individual differences must be recognized and provisions made in the total school program to ensure that the students can learn through the material from which they are asked to read.
5. A sound, well-balanced program of skill development must be developed that will ensure student growth.
6. Adequate materials and equipment, varying in type, interest, and range of ability must be available and used effectively.
7. There must be a continuous appraisal of the effectiveness of the program, including sound testing procedures.
8. Well-trained people in the area of reading must be available to work with special groups of students and to aid other teachers.

Defined Objectives

The reading program should have some direction if it is to succeed. There must be a list of expected outcomes that can be defined in such a way that avenues of action toward the objectives are obvious. Some objectives that may be formulated are

1. To determine the current status of reading achievement in our school now and to adjust to the range of achievement.
2. To formulate the best possible reading improvement program within the limitations of our school organization.

At the start of any discussion, the group of discussants should limit the list of objectives to those that can be reasonably carried out within the school year. Although long-range objectives are desirable, the specific and immediate objective should be realistic. The rewards of participation in any discussion group involving objectives must be immediate, or any momentum which has been built will be lost.

Coordinating Efforts

No program can succeed without a positive and active relationship between the coordinators of a program and classroom teachers. The kind of rapport established will determine the success or failure of the program.

In establishing the efforts to innovate a reading program, it is important that the following guidelines be considered.

1. The person working with the teachers in either a reading teacher capacity, supervisor, curriculum coordinator or content-area specialist must be respected by the teaching staff. It is probably best for the success of the program if the person has had experience as a secondary school

teacher. The experienced person has the background to say, "It can be done because I've done it."

2. The teachers who are interested in the program and secure enough to want to make changes should be the first to work with. It is foolhardy to force all teachers to change. A slow, steady development where success is assured is preferred to the bull-in-the-china-shop approach.

3. Limit the scope of what can be done to a small but vital area.

4. Provide for released school time for those teachers who are making some changes in their programs. Teachers cannot be expected to make drastic changes in the program without the time needed to select and prepare materials, discuss procedures, and think.

Appraisal of Reading

Before any evaluative measures are selected, it is essential that the objectives of the reading program be clearly formulated. It is only after the objectives have been discussed and agreed upon and specific needs identified that evaluation and particular tools can be determined.

Individual Differences

The treatment of individual differences is well known in the field of education. It is untrue, however, that common sense tells you how to work with the range of individual abilities within any given school. If common sense is the answer, it is amazing how uncommon it becomes when one observes teacher performance.

If teachers are to work effectively with individual differences, they must be given the materials to allow individual work to be done, and must be shown how to organize the classroom for their use.

Balanced Program

A balanced program that provides for the need of all the students in a school is a must for the program that is truly doing a job. No one should be left out of the reading program. There should be a balance which allows valuable instructional aid for the advanced reader as well as for the less able.

Materials

The materials available to the students and teachers have a great deal to do with the success of the program. They should be selected and evaluated for the contribution they can make in helping to achieve the objectives of the reading program. Materials of all types and descriptions should be used for skill development and enjoyment at all levels of ability. A reading program that does not have access to an abundance of materials is denying the students a chance to practice the skills which they are learning.

Testing Procedures

The testing program is essential to insure that the stated objectives are being met by the program. Without this overall evaluation it will be impossible to determine the common strengths and weaknesses, or the reading levels of the school population. Students who need to be identified for further diagnosis and possible remediation cannot be found without such a program.

Well-Trained People

The success of any program depends upon the people who are responsible for its operation. One way of assuring the professional competency of the reading specialist is to establish some standards for professional training. Listed below are the qualifications for reading specialists as established by the Professional Standards and Ethics Committee and approved by the Board of Directors of the International Reading Association.

QUALIFICATIONS*

A. General (Applicable to all Reading Specialists)

Demonstrate proficiency in evaluating and implementing research.

Demonstrate a willingness to make a meaningful contribution to professional organizations related to reading.

Demonstrate a willingness to assume leadership in improving the reading program.

B. Special Teacher of Reading

Complete a minimum of three years of successful classroom teaching in which the teaching of reading is an important responsibility of the position.

Complete a planned program for the Master's Degree from an accredited institution, to include

1. A minimum of 12 semester hours in graduate-level reading courses with at least one course in each of the following:

    (a) *Foundations or survey of reading.* A basic course whose content is related exclusively to reading instruction or the psychology of reading. Such a course ordinarily would be first in a sequence of reading courses.

    (b) *Diagnosis and correction of reading disabilities.* The content of this course or courses includes the following: causes of reading disabilities; observation and interview procedures; diagnostic instruments; standard and informal tests; report writing; materials and methods of instruction.

*Reprinted with permission of the International Reading Association.

(c) *Clinical or laboratory practicum in reading.* A clinical or laboratory experience which might be an integral part of a course or courses in the diagnosis and correction of reading disabilities. Students diagnose and treat reading disability cases under supervision.

2. Complete, at undergraduate or graduate level, study in each of the following areas:
   (a) *Measurement and/or evaluation.*
   (b) *Child and/or adolescent psychology.*
   (c) *Psychology, including such aspects as personality, cognition, and learning behaviors.*
   (d) *Literature for children and/or adolescents.*
3. Fulfill remaining portions of the program from related areas of study.

C. Reading Clinician

Meet the qualifications as stipulated for the Special Teacher of Reading.

Complete, in addition to the above, a sixth year of graduate work, including
   1. An advanced course of courses in the diagnosis and remediation of reading and learning problems.
   2. A course or courses in individual testing.
   3. An advanced clinical or laboratory practicum in the diagnosis and remediation of reading difficulties.
   4. Field experiences under the direction of a qualified Reading Clinician.

D. Reading Consultant

Meet the qualifications as stipulated for the Special Teacher of Reading.

Complete, in addition to the above, a sixth year of graduate work including
   1. An advanced course in the remediation and diagnosis of reading and learning problems.
   2. An advanced course in the developmental aspects of a reading program.
   3. A course or courses in curriculum development *and* supervision.
   4. A course and/or experience in public relations.
   5. Field experiences under a qualified Reading Consultant or Supervisor in a school setting.

E. Reading Supervisor

Meet the qualifications as stipulated for the Special Teacher of Reading.

Complete, in addition to the above, a sixth year of graduate work including
   1. Courses listed as 1, 2, 3, and 4 under Reading Consultant.
   2. A course or courses in administrative procedures.
   3. Field experiences under a qualified Reading Supervisor.

STARTING THE PROGRAM

There is no one way to organize a reading program. No two schools will find the same plan effective because of the many factors which may be interacting—i.e., school size, philosophy, range of student ability, training of teachers, administrative leadership, facilities, and teacher leadership. There are however, four requirements that are fundamental to the success of any program.

1. A core of highly respected staff members must be ready and interested in developing the best possible reading program. It is very unlikely that all of the staff members will be interested, but a small group of teachers can create the climate that will facilitate the program.

2. The school administrators must be willing to give enthusiastic support to the program. The leadership they can give is essential to organize and extend the program.

3. Parents must be informed and active interest on their part should be encouraged.

4. Adequate provisions must be made to ensure continued financial support of the program. A minimum outlay of $2,000 is required to operate the beginning phases of the program.

The most successful programs have a reading committee composed of representatives from all areas of the curriculum. If the program is to be accepted, membership should be composed of representatives from the administrative staff, library, guidance, and the content areas.

Specifically, the committee should (1) help and encourage teachers to extend the reading program throughout the school, (2) aid in planning in-service work, (3) aid in public relations for the program, (4) serve as a review board to evaluate and improve the program, and (5) promote communication about the program throughout the school.

The following is a list of some possible organizational plans for reading programs in the secondary schools.

1. *Planned Reading Unit Within Regular English Course.* This type of organization should be planned with the English Department staff and not imposed upon them. This type of plan is probably the most common in the secondary schools at the present time.

2. *Voluntary Developmental Reading.* This program is usually handled by a reading specialist or other teachers who have an interest and willingness to assume leadership in developing such a course. The course is usually set up on a five- or nine-week basis during the school year or a rotation basis. Students are usually accepted on a first-come, first-served basis with no graduation credit allowed. This type of course is usually very popular with the college-bound students.

3. *Combination of Voluntary Developmental Reading and Unit Within Regular English Course.* In this organization a school may offer a unit of work on improving reading skills within an English course and required of all students at their achievement level. This is often followed up with a voluntary developmental reading program of greater difficulty for college-bound high school seniors.

4. *Compulsory Reading Course.* Under this plan all students at selected

grade levels (usually grades 7, 9, and 11) take reading as an extra subject. This is accomplished by shortening each period in order to create another for this purpose or by scheduling the study periods of students for reading instruction.

5. *Special Course for Slow Readers.* In some schools this course is substituted for the regular English course. The course consists mainly of reading and improvement of steady skills and continues for as long as the student needs help.

6. *Reading Center.* The Reading Center is often a fairly elaborate complex of offices and classrooms consisting of rooms equipped with mechanical devices, laboratories, textbooks, library books, and magazines at several levels of difficulty. A reading specialist is usually in charge to work with students and to provide in-service training to teachers. Special classes are usually arranged to meet the needs of the slow, average, and superior readers.

PUTTING THE PROGRAM INTO ACTION

Putting the program into effect can be accomplished only after some foundations are laid and when need for such a program has been realized by the majority of the school staff. Regardless of the need for such a program and enthusiasm of some members of the staff, it should be realized that a period of about five years will elapse before any noticeable or worthwhile change will result.

For schools beginning a developmental program it is wise to start with a class composed of students with above average ability who are not working up to their capacity. There are several reasons for taking this group first. The more able students will make more rapid progress, and such results will indicate to the staff that the program is worthwhile. The climate for accepting the program as a developmental need for all students and not merely for the "dumb" ones will be obvious to students and staff alike. The teacher(s) working with the more able student will not have to be as highly trained as if they were working with severely retarded readers. The program can start as the staff is being trained.

Setting the Stage for In-Service Work

The in-service program is a learning activity and should be as carefully thought out as any lesson that may be conducted in a classroom. One of the first steps in a good lesson is the motivation of the pupils and the presentation of the concepts and ideas they will need in order to profit from the instruction. The same is true of the in-service program. The participants must be brought to the point where they can identify their problems, understand their exact nature, and be willing to do something about them. This is not an easy task to accomplish.

The process of bringing a staff to the point of acceptance of a problem may be long and bumpy and does not necessarily mean that anything will be done about it even when identified. A high school staff, for instance, may be willing to admit that a problem in reading exists yet be unwilling to change any of its teaching procedures to reduce or correct the problem.

The in-service program must develop in stages. The first of these is the identification of the problem or problems. In the elementary program some problems will be obvious to the teachers and they will want to discuss them, whereas others may not be obvious to the teachers but of great concern to the administration. At the high school level the initial difficulty may be in getting teachers to recognize that they have some responsibility in the problem.

Some ways in which in-service leaders may guide teachers toward a recognition of the problems are these:

1. Send to all or a selected group of teachers magazine articles on reading instruction.
2. Discuss standardized test results with the staff to emphasize spread in achievement and need for varying instruction.
3. Send several teachers to visit a school where teachers are working on the improvement of reading instruction.
4. Invite a classroom teacher from another school to discuss with the teaching staff the problems encountered in his school, and his school's efforts to find solutions.
5. Encourage a small group of teachers to try some different kinds of material or practices. Other teachers will also try the idea if it works effectively.
6. Give support and help to any teacher who is trying to find effective ways of teaching children with a wide range of reading abilities.

The initial stage is one of stimulating discussion among staff members, using test results where applicable to emphasize and to clarify the problem, and to encourage interested staff members to try new ideas.

The second stage, after acceptance and identification of the problem, is to initiate change that will result in improvement. This is by far the longest stage and in some cases may be the most difficult. As stated previously, a plan for the improvement of instruction is necessary and must be realistic in terms of the staff and resources available. The plan must allow for modification and variation. The most important factor in this stage is change in the classroom.

Many teachers avoid trying something new or different unless they are reasonably sure that the idea will work. Talking and discussing with teachers in generalities, then, is one of the surest ways of guaranteeing that stage 2 will never succeed. Teachers need to be shown through actual demonstrations how to use new techniques and materials. If at all possible, demonstrations should be with children from the school or system involved. Then the teacher is not likely to say, "That's a good idea, but it wouldn't work with my students."

If new ideas are to be tried, the teachers must be given practical help, material to use, encouragement, and most important, security. In carrying through this stage of the program some means that may be used to advantage are listed below.

1. Demonstrate the idea in the classroom with the children.
2. Provide materials and show the teachers how to use them.
3. Encourage the teachers to exchange ideas and comments on the effectiveness of the idea or material in their classrooms.
4. Provide reading specialists and special teachers to go into classrooms to help to demonstrate and carry out the program.
5. Provide adequate time for teachers to formulate a classroom plan for implementing new ideas.

The third stage involves an extension and elaboration of the developments started in phase two. The developed momentum needs to be continued with further in-service work, such as experimentation with materials and varying forms of instructional organization. Some of the ways in which the third stage can be continued are listed below:

1. In-service course work sponsored by a local university and the school system.
2. In-service work through committee assignments.
3. Planned in-service work with special groups of teachers.
4. A school or system bulletin on activities going on in other places and within the local unit.
5. Research activities with small groups of teachers.

The three stages, although discussed separately for clarification, may be in evidence concurrently in any given school system. The elementary program may, for example, be in stage 3, while the secondary program is in stage 1. And different groups of teachers may be in different phases at the same time.

THE TESTING PROGRAM

Test results may be used as a basis for starting an in-service program in reading. Or they may aid in the long-range evaluation of the effectiveness of a reading program, and, thus in-service work in reading. For example, an analysis of reading-achievement test scores and intelligence test scores, may reveal that for many children in elementary grades there may be wide gaps between reading-grade placements and intelligence-grade placements. In another situation, junior high or high school students may have a very low level of achievement in certain of the locational skills. In both instances this knowledge might generate an interest in reading improvement.

Throughout this chapter references have been made to the importance of testing and evaluation procedures in organizing and administering a secondary school reading program. It was pointed out that testing and evaluation procedures are important in planning the direction the program should take, and that they are also needed throughout to determine how well program objectives are being met. In this section a closer look will be taken at specifics of the testing and evaluation of reading.

Evaluation of Student Needs

Schools differ in the kind and amount of testing necessary to formulate a plan of operation in developing a reading program. However, a plan must be evolved and testing must be done.

In arriving at a decisions in these areas, the reading skills needed for success at various levels of the curriculum should be considered. Information is collected concerning the skills needed by students in order to perform the learning activities established by the curriculum. Once this has been accomplished, an investigation can be made to find instruments (tests) that will provide the information most effectively.

A fundamental concept in testing which is appropriate to any discussion of the reading program is that while the testing should go not further than necessary it must provide enough information upon which to operate. If this concept is followed to its logical conclusion, one would: (1) start with a group test for screening purposes, (2) evaluate in a group setting specific skills found to be weak for certain students on the survey test, and (3) evaluate the students who manifested severe reading difficulties on the survey test with an individual diagnostic test.

The group test administered to the total school population may provide the basic information upon which some decisions can be made. For example, it may be found that on a vocabulary subtest the school population as a whole is performing below the national level and below the general comprehension level of the school. This may indicate that the school has not been placing enough emphasis upon vocabulary development in the various content area subjects. Also, in light of the trends that can be seen from one grade level to the next, decisions can be made as to where the reading program might begin on the secondary level.

Naturally there will be some students whose performance on a group test will be confusing and misleading. These students should be given a group diagnostic test of specific skills in order to identify the specific problem areas. Once this information is obtained, it may lead to some regrouping of the students, a special course to develop the skills, or some other appropriate action.

There will still be some students for which the first two evaluations do not provide adequate information. It should be for these students that the time-consuming individual diagnostic measures should be reserved.

Any testing done for evaluative purposes must be used to aid in making decisions concerning the curriculum. If it is not, then the time and money spent in testing have been wasted. If the school is in the position where only the information that can be gained from a group survey test can be used, with no hope of reorganizing based upon the group diagnostic or individual tests, then evaluation should not continue after the initial group survey.

If one objective for using tests is to determine the needs of the students in order to guide the instructional program, certainly a second objective of testing should be to evaluate the success of the instruction. Evaluation at the beginning and end of the school year is essential if the teaching staff is to make any judgment concerning the impact of the program in correcting the weaknesses identified.

Specific Tests for Specific Needs

In deciding which areas should be tested, the individual school staffs must consider the curriculum of the school and the type of students being served. Once the areas have been identified, Buros' *Mental Measurements Yearbook* becomes an invaluable source of information.

The wise thing to do first is to collect and read what the publishers say they are trying to evaluate in their tests. If a test is found which appears to meet the needs, one would probably then want to consult the *Mental Measurements Yearbook*. In the *Yearbook* can be found information describing and evaluating the test by an expert reviewer. The reviewer will in most cases discuss the characteristics of the test, the results of research concerning the test, and its strengths and limitations.

Standardized Tests

Standardized tests provide for the individual teacher and the staff as a whole a systematic way of observing reading behavior. These tests call for the students to make use of some specific knowledge, understanding, or skill related to the reading process. Some of the commonly used standardized reading tests available for group evaluation are listed below.

Cooperative Reading Comprehension Tests. Cooperative Test Division, Educational Testing Service. Grades 9-12. Measures vocabulary, speed of comprehension, level of comprehension. Approximately 40 minutes. 3 forms.

Diagnostic Reading Tests. Committee on diagnostic Reading Tests. Grades 7-13. Consists of survey section; vocabulary in specific fields; auditory and silent comprehension; rate of reading; reading of social studies and science materials; and word attack, silent and oral.

Gates-MacGinitie Reading Tests. Teachers College Press. Grades 7-9. Measures speed, vocabulary, and comprehension. 3 forms.

Nelson-Denny Reading Test. Houghton Mifflin. Grades 9-12. Measures vocabulary, comprehension and rate. 2 forms.

Sequential Tests of Academic Progress. Educational Testing Service. Grades 7-14. Measures listening and reading comprehension. 2 forms.

Spitzer Study Skills Test. World Book. Grades 9-12. Measures skills in using a dictionary; using an index; locating sources of information; understanding tables, graphs, and maps; and organization of facts in note taking. 2 forms.

S.R.A. Reading Record. Science Research Associates. Grades 8-13. Measures rate, comprehension, paragraph meaning, directed reading, map-table-graph reading, index reading, sentence meaning, technical vocabulary and general vocabulary. 30 minutes. 1 form.

Traxler High School Reading Test. Bobbs-Merrill. Grades 10-12. Measures reading rate, story comprehension, understanding of main ideas in paragraphs.

Characteristics of Reading Tests

There are certain statistical properties one should look for in any instrument. It is appropriate at this point to review very briefly a few guidelines and concepts to aid one in selecting a good reading test.

Test characteristics are usually discussed in relation to essential information on validity, reliability, and norms. Following is a brief discussion of some of the basic concepts and definitions needed to understand the statistical properties of reading tests.

Validity is defined as the extent to which the test measures what it purports to measure. Four types of validity are usually distinguished.

1. *Content validity* refers to the testing of the complete knowledge or a sampling of the knowledge. For example, if one wanted to determine if students know the names of the twenty-six letters in the alphabet, one could test all twenty-six and have all the information available. If on the other hand one wished to determine a student's understanding or comprehension of what he reads, the problem would be vastly different. One cannot expect to measure all the skills involved in comprehension in one session; a sample must be taken from the general content of reading comprehension. The criteria for selecting a comprehension test then would be to determine what kind of reading material one wants to evaluate and what kinds of questions one wants the student to answer. If the test measures what one wants to evaluate and is a good sample of what is called comprehension, then the test is considered as having high content validity.

2. *Concurrent validity* is concerned with the degree to which the test results are related to the actual performance of the students in the classroom. One would expect to find, for example, a significant relationship between the results from a reading comprehension test and the students' ability to understand material read in the classroom setting.

3. *Predictive validity* is concerned with the accuracy of the test scores in predicting performance at some later time. For example, a vocabulary test may predict how well a student will understand and effectively use context skills in his future reading.

4. *Construct validity* can be used when no other validity information is available. One may have to use his own judgment and experience in order to determine if a given test will or will not give the kind of information he needs.

Reliability. The user of a reading test must also concern himself with one or more of the following kinds of test reliability.

1. The *coefficient of internal consistency* shows the consistency of performance on serveral parts of the same test during a specific period of time. It is usually computed by treating each half of the test as separate tests (split-half correlation) or by item analysis.

2. The *coefficient of equivalence* shows the consistency of test performance on different forms of the same test. It is usually based on the correlation between performances on Form A and Form B of the same instrument given at nearly the same time.

3. The *coefficient of stability* shows the consistency of performance on a test over a period of time. It is based on the correlation between performance on the test initially and a retest after a time period lapse.

In order to use the information provided in most technical manuals on tests wisely, several other guidelines concerning reliability should be considered.

(a) If the test has a speed factor to it, then a coefficient of internal consistency may be misleading.

(b) Reliability coefficients will increase as the ability range of the people tested increases.

(c) The test coefficients reported in a manual are appropriate only inasmuch as the local school population is similar to the group upon which the test norms were based.

(d) The Standard Error of Measurement must be known and interpreted correctly if the test is to be of value. It can best be used to make a judgment about various scores within tests, but not between tests. The Standard Error of Measurement is most frequently reported in score units or months.

(e) For any group test, the average scores of the group are more reliable than individual scores. One should be extremely cautious about making judgments about individual students based on group reading tests.

Norms provide a comparison group against which one can judge the performance of the group tested within a given school. Therefore the interpretation of the test results for a given group is only as good as the comparison group upon which the test was standardized. For example, if the test was standardized on a small select group of students in a private clinic for youngsters having problems in learning to read, the normative data would be of little or no use unless a given population in a school was similar. Test users must relate the publisher's information on norms to (1) the characteristics of their own school, (2) the objectives of the curriculum, (3) the purposes for testing, and (4) the use to which the test results will be put in the school setting.

Using Test Results

In one school system in the Midwest an anlysis of the achievement test results over a period of years indicated that the range of ability of students in reading achievement decreased from grades 7-12 in comparison to the range in grades 1-6. The conclusion reached concerning this phenomenon was that since formal reading instruction in the system stopped at grade 6 it was not unexpected to find the range of ability actually decreasing. After evaluating the test results, the system put into effect an organized reading program to meet the needs of all the students as long as they were in school. A reevaluation after a four-year period provided the school system with the information it needed to further support the program. The results showed that with instruction the students made continuous growth in the development of their reading skills.

In another school situation the results indicated that in comparison with the test scores in vocabulary and comprehension, the students who achieved well had a much lower rate of reading. After careful evaluation it was found that the students were reading much of the material at the same speed, regardless of the difficulty of the material or the purpose established for reading. Some work in speed reading, along with versatility in selecting the speed and continued emphasis on comprehension, resulted in noticeable improvement.

Both of the preceding examples demonstrate how school systems can use test results to good advantage. Problem areas were identified and programs instituted to deal with the problems. In addition, it should be noted that in both situations follow-up evaluation was a part of the process.

In evaluating a new program certain growth-evaluation should be considered. One concept deals with determining what *normal growth* is. For example, if a reading program was evaluated at the end of a nine-month school period and found to show twelve months' growth according to the test norms, enthusiasm might be premature. It could be that the standard error of the test is three months. In other words, the students may have made three months gain over what would normally be expected, or they may have actually made only six months' gain.

THE PRINCIPAL'S ROLE

Effectiveness of the principal is determined in part by his skill in improving instruction and in part by his ability to furnish competent supervision. This implies that the principal has a knowledge of reading instruction in his school, in part, through personal observation of teachers in the classroom setting. Through this supervision he gains knowledge of each teacher's program, including the materials and methods used. This implies further that the principal has more than a superficial knowledge of the reading skills to be taught, the continuity from level to level, the ways in which teachers make adjustments for individual differences, and the effectiveness of the total program. The principal certainly cannot be an expert in all areas, but he must have a reasonably good idea of what constitutes a good reading program.

    As in the case of the teacher, the principal's responsibilities are numerous in carrying out effective in-service training programs in reading. A principal who assumes responsibilites for in-service programs takes the following actions:

1. He builds a background of understanding about what constitutes a good reading program, and, if weaknesses in this knowledge exist, he takes steps to build up a background of understanding.

2. He initiates or encourages others to start in-service programs in reading if his school does not have such a program.

3. He encourages teachers to express freeely their opinions about reading instruction in conferences with him and in faculty meetings in which the reading program is discussed.

4. He takes whatever action is necessary to get all of his teachers involved in existing in-service activities.

5. He takes the responsibility for setting up an organizational pattern for accomplishing things in in-service programs or gives active support and help to delegated in-service leaders in seeing that improvements grow from the programs.

6. He shows the teachers that he is vitally interested in the program by attending in-service meetings and taking active parts in programs and in discussions.

7. He involves teachers in the selection of materials and methods of reading instruction.

8. He uses his administrative position to help in obtaining materials when in-service study groups recommend such material and equipment.

9. He arranges for substitute teachers or modification of school schedules, when feasible, to free teachers for such in-service activities as visits to other teachers' classrooms for observation.

10. He respects the opinions of his teachers, but on any topic on which decisions must be made he also uses his own knowledge as well as the recommendations of his teachers.

SUMMARY

Junior and senior high schools which hope to meet the needs of all of their students must have both developmental and remedial reading programs. These programs should have the following characteristics:
1. Well-defined, realistic objectives.
2. Coordinated efforts of the entire staff.
3. Appraisal of reading abilities.
4. Provisions for individual needs.
5. Well-balanced program of skill development.
6. Adequate materials and equipment.
7. Continuous evaluation of program effectiveness.
8. Well-trained people in the area of reading.

Each reading program will be unique as each school has different needs; however, every program must have a core of interested, enthusiastic staff members, a cooperative, supportive administration, informed parents, and continued, adequate financial support.

When the program is activated, a three-stage in-service program must be started where problems are identified and accepted or change initiated, and where later extension and elaboration can be accomplished. This third stage will depend on the progress of the first two stages, especially the second in which continuous evaluation should be occurring. This evaluation will largely take the form of testing. Student testing must be done in accordance with student needs and progress. Their needs and progress must then be evaluated so as to serve as the basis for furthur program development.

ADDITIONAL READINGS

Astor, M. H. "Reading Test or Counseling Interview to Predict Success in College?" *Journal of Reading*, XI (February 1968), pp. 343-345.

Atwater, J. "Toward Meaningful Measurement," *Journal of Reading*, XI (March 1968), pp. 429-434.

Bennett, R. A. "Building a Total Reading Program," *Journal of Secondary Education*, XLII (November 1967), pp. 321-327.

Corbin, D. D. "Total Reading Program for Secondary Schools," *School and Community*, LIV (April 1968), p. 28.

Crisculo, N. P., Jr. "Attacking the Reading Problem in the Secondary School," *Journal of Secondary Education*, XLIII (November 1968), pp. 307-308.

Dawson, M. A. "Looking Ahead in Reading," *Reading Teacher*, XXI (November 1967), pp. 121-125.

Fry, E. "Do-It-Yourself Terminology Generator," *Journal of Reading*, XI (March 1960), p. 428.

Geerlofs, M. W., and M. Kling. "Current Practices in College and Adult Developmental Reading Programs," *Journal of Reading*, XI (April 1968), pp. 517-520.

Hays, G., and L. J. Phipps. "Multi-level Reading Material Needed," *Educational Magazine*, XXXIX (June 1967), p. 286.

Hayward, P. "Evaluating Diagnostic Reading Tests," *Reading Teacher*, XXI (March 1968), pp. 523-528.

Kender, J. P. "How Useful Are Informal Reading Tests?" *Journal of Reading*, XII (October 1968), pp. 37-38.

Lebow, Helene, and Valentine Seveger. "The Developmental Reading Program at the Secondary Level," *Academic Therapy Quarterly*, XIII (1966), pp. 185-187.

Littrell, J. H. "Teacher Estimates Versus Reading Test Results," *Journal of Reading*, XII (October 1968), pp. 18-23.

Martin, M., et al. "Teacher Motivation in a High School Reading Program," *Journal of Reading*, XI (November 1967), pp. 111-121.

O'Connor, J. R. "What Skills Do Reading Tests Measure?" *High Points* (Spring 1967), pp. 23-25.

Schiffman, G. B. "Total Language Arts Commitment: Kindergarten Through Twelfth Grade," *Reading Teacher*, XXII (November 1968), pp. 115-121.

Sodes, D., and J. E. Terrell. "Communication Skills Projects: A Community Action Program," *Claremont Reading Conference Yearbook*, XXXI (1967), pp. 156-158.

Weidig, P. D. "Reading Teacher Extends Her Role," *Instructor*, LXXVII (February 1968), p. 86.

REQUIRED READINGS FROM BOOK OF READINGS

II. Organization and Administration of Secondary School Reading Programs
Developmental Reading in Junior High School—U. Berkley Ellis.
Reading and Study Skills Program—Sally Berkey and Irwin H. Fields.
The Reading Laboratory—Ralph P. Sherlock.

IV. The Evaluation of Reading
The Role of Testing in Reading Instruction—Frederick B. Davis.
Some Pitfalls in Evaluating Progress in Reading Instruction—Arthur S. McDonald.
Assigning Grades to Students in Special Reading Classes—Albert J. Kingston.

chapter 3

Comprehension Skills
in Reading

In the summer 1959 issue of the *Harvard Educational Review* William G. Perry reported a study of 1,500 Harvard and Radcliffe freshmen and their approaches to reading a chapter from a history book. Among his findings were the following:

1. Over 90 percent of the students stated that they had simply started at the beginning and read straight ahead.
2. The students' ability to answer a multiple-choice test on details was excellent.
3. Only 150 of the students made any claim to having used the author's marginal glosses or to having looked ahead and read the summary at the end of the chapter.
4. Only 1 percent of the total group was able to write a short statement about what the chapter covered.

Perry concluded "... After twelve years of reading homework assignments in school, they had all settled into the habit of leaving the point of it all to someone else. ..."

The results of the Perry study should indicate at least two things to educators. First, it should raise the question that if some of the finest readers in the country are this purposeless in their reading, what are junior and senior high students doing? Secondly, it might be argued that secondary school teachers aren't doing a very effective job of teaching students certain important comprehension skills involved in making effective use of a textbook.

DIFFICULTIES PRESENTED BY TEXTBOOKS

The primary purpose for reading in the content areas is to get information from the printed page. In order to get information, the student must be able to bring some meaning to the material so that he will be able to see the similarities between what he knows and what he reads in the book. He must also be able to generalize or evolve principles from his past experience in relationship to the new. These tasks are not easy, and are not uniformly distributed either within individual students or among students. The processes which are involved in concept formation cannot be inferred from mental age or vocabulary, but rather from the cumulative experiences of the individual that have had meaning for him.

The "loading" of concepts found in a single paragraph of most subject-matter textbooks may be so difficult in their complexity that little more than a very general type of understanding is impossible. As an example, the following paragraph has been broken into concepts by diagonal lines (/).

The surface/ of the sun/ is a turbulent mass/ of hot gases/ with a temperature/ of about 10,000°F. Tremendous explosions/ take place on the surface/ which send great bubbles of gas/ miles up/ to form sunspots./ These explosions/ may also cause gigantic bursts of gases/ known as prominences./ The smallest prominence/ is called a spicule./ They rise/ to only a few thousand miles/ above the surface/ of the sun and last for only about five minutes./ Some of the larger prominences/ shoot upward/ for half a million miles/ into the atmosphere/ with what appears to be pulsating shock waves./ Many prominences last for hours/ before they sink back/ to the surface or shoot off into space./

Without an adequate background of information and concepts, how many students would have an idea of what a "turbulent mass of hot gases" really is, or how many would have a concept of million of miles or thousands of miles? The number of types of concepts involved in this one paragraph should make one aware of the problems students face with the textbooks they use each day.

Some of the vocabulary may also cause a problem because words with commonly known meanings may be used in a way unknown to the reader. For example, a student may view "great bubbles of gas" as being something like the bubbles on the Lawrence Welk Show or those from a glass of ginger ale. The "sunspots" also may create images and ideas quite different from those intended.

The textbook is not an easy tool to use. If it is to be used effectively, the student must know its strengths and weaknesses, as well as how to use it to full advantage. Most students do not acquire the skills of using a textbook by themselves. The teacher must help. It is the teacher's job to be aware of the possible problems that will arise in textbook use and employ every means, insight, experience, and teaching skill to facilitate the learning process with a minimum of confusion.

EVALUATING STUDENTS ABILITIES TO READ TEXTBOOKS

A textbook can and certainly should be used in a variety of ways. It can be used to provide information for a student or to reinforce material already learned. A text can usually go into more detail than class discussion may permit such as giving concrete and specific examples to illustrate a concept. Another valid use of a textbook is to provide a common background of information from which a teacher can develop lessons.

In making use of a textbook for whatever reason, a teacher must be aware of several factors. Perhaps most fundamental of all is the fact that there is absolutely no sense in asking a student to read from a text in which a teacher knows the student is incapable of pronouncing the words or understanding the material. Yet it is not unusual to find several divisions of a class using the same text, even though the sections are grouped according to ability.

Forcing a student to read a textbook which *we* know he cannot read and *he* knows he cannot read is certainly doing nothing to develop the skills and abilities that we profess to be teaching. A lack of reading ability and the frustrations that accompany this lack are often contributory causes to school dropout.

The first thing that teachers should do in their classrooms at the beginning of the school year is to find those students who can make use of the textbook and those who cannot. One of the ways this can be done is to take a typical selection from the text to be used in a class. A selection of 250 - 300 words should be adequate. The student will read this material silently.

The teacher should prepare questions that check factual recall and the students' attention to relationships and associations they should be making as they read. As an example, two sets of questions are given here, following a selection from *Living World History*, by T. Walter Wallbank and Arnold Fletcher.

England's New Liberty Confirmed

Charles II was called the "Merry Monarch." He was quite willing to let his subjects have a good time. And after the gloomy days of the Puritans, the English people were ready for fun. They went as far in the direction of amusement as the Puritans had gone in the direction of gloom. The period is called "the Restoration."

Charles was really a crafty and clever king, although he pretended to be interested only in a good time. He had both brains and common sense, and was quite a wit. Actually he hoped to restore the Roman Catholic religion and royal power. But some people suspected his plans. The old issues of religion and royal despotism were emerging once more.

This controversy led to the formation of modern political parties. The *Whig Party* supported Parliament, while the *Tory Party* stood for the power of the king. For the first time in modern history, parties took part in political campaigns, had slogans and party machinery. In the contest that followed, the Whig Party was defeated. Although Charles II sensed the danger of pushing his power too far and so governed with moderation, he was quietly increasing his authority. When he died in 1685, the liberties fought for in the Puritan Revolution were again in danger. Everything depended on the next king.

Fortunately for English liberty, the next king was as stupid as Charles II had been clever. He was James II, brother of Charles, an ardent Roman Catholic and believer in divine right. Soon the nation was alarmed by his open contempt for Parliament and his support of the Church of Rome. In the face of this threat, the Whigs and Tories forgot their differences and joined in a revolution. Mary, the Protestant daughter of James, and her husband, William, the ruler of Holland and foremost statesman of Europe, were invited to accept the English throne. There was no fighting; William and Mary landed in England in November 1688, and James II fled to France. The threat of tyranny had been removed by what the English call their "Glorious Revolution."*

Factual Recall Questions

1. Why was Charles II called the "Merry Monarch"?
2. What two political parties were formed?
3. Who became king after Charles II?
4. What was the revolution called in which William and Mary became rulers of England?

Interpretation Questions

1. Why was the period in which Charles II reigned called "the Restoration"? What was he restoring?
2. The Tories and Whigs joined each other to dethrone James II. Can you name two modern-day groups that joined together for a common purpose and tell why?
3. Why should the Parliament be upset that James II supported the Church of Rome?

If a teacher wants further information about the student's understanding, she may wish to check on his ability to understand words presented in context. This can be done by presenting several sentences from the selection and asking the students to rewrite the sentence using a synonym or phrase for the word(s) in italics:

1. The old issues of religious and royal *despotism* were emerging once more.
2. Although Charles II sensed the danger of pushing his power too far and so governed with *moderation*, he was quietly increasing his authority.
3. He was James II, brother of Charles, an ardent Roman Catholic and believer in *divine right*.
4. The threat of *tyranny* had been removed by what the English called their "Glorious Revolution."

*From T. Walter Wallbank and Arnold Fletcher, *Living World History* (Glenview, Ill.: Scott, Foresman and Company, 1958), p. 374. Copyright © 1958 by Scott, Foresman and Company.

After this evaluation has been done, the teacher may wish to investigate further those students who did poorly on the silent reading. Those few students who would fall into this category can be asked to read orally from the material immediately following the portion used for silent reading. If a student hesitates over a word for more than five seconds; fails to pronounce, mispronounces, or miscalls five or more words per 100 words (other than proper names), the material is too hard for him. It is impossible to comprehend material in which new ideas and concepts are developed if the words by which these are developed are stumbling blocks in themselves.

In almost every classroom there will be a few students who will be unable to read the textbook. It is the job of the teacher to find material which these students can read. Regardless of the level or subject matter, teachers should all be involved in the development of the skills necessary to learn. If the students are to learn not only how to read but the content or subject matter itself, they must have the required skills and materials.

If students are incapable of reading the text material, there are several possible solutions. Library books or other textbooks that contain the same information but which are written at a less difficult level can be used. Another solution is to have the textbook material read orally to the students. However, this is not a very satisfactory solution since students are only given information without being helped to develop independence in acquiring information through their own skills. The best solution is to provide them with materials they can read. The school librarian should be able to help in the selection of reading material at appropriate levels.

SELECTION AND USE OF A TEXTBOOK

Teachers who have a hand in selecting textbooks as well as students who are asked to use them should be aware of the characteristics and organization of such books. The outline that follows can be used by teachers as a guide in textbook selection, or can form the basis for a series of lessons to help students make maximum use of the textbooks chosen.

I. Readiness
   A. How is the book written?
   B. How can one discover the author's plan of organization?

II. Parts of the book
   A. Where can we find out about the author?
   B. Where can we obtain the "point of view" of the author? (Preface)
   C. Where can we obtain the author's overall plan? (Table of Contents)
   D. How is the book divided into parts or divisions?
   E. Where can we find out about specific subjects in the text? (Index)
   F. Where can the pronunciation of a word be found? (Glossary)

III. Individual characteristics of the texts (Questions here will vary to fit partic-
ular texts.)
- A. Does the author have an introduction to the parts or chapters?
- B. Does the author summarize at the end of each part, section, or chapter?
- C. What purposes do the headings serve? Are there different kinds of head-
ings? Where are they located and which are most important?
- D. Are there questions at the end of the chapter?

IV. Other considerations
- A. What signals does the author use?
- B. What is the value of the charts, diagrams, pictures, and graphs?
- C. How extensive is the new vocabulary, and is it introduced at the begin-
ning of each chapter or unit?

Students can also be helped to make more effective use of their textbooks
by being shown a systematic approach to textbook study. One of the approaches
most often used is the "SQ3R method" developed by F. P. Robinson (1941).
The five steps in the method are detailed below.

1. *Survey*. Much can be learned by looking through the entire assignment
to get a broad overview. The title should be read first and then the introductory
materials, if any. Then the student should thumb through the selection, noting
the main headings, subheadings, pictures, maps, and charts. This should provide
hints of the content of the lesson as well as indicate the general organization of
the material. Finally, in this first step, the summary should be read, and any
other aids at the end of the chapter should be given a quick glance.

2. *Questions*. As the student surveys the assignment, he should try to get
the key ideas by reading the title and section headings and by looking at the
pictures. A sure way to become involved with the author's ideas is to change the
headings and/or topic sentences into meaningful questions.

Headings such as "The English Stage a Revolution" tell the student what
the author is writing about, while the subheadings "James raises an important
issue," "Charles complicates the quarrel," "Civil War breaks out in England," tell
not only the sequence of events but also what is going to be discussed.

In the following paragraph (Wallbank and Fletcher, 1958), the topic sentence can be converted into the question. "What did James I do that showed he
didn't understand his subjects?"

> James I did not understand his new subjects very well. He had much book
> learning, but little common sense. Called the wisest fool in Christendom,
> he believed strongly in the "divine right" of kings and expected the
> English to believe in it, too. He told his subjects that "the State of Mon-
> archy is the supremest thing upon the earth." Kings, like gods, he thought
> "may make and unmake their subjects . . . are judges . . . in all cases and
> yet accountable to none but God only." This did not impress the English.
> After all, they had forced a king to sign an agreement to respect the laws

of the land over four hundred years before. So, as you might guess, James often quarreled with Parliament.*

3. *Read*. The third step is to read the lesson. If steps 1 and 2 have been done well, the student will find himself reading the material rapidly and with specific purposes and questions in mind. He should not try to read each word, but should concentrate on getting the main idea and the primary facts that support the idea. The student should not try to memorize at this point.

As an aid for review later, the student should be encouraged to make notes. This can be done effectively on one side of a 3 X 5-in. card, listing the important supporting details on the opposite side. This procedure should be followed on one section at a time and only after the entire section has been read. It is impossible for the student to write down the details as he reads because he really can't make a valid judgment of those details that are of primary importance and those of secondary importance until the whole section has been read.

4. *Recall*. Using the questions on the 3 X 5-in. card, the student should try to recall the important supporting facts for each of the sections read. This should be done immediately after the entire assignment is read. If the student is unable to answer one of his questions, he should turn the card over and look at his notes or refer back to the book.

5. *Review*. Before the next class meeting and certainly before a test, the student should study his cards. If steps 1 - 4 have been done faithfully, the student will be able to review the assignments quickly and effectively.

IMPROVING READING SKILLS THROUGH THE ASSIGNMENT

Scene: A typical high school classroom. A bell rings, signaling the end of the period.

Teacher: Before you go, your assignment is to read the next chapter in your text. Tomorrow, when you come in, we'll talk about it.
Bob: What did he say?
Fred: Read the next chapter.
Bob: Oh.

Unfortunately this scene is not too unfamiliar; in many cases it is the rule rather than the exception. When assignments are given as the teacher in the example did, the textbook is not being used effectively. Reading problems are being created in some cases where they have not existed previously.

Subject-matter teachers can help to solve their students' reading and study

*Wallbank and Fletcher, *ibid*., p. 370.

difficulties by giving thought to the assignments they make. A good assignment tells the students three things:

1. What he is to do. (Content)
2. Why he is to do it. (Motivation)
3. How he is to do it. (Skills)

Content. In helping the student to decide what he is to do for the assignment, it is important that the teacher indicate exactly the purpose for the reading. For example, the teacher may want the student to read and to compare two events, react to the material, find factual information, interpret, generalize, or draw a conclusion. There are many purposes the teacher may have in mind, but unless the student is told what he is to get from the material he cannot be expected to read with understanding. Students are not mind readers.

If a student is asked to read in order to compare events that led up to two different revolutions, he is being required to do a type of reading that is going to take some time. If on the other hand he is asked to read in order to find the answer to some factual information questions, he should be able to read more rapidly. In too many cases teachers do not take into consideration the type of assignments given and the various demands made upon the student's time and his ability to use the skills required.

Every teacher knows how rewarding it is to have an assignment completed by a group so that the next day is a wonderful teaching experience, because the students had obviously read the material and the discussions were lively and informative. At the end of such a day, the teacher hopefully gives another assignment expecting the same results, but the following day is a complete loss. At this point the teacher should stop and ask, "Did I ask the same type of questions the second day as I did the first? Perhaps the inability to answer the questions was not the students' fault but mine." The students may have read the same way both days but the teacher did not ask the same kind of questions. Without knowing the teacher's purpose in having them read the material, perhaps all the students did was *read*. If demands for mastery of content material are to be made to students then *it is vitally important that they be informed as to what they are expected to produce.*

Motivation. In making any assignment it is important that the teacher show the students how the assignment relates to the larger objectives of the ongoing work, how it connects with what he has gone on before, and how it will prepare for what is to follow. It is generally felt by reading educators that two of the most important factors in comprehension are the ability to organize and the ability to make associations as one reads. It is the job of the teacher to help the student to develop these abilities by demonstrating whenever possible the *usefulness* of what he is to do. "Usefulness" should be thought of in a broad sense to include such matters as pleasure in reading a play or novel or the importance of some piece of historical information to the understanding of a current problem.

Skills. The teacher should let the students know how *thoroughly* they should read or study by indicating clearly what kind of recall is expected of them. The following are some types of recall of which the teacher should be aware:

1. Thorough recall—remembering the important facts without aid.
2. Recalling only the main points.
3. Reading to recall points connected with only certain topics.
4. Aided recall that is adequate for true-false or multiple-choice quiz.
5. Recall accompanied by inference or critical thinking in order to partici-pate in class discussions.

Many of the students will need help with the techniques they should use to study and read for various kinds of questions. The teacher should not expect the same level of ability in using the skills in reading from all of the students. In many instances the teacher should not only indicate the skills to be used but should also give some help with their use. New or difficult skills should always be demonstrated by doing part of the assignment with the students.

WORD-MEANING PRINCIPLES

Vocabulary is highly related to comprehension. In order to comprehend, the student must be able to bring an extensive knowledge of word meanings to the printed page. From his many experiences with word meanings he must be able to select and apply the appropriate meaning to fit the context of the material.

Although more specific plans for developing students' reading vocabularies are discussed in another chapter, it is appropriate here to present certain general principles which should guide the content-subject teacher in the development of vocabulary:

1. The new vocabulary load is greatest at the beginning of a text.
2. Students in the secondary schools are exposed to more new vocabulary words in content areas than they would be expected to learn if they were taking a foreign language.
3. Depth of understanding is more important than quantity with little understanding.
4. Most words have more than one meaning.
5. The specific word meaning is a function of the context in which the word appears.
6. The number of meanings a student has for a word depends upon the quantity and quality of previous associations with the word.
7. People think and communicate with each other primarily through words.

READING FOR THE MAIN IDEA

The ability to identify the main idea is basic to understanding and interpreting material. Without this ability it is impossible to outline, to see the relationship of details to the whole, and to comprehend accurately.

The teacher can help his students by guiding them through the following procedure:

1. Read the first sentence of the paragraph carefully. In the majority of cases, it does contain the main idea.
2. If this is the topic sentence of the paragraph, decide what the paragraph is going to be about.
3. See if the rest of the paragraph bears on this topic by skimming for ideas and words.
4. If it does bear on the topic, then it is the topic sentence. Put the idea into your own words.
5. If the first sentence does not contain the main idea, see if you can determine what the author is trying to say.
6. See if you can find a phrase or sentence that expresses this idea. The topic sentence may be found near the beginning, in the middle, or at the end.
7. If the topic sentence cannot be found, try to find a few key words or phrases. Put these together to see what they say. You will probably have to make your own topic sentence.

In the development of this skill, the following exercises listed in order of difficulty, may be helpful for students.

1. Have students read a short selection and select the best title from several given.
2. Have students read a short selection and give it a title.
3. (a) Take a short paragraph from the text and put each sentence on a strip of construction paper large enough to be seen by the class.
   (b) The strips should be put on a corkboard in mixed order. Ask the students to arrange them into a well-organized unit.
   (c) Ask the students to find the topic sentence and then discuss with them why they preferred one organization over another.
   (d) Look in the textbook and find how the author originally wrote the paragraph. Discuss why the author might have used his organization rather than another.
4. (a) Select several other paragraphs from the text and put them on a Ditto sheet in a mixed order. Cut the sentences into strips.
   (b) In groups of three or four, have the students organize them into paragraphs.
   (c) Have each group read their organization and discuss the variations from group to group.
   (d) Check the paragraphs in the book to see how they are written.
5. Give the students practice in writing topic sentences for paragraphs.
6. Help the students make direct applications in the textbooks they are using.

Using geometric shapes in helping the students to visualize the topic sentence placement can be extremely effective. The following are examples of the five locations in which topic sentences may be found and the geometric shape that explains the placement:

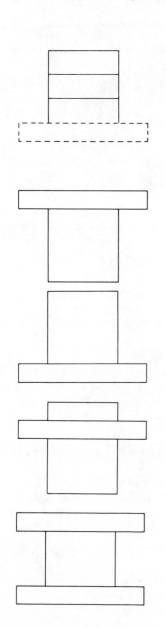

An important part of dental care is a regular checkup with your dentist. It is also very important to regulate the amount of high-sugar foods that you eat. Finally, as they say on television, brush after every meal.

(This paragraph contains no topic sentence. All details point to one main topic, which is unexpressed. The students can write a topic sentence for this type of paragraph.)

The early settler's diet consisted mainly of wild game. The New England woods abounded with deer and all varieties of wild birds. Many times, the colonist's tables bore squirrel and raccoon, as well.

We have found excellent performance and high gasoline mileage with our car. The finish is of excellent quality and just sparkles without a waxing. *As far as we are concerned, our 1932 Buzzard is the best automobile on the road.*

We have found one fact to be very true. *Being "owned" by a Siamese cat is a wonderful thing.* They're loving and independent; clean and playful; and insist on sleeping in your lap when you're trying to read a newspaper.

A political convention can be very confusing. All of the lights, signs, balloons and noise make one wonder what is going on. One thing is certain however. *It is the truly democratic way of selecting the "Peoples Choice."*

READING FOR DETAILS

Reading for details is an essential skill in the reading of any content subject.
Without the knowledge of the important details, there can be no real understanding of the main idea. Details are the foundation of the main idea, the
backbone; they give support to the main idea. For example, the key sentence
might be, "The American Revolution now changed into a worldwide conflict."
This statement, by itself, tells very little. The remainder of the sentences in the
paragraph give the details which support the statement.

It is helpful to learn how to recognize details that support the main idea
quickly and efficiently. The following are some of the reading skills, listed in
gradation of difficulty, that would be helpful to students. These are the ability
to use:

1. Guide words or signal words. The authors provide many clues to the
   number of details by writing "first, second, or third"; or by using the
   numbers (1), (2), (3), or the letters (a), (b), (c). Other signal words and
   phrases to meaning often used are *therefore, because, but, however,
   besides, as a result, generally*.
2. Details that list specific facts, a sequence of events, or important facts
   that support.
3. Details that explain or support a topic sentence that is a generalization
   or a conclusion.
4. Details that give examples or illustrations to support the main idea.
5. Details that contain subtopics.
6. Details that have little value or no value and should be discarded.
7. Main ideas which anticipate the details.
8. Unrelated details in a poorly organized paragraph.

A good reader comprehends the organization of what he reads and thinks
in a pattern that will help him to remember. He sees relationships between the
main idea and the details in the paragraph and the paragraphs in the larger unit.
He uses his information from many sources to help him draw conclusions and
make adequate summaries.

There are many activities that help students to learn how to organize what
they read. The following are some suggestions.

1. Have students group objects according to categories.
2. Have students list events or people under headings, such as history,
   mathematics, science, or English.
3. Have students organize ideas to show how they are related to each
   other by placing the topic sentence over to the left on a page with the
   other sentences under it.
4. Have students select from a list of sentences those likely to be topic
   sentences and those that are sentences containing details.
5. Have students make a topic sentence for a group of ideas after seeing
   how they are related.

It is also vitally important that the students see the author's plan of organization for a chapter, unit, or paragraph. Some of the most common organizational schemes are

1. *Organization according to time sequence.* This organization is probably most common in the study of history.
2. *Organization according to contrast.* In a history or a science text there are often found paragraphs contrasting events in two locations, forms of government, or the like. This organization is also found frequently in biology texts or other scientific works.
3. *Organization on a cause-and-effect basis.* This type of organization is found in all of our reading and deserves consideration in every area.
4. *Organization according to a main idea with supporting details.* Although this general pattern may apply to all of the previous patterns (1) through (3) are probably obvious to the reader and should be thought of in these organizations for ease of studying and understanding. This pattern (4) might be further broken down into opinion-reason, conclusion- proof, or question-answer.

OUTLINING

Outlining is another way of organizing information. But it is impossible to outline without an understanding of organization and the relationship of details to a main idea. There are many students who find outlining an exercise in frustration and confusion because they don't see its purpose and don't know what they are doing, or why.

If the material is organized with the topic sentence clearly stated first and the supporting details following, the majority of students will have few problems. The problems begin to arise when the students find variations from the "lead-topic-sentence" organization. If the student reads material in which the topic sentence appears anywhere but at the beginning, he will have to reorganize the paragraph in his mind to fit the outline form. Unless the student *has* a firm grasp of the skills of organization he will such mental restructuring an impossible task.

Many of the problems students have with reading skills are the result of lack of information. A student cannot be given poorly organized or difficult paragraphs and be expected automatically to make a good outline. Initially, exercises should include simple, well-organized paragraphs that can be outlined easily and which follow a logical pattern of thought.

Teaching students to outline might include the following plan of exercises:
1. Teach reading for details and organization *first*.
2. Help students to select various details from a paragraph and write them into an already prepared outline. Example: I. ? ? ?
   A. (Detail supplied)
   B. (Detail supplied)

Example: I. (Supplied)
    A. ? ? ?
    B. ? ? ?
3. Give students a skeleton outline with a selection and have them fill in all the parts.
4. Assign students to make their own outlines from a paragraph.
5. Have students recast an outline on a different basis of organization.

EXAMPLES OF TEACHING PLANS

The following detailed teaching plans on the introduction of a textbook, organizational skills, main idea, outlining and reading maps are presented to aid you in seeing how these skills could be taught through a content area. These plans represent a sample of the type of things that could be done in using the textbook *History of Our United States* by Eibling, King, and Harlow (River Forest, Ill.: Laidlaw Brothers, 1965).

LESSON I. INTRODUCE TEXTBOOK

Purpose: To give students an opportunity to get acquainted with textbook. To assist students in recognizing aids to study in their text and in how these may be used.

Method: Class discussion, work sheet for follow up activity.

Procedure: 1. Pass out textbooks. Give students an opportunity to look through textbooks. As they look through the books ask them to see how many parts of the text they can find that will help throughout the year in using this as a basic reference. Also look for parts of the text which should be used throughout the year.
2. After the students have looked through the textbooks, ask them to name the parts of the text that should help them in using the text. As these are mentioned, they should be listed on the board. The following should be mentioned in class discussion, elicited by questioning on the part of the teacher, or added by the teacher.
    A. Title page
    B. Copyright page
    C. Table of Contents
    D. Table of "Maps for You to Use"
    E. Dictionary of Historical terms—Pronunciation Key
    F. Index
    G. Charts
3. After these have been listed on the board, take each in turn, have pupils turn to the part under discussion and ask pupils what

information is found on each page or in each section. As each aid is discussed, be sure that pupils recognize the following. These may be expanded upon, depending upon the class and their response.

A. Title page
  1. Title means name of book—usually printed in large or distinctive type.
  2. Authors—the information listed about each author gives an idea of their qualifications.
  3. Publishers—the company who publishes the book.
  4. Edition—in the case of this text it is the second edition so this book has been published before. Probably it has been revised and brought up to date since the first edition.

B. Copyright page
  1. Location—usually back of title page; may be included at times on the title page.
  2. Copyright
     (a) Tells who owns the material in the book and protects the owner of the material, as no one can reproduce the material in any form without permission.
     (b) Date—tells when the copyright was issued.
     (c) To obtain the copyright, two copies of the material are sent to the Library of Congress in Washington.
     (d) Everytime the material is substantially changed a new copyright date is given.
  3. May include acknowledgments telling who made drawings, historical cartoons, where the sources of photographs and charts are acknowledged, who drew the maps, who read or proofread the scripts.

C. Table of Contents, pp. 5 - 7.
  1. Give authors' plan for book.
     (a) How many units—main parts
     (b) How many chapters—gives headings
     (c) Page number for the beginning of each unit and chapter
  2. Include listing of special sections with page on which each begins.
  3. Unit titles and chapter titles get name from main idea of each section. Give clue as to what to expect.
  4. Topics appear in the order in which they are in the text.
  5. Provide quick way to get overview of topics covered in this particular book—helps you decide if it includes information which you want.

D. List of Maps, p. 8.
  1. Maps appear in this list in order found in text.
  2. Title gives some idea of what to expect on the map.

3. Will find many different types of maps.
4. Have pupils turn to the following pages to see samples of the different kinds of maps: p. 31, elevation and rainfall; p. 82, original colonies, outlines; p. 281, early roads; pp. 226 - 227, how the United States has grown; p. 218, products map.

E. Index
1. Alphabetical listing of topics with pages on which each is found.
2. Found at back of textbook.
3. Explanation given at top of the first page as to the meaning of abbreviations used in the index.
4. Helps you find quickly information on a specific topic.
5. As a class look at the following topics in the index and discuss as to the specific information given.
   (a) *Oregon Trail:* lists pages on which find information; also gives two abbreviations.
       (1) *Ill. 308*—have pupils turn to p. 308, where they find an illustration.
       (2) m. 307: turn to p. 307, find a map showing trails west, including the Oregon Trail.
   (b) *George Washington as president:* have to look under Washington—find sub-topics with pages Example: as Pres. p. 203, 204, 221
   (c) *Arapaho Indians:* find parentheses around pronunciation. Here could have pupils refer to pronunciation key on page 643. For pupils appearing to have little knowledge of use of this key, a lesson could be presented later to those specific pupils.
   (d) *Friends Society:* find these words, " *see Quakers.*" This is a cross reference, means to look under the topic listed (it is a synonym). Sometimes the text will not give a cross reference; you will have to think of a synonym and look for it.
   (e) *Morse code:* look on p. 380 to see what *cart* stands for (cartoon).
   (f) *National forests:* see p. 434 to see what *c* stands for (chart).
   (g) *Battles:* tells you to "see battles" so look by name.
   (h) *Atomic energy:* after listing, says *"see also,"* meaning to look for more information under the topics listed after *see also.*

F. Dictionary of Historical terms, p. 643
1. Alphabetical—just like a dictionary.
2. Includes words found in book and events referred to in

books—many are found in dictionary but not defined in relationship to history.

3. Examples:
   (a) Look up *stock*. Is this the only meaning it has? May compare this with definition in a dictionary. Why is this the one included here?
   (b) Look up *Western movement*. Would you find this in a dictionary? Why? What would you find?

G. Charts, pp. 639 - 642

1. Look at each and discuss how headings are used and how to read each.
2. Discuss the following questions and help students see how to locate the answer to each question.
   (a) What year did Georgia enter the union?
   (b) How many territories and possessions does the U. S. have?
   (c) What is the capital city of Florida?
   (d) Who was Dwight D. Eisenhower's Vice-President?
   (e) How many representatives does Georgia have? (I do not ask questions about electoral votes until this has been studied in class.)

Probably these lessons would cover at least two days, maybe more, especially with slower classes. Divide the discussion of specific parts up covering A - D on one day and E - G on the second.

For the slower students, give more sample exercises in class and in some cases would go over the entire worksheet with the students working as we discussed it. With average and above average classes, have them do these on their own, then later discuss the findings in class.

For above average students, have samples of other texts on the same topic and have them compare these as to each part of the outline and especially as to contents to see the difference in the topics and order used.

Following is a worksheet sheet suggested for use after having discussed the above information in class.

Worksheet. Lesson I

1. Which of the three authors would you think was responsible for being sure the historical facts were accurate? Why?
2. To which of the publishers offices would we write if we wanted more information on the text? Why?
3. What was the copyright given for this book?

Method: Class discussion, group participation in class, individual work
Procedure: 1. Look at introductory page of Unit I.
         A. What is the title of Unit I?

    B. What do you expect this unit to be about from what is listed on this page?

    C. How many chapters are in this unit?

    D. What are their titles?

    E. How do you expect these two chapters to be different?

2. Read the paragraph at the bottom of the introductory page. Discuss why a torch was used. What is the correct title of the statue? What do we usually call it? What do you think *oppressed* means? What gives a clue to its meaning?

3. Show that the subtitles of the chapter are given at the top of the first page of the chapter.

4. Show how the subtitles of the chapter are printed in all capital letters with a number before them. Subtopics under the subtitles are printed in heavy print.

5. (a) Have the class look at the pictures in the first section of the chapter. (1. Our Freedoms Have Endured.) Read the sentences under these. Look at the end of the chapter. You may want to read the questions at the end under "Reviewing Chapter I." These may help give an idea of the important topics to look for in the chapter. Also look at the list of words "What Do They Mean?" (It is assumed here that time has been spent in vocabulary development before this activity.)

    (b) Have the class preview part 1 of the chapter by looking at the subtopics. Can you see how the subtopics are related to the subtitle? Yes, the subtopics under part 1 seem to name the freedoms that have endured. The first section "sets the stage" by describing the "climate" for freedom.

    (c) What do you think a "climate for freedom" is? Read this first section to see what this climate is.

    (d) Does "climate" in this section have the same meaning that climate has when we talk of weather? How is it different? How is it similar? What made the "climate for freedom?"

    (e) Each of the following subtopics in the chapter describe the basic freedoms of our country. Suppose you make each subtopic into a question.

6. Who drew the historical cartoons?

7. The text contains ___ units and ___ chapters.

8. To what page would you turn to read the chapter "Passing of the Frontier?"

9. What is the title of the chapter in which you would expect to find information on the settling of our first colonies in America?

10. On what page would you find a copy of the Declaration of Independence?

11. On what page would you find maps showing railroads?

12. To what page would you turn to see a map with the location of the first colonies in America?

13. To what pages would you turn to compare the size of the United States in 1783 with its size in 1853?

14. To what page would you turn to find an illustration of President John F. Kennedy?

15. To what page would you turn to find a map of the Santa Fe Trail?

16. What two aids could you use to help you find the map of the Santa Fe Trail?

17. To what other topics would you look in the index to find additional information on atomic energy?

18. What does the letter *c* mean before a page number in the index?

19. What two aids could help you find the pronunciation of certain words?

20. Which two aids in the text are in alphabetical order?

21. How many states entered the union before Ohio?

LESSON II. ORGANIZATION

A. Suggested Means of Study—Main Idea Organization

Purpose: To help students note organization of material.

To guide students in one method of study.

To help students become aware of study aids included in text.

For example: What is the right to know?

What is freedom of speech?

What is the right to petition?

What is freedom of the press?

(Write these on the board.) As you read each subtopic listed, read with the specific question in mind and see if you can find an answer to each as you read. As you finish each section, see how you would answer the question for that section and how much you recall of what you read in that section. Then go on to the next.

(f) When the students have finished the above part, go back to each question on the board and have students share what they found in answer to each question.

(g) Explain that what they have done is similar to a study method which some people call SQ3R. You have surveyed the chapter. You have raised questions about the subtopics, read the subtopic areas, then recite to yourself what

you read. Then we reviewed together by seeing what you
remembered of each subtopic. This material was organized
in a main idea form of organization and when material is
organized in this way you can use this means to help you
study.

(h) Assign the last four subtopics (pp. 16 - 20) and suggest that
students use the same means for study individually, then
discuss in class how this seemed to work or not work for
them. Check comprehension by oral or written questions.

B. Time-Sequence Organization

Purpose: To help students recognize time-sequence organization and how to
follow such organization.

Method: Class lecture, class discussion, independent work.

Procedure: 1. We have looked at one type of organization which our textbook
uses, that of main-idea organization. One of the most common
kinds of organization we can expect to find in history is time-
sequence organization. Why would you expect this to be true?
Let them discuss: "Yes, history relates events from the past and
often the dates when these events occurred are of importance in
understanding later events or are useful to know in summarizing
or reviewing."

2. The English colonies were settled in a period of 125 years and
were made all along the East Coast. The first section of this
assignment told why the English came to America and the types
of colonies which were established.

3. Beginning of page 69 with "The First Colony—Virginia" you
find each colony discussed and with each the date when it was
settled, is included. Glance over pages 69 - 81. Look only for
dates, not at the words. Try to get an idea of what years are
covered.

4. When they finish, discuss the dates they noted. As they recall
dates they remember, list on the board. The dates go from 1607
to 1764. Many times you find 1610, 1619, 1620. There are few
dates in the 1700's listed.

5. Now read the same section, noting especially the name of the
colony and the date when it was settled. When you finish, I'll
ask you to fit the colonies into a *time line* which you can use to
review and to organize the information as you study.

Time-Line Exercise

A time line is a chart of dates with important or key words placed by these
dates to help us remember when events happened and see them in relation to
one another.

Place the colonies listed at the right into the correct location on the time line to show when each was settled

1607

1620

1623
1624

1630

1633   Connecticut
1634   Delaware
                                        Georgia
1636   Maryland
                                        Massachusetts
1638   New Hampshire
                                        New Jersey
                                        New York
1650   North Carolina
                                        Pennsylvania
1653   Rhode Island
                                        South Carolina
                                        Virginia

1670

1682

1700

1733

LESSON III. ORGANIZATION, MAIN IDEAS, OUTLINING

A. Topic Sentence

Purpose: To aid students in recognizing of paragraphs, specifically to recognize the topic sentence.

Method: Class discussion, class participation, small group work

Procedure: 1. Have the following paragraph printed on cards with one sentence
                 on each card. Have these mixed up and have the students suggest
                 the order in which they think they belong. Compare with the
                 actual paragraph in the text. Observe that it could be arranged in
                 any of several different patterns and still make sense. Notice that
                 one sentence in the paragraph gives the main idea or topic and
                 the rest of the sentences add to this. This sentence is the *topic
                 sentence.* Sometimes it may come at the beginning, the end, the
                 middle or in other places.
                 (From page 48, *History of Our United States*)

                      The people of Spain gave the returning explorers a won-
                 derful welcome. The king and queen invited Columbus to sit
                 beside them and tell them about his experiences. Columbus was
                 given a title and other honors. He displayed the Indians and
                 other things he had brought from across the seas. His backers
                 agreed that he should make another voyage at once to look for
                 gold, silver, and spices.

              2. Look together as a class at paragraphs in a portion of Chapter
                 three and discuss where the topic sentence is in each. When you
                 feel that the class has an understanding of what they are looking
                 for, give out the following sheet of sample paragraphs and ask
                 the students in groups of three or four to determine where the
                 topic sentence is in each. Then discuss in class together.

              3. Assign a small portion of the chapter to be studied for home-
                 work and ask students to look for the topic sentence in each
                 paragraph as they read.

Lessons A and B

1. Of great importance to seamen in navigation was the invention of the
   astrolabe and the magnetic compass. The astrolabe was a circular instrument with sights. With it a seaman could learn the latitude of his
   position by measuring the angle between the horizon and a heavenly
   body, such as the sun or the North Star. The compass enabled a seaman
   to steer in one direction and thus keep on his course. Such instruments
   took much of the guesswork out of sailing unknown seas, and sailors
   were more willing to sail beyond the sight of land. General use of these
   instruments led to more precise geographical knowledge and to more
   accurate mapmaking. (p. 44, *History of Our United States.*)

2. About the time that Columbus made his last voyage, a letter printed in
   Europe contained the claim of a merchant from Florence that he had
   made four voyages to the New World. The writer, Americus Vespucius,
   said that on the first voyage, in 1497, he helped to explore the coast of
   a new continent (South America). Word of this claim came to a German geography teacher named Waldseemüller. When he issued a new
   geography, Waldseemüller put in it a map which showed the islands
   explored by Columbus. South of these he indicated a new continent,
   which he named America. The name was accepted and was later used

for both the northern and southern continents. Thus Columbus lost the honor of having the New World named after him. (p. 49, *History of Our United States*.)

3. Adventurous young men sailed out from these bases to other islands and to the mainland. Traveling in boats, they explored the land along the waterways. On horseback and afoot they pushed through the tangled tropical forests, hunting for gold, spices, and other treasure. As they explored, the Spaniards listed on their maps the mountains, streams, and villages they found. Their achievements were costly, however, for many died of starvation, fever, and the wounds made by poisoned Indian arrows. (p. 50, *History of Our United States*.)

4. Ten years passed. The French were still thinking about a waterway to Asia. They chose Jacques Cartier to look for a northwest passage. Cartier had been to the fishing banks near Newfoundland, so he took the fishermen's route that far. Sailing around that island, he discovered the Gulf of St. Lawrence in 1534. In 1535 he sailed up the St. Lawrence River as far as the site of Montreal. He came again in 1541, but failed to establish a lasting colony. (p. 55, *History of Our United States*.)

B. Recognizing Details Which Support Topic Sentences

Purpose: To help students learn to recognize details which support topic sentences and ways in which they do this.
Method: Class discussion, groupwork
Procedure: 1. Look again at paragraphs used in lesson A.
2. Look at them paragraph by paragraph and discuss how each is organized.
   1. Main idea—two subtopics with details dexcribing each subtopic.
   2. Details follow sequence and build up to topic sentence at end.
   3. Details supporting main idea.
   4. Sequence of events, year by year

C. Organization

Purpose: To help students determine how paragraphs or sections of text are organized in order to learn to better interpret and organize ideas.
Method: Review Lessons A and B. (It is assumed that this set of Lessons A - E would be used over a period of several weeks, depending on the ability of the class and how well each lesson progressed.) Class discussion, small group work.
Procedure: 1. Give mimeographed copies of sample paragraphs and sections from text to students.
2. See if they can recognize topic sentences. Note that the last two selections consist of several paragraphs and the topic for them is in boldface type. Then the topic sentences of the paragraphs are supporting details which in turn are supported by details.
3. Take them paragraph by paragraph and discuss.

1. Main idea with supporting details.
2. Main idea with supporting details which can be recognized by full signals (numbers).
3. Time sequence.
4. Comparison-contrast with main ideas supported by details.

D. Outlining

Purpose: To help students see how recognizing organization can aid in outlining.

Procedure: 1. Have sentences used in Lesson C printed on cards which are backed with flannel for use on flannelboard (or prepared in some way so they can be displayed before students and moved from place to place). Have one sentence on each card.
2. Take them paragraph by paragraph. Ask students to point out topic sentence. Place at top of flannelboard.
3. Have students select supporting details. Place these beneath topic sentence, slightly indented so it looks like an outline.
4. Continue with other paragraphs. Then give them samples of similar paragraphs to see if they can follow same procedure on their own.

1. Champlain was a successful colonizer partly because he was so friendly with the Indians. He secured their confidence by treating them as equals, by learning their languages, and by living in their villages. He encouraged his young men to treat the Indians fairly at all times, to trade with them, and to marry Indian women. (p. 55, *History of Our United States*.)
2. Jamestown almost failed in its first year. The suffering of the men was due to several causes. 1) *They ran out of food* and raised little. Newport and Captain John Smith obtained corn and venison from the nearby Indians, but this was not enough. 2) *Disease struck the camp.* Many died from malaria. 3) *The search for gold* took men from the work of raising food, building shelters, and preparing for winter. 4) *Fire destroyed most of the camp* in January of 1608. 5) *The London Company wanted returns on its investment.* Twice during 1608, Newport had the men gather cargoes of sassafras, lumber, and naval stores, which he took to England. 6) *Fear of the Indians* kept the men from working outside the stockade. (p. 69, *History of Our United States*.)
3. NEW FRANCE GROWS SLOWLY. The French were slow to recognize the opportunities offered by the New World. Verrazano claimed the east coast of North America for France in 1524. You have seen that Cartier came to the St. Lawrence region in 1534, and again in 1541, but he failed to start a successful colony. No other Frenchmen attempted colonization during the 1500's.

French fishermen who came to the fishing waters off the eastern coast started the fur trade. They met the Indians and traded for furs when they went ashore to dry their fish. Realizing that profits could be made on furs, French merchants told their king they would set up colonies in New France in return for fur-trading rights.

As a result of this offer, in 1604 a colony was started in Acadia near the Bay of Fundy, and in 1608 Samuel de Champlain founded Quebec, the first permanent settlement in Canada. Montreal was founded as a missionary center in 1642. Then, in 1663, the French king decided that New France must have more colonists. He took the government from the trading companies and made New France a royal colony.

4. DIFFERENCES IN POLICY. The English had more power in America than the French. This was in part due to a difference in their colonial policies. The French had one kind of colonial system; the English had another. The French did not look upon America as a place to settle, to raise families, and to build a new life. They thought of it more as a place where adventurous young men might seek their fortunes in fur trading and then return to France. The English came to the New World determined to make it their home. Whole families came to the colonies fully intent on building and staying. Consequently, the English colonies were more stable from the beginning.

The main occupation of the French in America was fur trading; the English for the most part, made a living by farming. Farming is a more settled way of life than trading. As you saw in the New England town, farmers tend to develop a solid family and community life. Champlain realized this and tried to get many Frenchmen to farm along the St. Lawrence and Mississippi, but not many farmers came. As a result, the French colonists had to buy much of their food from the English colonists.

Geography helped to slow up the development of New France in another way. The river valleys in which the French settled were fairly level. The people could spread out easily. Consequently, their settlements were scattered more widely than the English towns. New France itself stretched from the snows of Canada to the canebrakes of Louisiana. The English colonies covered a more limited area along the Atlantic. Imagine how long it must have taken for a message to go from Quebec to New Orleans by canoe and sailing ship!

There was a great difference in the government of the colonies too. The French were used to being ruled. The English were used to having at least some voice in their government. Consequently, the French colonies were governed entirely by agents of the king and in the best interest of the mother country, without opposition from the settlers. In case of war with England, the French government could expect that the majority of her colonists would fight wholeheartedly for France.

As you have seen, for the most part the British colonies were allowed to govern themselves and to place their own interests first. Each colony developed more or less independently. Therefore, it was not always easy to get the Thirteen Colonies to work together as a team for England.

E. Key Words From Outline to Shorten Outline

Purpose: To help students see how sentence outlines may be shortened as a means of taking notes on material. (Later lesson may teach the student to look for key words to make outline rather than making sentence outline first.)

Procedure: 1. Take same paragraphs used in Lessons C and D. Place them one at a time on the board as they were in the outline form.

2. Do we need all those words to give us the meaning? No. What words are necessary? Decide in class what words could be used to mean same thing.

3. Go over each paragraph together doing this.

4. Have students do the paragraphs that they outlined in Lesson D in the same way these were done in class.

LESSON IV. REVIEWING USE OF MAPS

Purpose: To aid students in recalling and reviewing map skills which it is hoped they began to develop in grades 5 and 6. To aid students in recognizing how maps can be of aid in understanding the material in the text.

(For those students who appear to be weak in these skills, all or some of the following books might be utilized for individual or small group study.)

Method: Class discussion, group activities

Procedure: 1. Turn to list of maps on page 8.

Ask students to look at this list and to think of other books they use to see how many different kinds of maps they can think of and what kinds of information maps can give.

2. List kinds of maps. This list might include the following kinds:

A. Boundaries
   World
   Countries
   State
B. Geographical features—mountains, plains, rivers
C. Roads, Railroads, Trails, River Routes
D. Weather
E. Products
F. Battles

3. Have students turn to page 217 in text. Is this a map? Yes, it shows the location of lots in a township. Have class suggest different types of maps that could be drawn. If possible use one of the types they suggest in the following discussion. Use something that they are all familiar with. Might be their school area, or a classroom.

We could draw a map of our classroom to show the location of desks, tables, bookshelves, etc. How large should we draw it?

How would someone who had never seen the classroom know how large the room was from the map?

Yes, you have to have a *scale*. This means we let a certain length such as one inch, ¼ inch, etc. represent one foot, one mile, and so on.

Look at the map on p. 24. How do we know what size North America is? Yes, there is a scale of miles.

Turn to the map on p. 290. Does this use the same scale of miles? No. Why? It only shows part of the United States to show certain trails. If it used the same scale as the map on page 24 the traisl would be too small to see well.

4. Look at the map on p. 31. What kind of map is this? What two kinds of information does this map give us? (Elevation and rainfall.)

   How does it show this information? (Symbols—color, lines, dots, etc.) How do we know what each symbol stands for? (Legend—explain or show each.)

5. Look at map on p. 307. Doesn't use a legend. Expects you to know some of the symbols and labels the trails and other points of importance.

6. Look at map on p. 351. Just looking at it, does this map mean a great deal to you? Probably not. We know it has something to do with the Civil War but until you read the information in the chapter that explains the battles and movements of Sherman, Grant, and Farragut, it doesn't mean much. If we just read about these, it probably would not be clear to us where each had gone. However, if we both read and study the map, the two together should make the information easier to remember and understand.

7. Look at map on p. 418. What products is this map showing? How do you know? (Symbols.) Which part of the United States produces the most oil? iron? coal?

8. We have looked at some different kinds of maps, and have seen some of the kinds of symbols that are used. There are many other symbols that we have not discussed that you may remember from other books. Have class list those that they remember.

9. Divide class into small groups of four or five students and have them complete the following exercises. Then discuss in class.

Note: It is realized that a single lesson such as this is not sufficient for teaching map skills. It would be much better to study and discuss various map skills as they are needed throughout the text. However these might be samples of what might be done. It also might be helpful to use some type of activity such as this near the beginning of the year to help students realize that maps do give information to supplement the text material.

MAP EXERCISES

To complete each exercise, turn to the map on the page indicated.

1. Page 31:

    (a) At what altitude would you say more of the land in the United States is?

    Sea level to 500 feet above sea level, 500 - 1,000 feet, 1,000 - 2,000 feet, 2,000 - 5,000 feet, 5,000 - 10,000 feet

    (b) How many inches of annual rainfall does the state of Georgia get?

2. Page 24:

    Approximately how wide is the United States from east to west at the widest point?

3. Page 71:

    Which European country claimed the most land in the New World in 1650?

4. Pages 226 - 227 and 322 - 323:

    Compare the size of the United States in 1819 with its size in 1853. By what four means was land added after 1819?

5. Page 374:

    Why do you think there are more railroads in the East than in the West?

6. Page 390:

    Approximately how far did cattle have to be driven if the cattlemen used the Sedalia Trail? The Goodnight Loving Trail?

7. Page 418:

    Which of the products shown on the map does Georgia produce?
    Which of the products shown on the map does Alabama produce?
    What industry would you expect to find around Birmingham? Why?
    Which state in the United States appears to produce the most oil?

8. Page 491:

    Which was the first territory added to the United States?
    When was the Panama Canal Zone annexed to the United States?

SUMMARY

A student must be able to bring his own background of information to the material he reads in order to get meaning from it. But even with a good background, the number of types of concepts and vocabularies of new content material often found in textbooks may present problems to a student. The teacher, partly by knowing how to select an appropriate text, can help alleviate the problems a student will face.

A textbook provides new information, reinforcement of material covered, examples and important details, and a common background for the students. But it is of no value if students cannot read it. For this reason, every teacher should, at the beginning of the school year, test the students to determine their ability to read the text. Those who cannot read and comprehend the text material should be given other material which is at their reading level but which covers the same material as presented in the original text. After receiving an appropriate textbook, each student should be taught to employ the SQ3R method so that they can make effective use of their respective texts.

When making an assignment, a teacher should always tell the student three things:

What they are to do. (Content)

Why they are to do it. (Motivation)

How they are to do it. (Skills)

When completing an assignment, a student must be able to identify the main idea or topic sentence, as it is basic to understanding and interpreting the material. Along with the main idea, a student must also be able to locate the details which form the foundation for and support the main idea. A teacher should aid the student in his search for these components in the content material and show him how to organize what he finds by teaching him how to outline. A brief study of the organization of his own textbook will give the student a good understanding of how an outline should be constructed.

REFERENCES

Perry, William G., Jr. "Students' Use and Misuse of Reading Skills: A Report to the Faculty," *Harvard Educational Review,* Vol. 29, No. 3 (Summer 1959), pp. 193 - 200.

Robinson, Francis P. *Effective Study.* New York: Harper & Row, Publishers, 1941.

ADDITIONAL READINGS

Cooper, David. "Concepts from Semantics as Avenues to Reading Improvement," *English Journal,* LIII (February 1964), pp. 85 - 90.

Stauffer, Russel G. "What is Adequate Comprehension and When is Comprehension Adequate?" *Journal of the Reading Specialist,* II (December 1962), pp. 20 - 23.

Strang, Ruth. "Secondary School Reading as Thinking," *The Reading Teacher* (December 1961), pp. 155 - 161.

REQUIRED READINGS FROM BOOK OF READINGS

VI. Developing Comprehension and Interpretation Skills
    Promoting Growth in Interpreting in Grades Nine Through Fourteen—James M. McCallister.

chapter 4

Developing Critical
Reading Skills

When asked to identify the ultimate goals and objectives of instruction most reading authorities eventually come around to a discussion of the importance of critical reading skills. Those same authorities feel that considerable time and effort should be devoted to such skills in a secondary school developmental reading program. Certainly the importance of having an informed and critical thinking citizenry cannot be overestimated.

What is meant by critical reading? Ennis (1962) said that critical reading meant judging or evaluating the correctness of what was being read. Huus (1965) agreed that critical reading required evaluation of printed material with some known standard or norm.

Huus further suggested that the reader has to have some knowledge of the facts being presented in order to evaluate them, as well as some knowledge of the author's qualifications for making the presentation. The student also needs to be able to look at the internal consistency, determine the accuracy, estimate the recency, and evaluate the perspective of the content in light of the author's style and tone.

Marksheffel (1966) stated that in critical reading the reader makes sound judgments. He said that such a reader is not born but is a product of a number of combined processes, forces, and time. He suggested that the purpose of the reader determines whether he will read critically or not.

Many other ideas about critical reading could be quoted, but those presented give the major points of emphasis. When an act of evaluation and judgment of reading material is based on some norm or standard that relates to the content or message of a printed passage to determine its accuracy, consistency, truthfulness, factual content, recency, value, tone, mood, bias, or other pertinent value, critical reading is occurring. During this process the reader will employ past experiences and personal values in order to evaluate the materials. If the reader is a "good" critical reader, he may achieve accurate perception of what is being said and why it is being said. If the reader is not a "good" critical reader, he may gullibly accept what is being said without doubting its truthfulness.

Critical reading is not a destructive process; on the contrary, it is constructive. It involves the emotional and intellectual interaction between reader and author. It involves the reader's ability in recognizing the author's intent or point of view, distinguishing fact from opinion, making judgments and inferences, as well as other advanced reading skills.

Critical reading skills are often thought of as being applicable only to those having high intellectual powers and much background experience. If one were thinking of certain advanced skills of critical reading, this might be true, but just as there are subtle ways of showing intent, stating a point of view, or presenting an opinion so that it appears to be a fact and making inferences, so also are there obvious ways. Critical reading skills, then, should not be thought of as being something that can be developed only for gifted students. They are just as important for the average and below average. In fact, they may be more important for this group because, without instruction, it is very likely such students will not acquire them at all. With less able students it is not a question of skill in reading poems by Cummings, novels by Goulding, or political essays by Schlesinger. Rather, one is talking about reading the newspaper and watching television.

THE NEED FOR CRITICAL READING

The primary reason for teaching critical reading skills is to enable readers to get more from the material they read. Because of the world in which they live, with its emphasis on mass communication, it is imperative that students evaluate and judge critically the material to which they are exposed. They must be aware of the techniques and methods by which ideas are developed, as well as the intent of these ideas.

Teen-agers are constantly being exposed to material in magazines which plays upon their anxieties. It is impossible to pick up a magazine written for this age group without finding articles and advertisements on remedies for acne, bad breath, inferiority feelings, weight problems, and the like. All of these have their appeal to a teen-ager who has an allied problem. If the teen-ager does not have specific information relating to his problem, he cannot read this kind of material critically and may find himself seeking "instant" cures instead of awaiting the natural course of events as he goes through the processes of maturation.

Skills need to be taught to make students aware of the means by which judgment can be swayed and behavior changed. In school and later in life they will be exposed to political ideas and arguments. If they are to be good citizens with a knowledge of the world and of the domestic situation they must be able to make valid judgments based on facts, not on emotions and prejudices. They must be able, for example, to read two different newspaper accounts of the same event and determine the points of view, how the facts are interpreted, and the purposes of the interpretation. They must be aware that a statement taken out of context may give a totally different impression from that of a statement in context. These skills are important and should be consciously taught by every classroom teacher, regardless of subject.

The question, "Why do we need to read critically?" can easily be answered by turning to the mass media. Any random sampling of printed materials will show a divergent manner of reporting and an equally divergent realm of ideas. Television and radio reporting are no exceptions to printed materials, and show similar trends. At present there is an increased degree of editorializing of news events. Television reporters say that they will report *what* is happening in an election and tell *why* it is happening. While the election returns are piling up the reporters discuss the issues *they feel* are related *to why* the votes are going as they are. Usually the accurate evaluation of such events may take weeks or months, if such action is ever to be fully understood.

There is a definite need for a student to learn to cope with editorial reporting on television or radio, or in print. He needs to be made aware that what is reported is colored by the reporter's or editor's interpretation. This interpretation is based on such things as the reporter's or editor's experiences or lack of experience, or biases, and by competition among the news media. The student should be taught to take several reports of the same event or incident and try to determine the facts or the real truth in what is being reported. The present diversity of ways to report facts and happenings will make a critical reader realize that many people are trying to sell their own ideas, outlooks, biases, or prejudices.

Further, when one considers human nature one realizes that if a writer wants the reader to agree with him he will use all possible methods, including false logic and appeals to emotion. These serve to reinforce what the writer thinks, and to give plausibility to the writer's argument. A politician who receives constant rebuffs on some pet project will usually adapt his ideas until he finds something that will be more appealing. He is primarily a realist who knows that eventually he must "sell himself" to his voters to be elected. A highly inflexible person may also have the dogged courage or lack of feeling to face rebuffs constantly.

Belief in the infallibility of the printed word has also caused some problems for the unwary reader or untrained student. Many students think that if a statement is printed in a book or newspaper it is necessarily true. This idea can be traced back to the fact that eons of knowledge have been gathered between the covers of books. It is quite often the case that someone says, "They wouldn't print that if it wasn't true." Some authors use this credulousness along with propaganda techniques to sell their ideas.

Clements (1964) has pointed out that newspapers, textbooks, magazines, and advertisements are concerned with the actions and beliefs of the people who read them. The reader who cannot critically evaluate the printed materials he reads may be sold ideas that are not consistent with his thinking, or be blinded to the truth. In advertisements he may be sold things he does not need or want because of a clever appeal to his emotions or his fears. As Clements has suggested, one must be careful when reading anything written by historians, journalists, ad men, or anyone who writes to sell a viewpoint. The student must be taught to detect such devices and know how to handle them objectively.

Artley (1959) has observed that ownership of many of the country's newspapers and magazines is being consolidated into the hands of a few publishers. This has put an even greater demand on teachers to see that students are taught to evaluate editorial policy. Piercy (1964) has also said that the purpose of the newspaper was to inform but that there has been an increasing trend for it to give opinions. She notes that this also places further burdens on those responsible for developing critical skills of evaluation with students. She says that "a youthful reader whose personal opinions are in the throes of being formulated can use guidelines." She suggests that the reader be given these guidelines through being taught to ask pertinent questions about the newspaper and its policies.

In addition to control of mass media by the few and the present tendencies of news media to editorialize, there is also the question of political censorship and the use of influence to control what news or what books reach the public. The Johnson administration was under fire for what was called a "credibility gap" in reporting information on Vietnam. William Manchester's book *Death of a President* (on the assassination of John F. Kennedy) also showed that under some circumstances influence can be brought to bear to suppress publication of a book or to control what will be printed in it. What is right for a country to report about its war activities, or what is fair for protection of a name is not the question here. That such controversies exist in the mass media is the fact for the student to recognize. With help he may be taught to face the fact realistically and objectively. Otherwise he may be caught in the emotional plea of the reporters and the biases represented there. As for the Manchester book, some reviewers called it a sensitive portrayal of a tragic event while others labeled it yellow journalism. A student must have skills which will help him evaluate either of these extremes of opinion and all those that lie between.

One might ask, "Is this relevant to a high school student?" "Is the high school student concerned with such adult matters?" All of the above facts do relate to the high school student. As was mentioned, the high school student's later adult personal opinions are now being formed, and he needs guidelines to help in evaluating all that he reads. It will also be noted later that the materials most teen-agers read are adult newspapers and magazines. If the student is now confronted with such contrasts in facts, divergent opinions, and varying reporting techniques, he must be concerned with them. If society is to remain healthy, teachers must also be concerned with these facts and the related needs of the students.

There is also a personality factor that must be considered. Gordon (1965) has discussed the tendencies of many students and adults to be intellectually lazy, to run with the herd. Following the course of least resistance by complacently agreeing with the opinions of others leads many people into blind conformity. Today in the mass media heroes and monsters are created overnight. When people blindly follow the mass media into such characterizations of national figures, the prejudices of the newsmakers become the prejudices of the people. In such cases people are nothing more than dupes of those who hold the power of the printed word.

Russell (1956) has pointed out that the first step of a totalitarian government is to seize control of all forms of communication. When this is done the people receive only the ideas and philosophy of those in control. Such was the case in Russia following Stalin's death, when the erstwhile dictator who had been depicted as a great hero, was now demeaned by his successors. The new power structure found it convenient and to their liking to destroy the earlier image of Stalin as a great leader of the people. Stalin's relative "goodness" or "badness" is not the point; the fact that the mass media of Russia was used to do the will of the power structure is the point. Hitler is another example of a ruler who used the controlled press to see that his will became law. Germans can still look back to the war years as the "dark night of their souls." Control of ideas is not the answer to today's problems. It is best that the newspapers and news media be allowed the right to express their divergent ideas. But it is also imperative that students be taught skills to handle such differing ideas so they will not become gullible readers.

CRITICAL READING AND THE SCHOOLS

Critical reading is a process that can be enhanced by teaching. Students can be helped to develop critical reading skills as well as general types of evaluation which will apply to all types of communication. Marksheffel (1966) pointed out that skills of critical evaluation should be developed in the first grade and in all following grades. Caskey (1963) has said that it is impossible to teach children at any level to read critically if the materials used are not within their understanding and interests. Aaron (1963), Russell (1961), Smith (1961), and Sheldon (1958) are samples of the interested authorities who feel that critical reading should be emphasized in the primary grades as well as all others.

Williams (1959) and Austin (1963) have said that teaching materials, while supposedly claiming to develop the critical reading skills, did not contain enough good materials to do the task, or that the materials were not being used adequately. Whether from lack of materials or their misuse, these skills are not being developed adequately in students at all grade levels. Austin suggested further emphasis be placed on the development of these skills at all grade levels.

Stauffer (1961) has discussed the atmosphere of the normal classroom and the fact that it tends to militate against the development of the evaluative and questioning skills. He feels that in an atmosphere where the teacher has complete and autocratic control, the student reactions tend to be more conforming rather than questioning and creative. Caskey (1963) has also said that a child must have freedom to question. A child in an atmosphere where he cannot make a mistake without facing ridicule and embarrassment will tend to take a passive role.

Gordon (1965) has also discussed the role of the teacher in developing skills of critical appraisal. She feels that the teacher should be responsible for encouraging ideas and skills of questioning. There should also be a deliberate effort to organize teaching in such a way that interpretation and not factual recall of printed materials was stressed. The natural curiosity of pupils should be channeled into problem solving instead of memorizing facts.

At the high school level a student should display more judgment. Supposedly he is maturing and the adult world expects him to have gained more sophistication in dealing with all materials he hears, sees, and reads. Wolf (1965) points out that such judgment is hopefully based on accuracy, validity, and worth. If students have been trained to interpret only factual materials, they will usually continue in this manner. Rogers (1960) reported in his study of high school sophomores and seniors that factual recall was noted to the exclusion of critical evaluation in materials designed to test critical evaluation. He also reported that high school graduates interviewed were no more inclined to interpret meanings or to react with sound judgment than the elementary school graduates. Gray (1956) in dealing with adults concluded that they, too, found it hard to recognize implied meanings or to draw conclusions. The adults functioned on a mechanical rather than a critical level.

Critical reading, then, is a skill area that should be developed within the schooling process. Smith and Dechant (1961) noted that it can be dealt with in two ways: incidentally or directly. Both of these approaches have their place in teaching, but each by itself is not complete. If the incidental way of teaching is used to the exclusion of a directed way, there may be gaps in the development of critical skills. If the directed way is used without capitalizing on the incidental occurrences, many good avenues for developing these skills are ignored.

OBSTACLES TO CRITICAL READING

It seems clear that the critical reading skills have not been taught effectively in the past for several reasons. There are at least five obstacles that have prevented the development of such skills: the use of a single textbook, the "halo effect" attached to the printed word, the desire on the part of school administrators and teachers to avoid controversial subjects, the emphasis on conformity, and the involvement of emotions and prejudices.

The Single Textbook

The use of a single textbook is one of the greatest deterrents to the teaching of critical reading skills. Even in a history book the author has selected and interpreted facts. If a student is exposed to only one interpretation and one selection of facts, he will undoubtedly accept them as true. If on the other hand several textbooks are used, the students will be able to compare facts, information, and conclusions which may very well be different.

In a class where American History was being taught to ninth graders, the students were reading an account of the Andrew Jackson inauguration. In one text it stated that he invited his friends from the woods to his inauguration and the party that followed. The text went on to say that the party lasted for several days. In another text, read by some of the students, the authors indicated that the inauguration party ended as a drunken brawl resulting in extensive damage to the White House lawn and necessitated the calling of the military to restore order. Needless to say, the students became very involved and rather upset. The incident made them look for further information and planted the idea that perhaps several sources were better than one.

The Halo Effect

Most teachers are very much aware of the importance students attach to the printed word. If in class students read a statement of fact and the teacher orally presents another statement opposing the first fact, it is a foregone conclusion that the students will accept the printed statement as truth. The reason is that students have not been made aware of the need for evaluating the purposes for which material is written and for making judgments of accuracy. It goes without saying that this can be extremely dangerous. An uncritical reader who cannot ask meaningful questions about the material he reads is ripe for many propaganda techniques and errors in logic that would otherwise be obvious. Some organizations put a great deal of time and effort into writing and publishing reading material because this is the way to influence people's decisions.

The Desire to Avoid Controversy

Critical reading and thinking skills cannot be developed without facts or issues that are open to controversy. In developing these skills there must be an opportunity to interpret events in various ways. If teachers are not willing to open their classrooms to a discussion of the social and political problems facing society there is a serious limit to the effectiveness of any critical reading program.

The Emphasis on Conformity

One of the characteristics of teen-agers is their desire to conform to their peers. It is this conformity, however, that can act as a barrier to critical reading and thinking. If teachers want their students to think for themselves they must create the atmosphere in the classroom that will allow, and make socially acceptable, a lack of conformity. It is important for students not to accept a "party line" without thinking about it themselves, merely because everyone else is conforming.

Emotional Involvement and Response

All students come to school with certain prejudices, emotions, and experiences. These may be so strong as to prevent an evaluation of the true facts. It is probably not the school's job to completely change these ideas, even if it could be done, but it is the teacher's job to make the students aware that these factors are involved in their evaluations of material read. Students can be brought to the point where they understand why they feel as they do. Emotional involvement cannot be erased from the critical evaluation, but it can be minimized.

CRITICAL READING EXERCISES

Some practice exercises in certain aspects of critical reading should serve to focus attention on the kinds of activities in which the critical reader engages. In the development of any of these skills it is important for the teacher to realize that learning takes place in the teacher-student and student discussion of the exercises. It is important that the students know *why* and ask questions.

Distinguishing Fact from Opinion

A *fact* is something that can be proven to be true or untrue, and an *opinion* is a matter of personal taste. The following is a list of possible exercises that can be used to help students learn to distinguish facts from opinions:
1. Display five advertisements on the chalkboard. Have students list five facts and five opinions about each.
2. Have each student list ten facts and ten opinions about himself. Have him do the same for someone else he knows well.
3. Have students read selected statements and label them as being statements of fact or statements of opinion. For example, the following type of statements might be used:
   (a) The greatest thing Abraham Lincoln did was to free the slaves.
   (b) Our country is composed of people from many nations.
   (c) "Do a good deed daily" is one of the Boy Scout rules.
4. Have students read orally, to the class, advertisements from which they have deleted all statements of opinion.

5. Have students select editorials from different newspapers, cross out all statements of opinion, and read what is left to the class.
6. Select passages from the textbooks used in class and ask the students to identify the statements of fact and statements of opinion.
7. Have students make a sampling of textbooks in the fields of English, social studies, science, and mathematics. Ask them to gather proof for a comparison of the amount of facts and the amount of opinions.

Teachers should point out to students that the object of most writing is to persuade or influence the reader. A statement of opinion in a piece of writing does not make it bad. It is a bad situation only if the reader is unaware that the author is sometimes expressing his own personal opinions, not facts.

Detecting Bias and Prejudice

Another important critical reading skill involves the ability to detect bias and prejudice in writing. This may involve recognizing how a writer's choice of words can slant his writing, and considering an author's qualifications and background. Sample exercises for developing this skill in students are as follows.

1. Give students practice in distinguishing favorable comments and unfavorable comments from comments that are neither favorable nor unfavorable. An example of this type of item follows:

> Comments About Governor Mack
>
> a resident of Jonesville
> never pays his bills
> a real American
> has beady eyes
> is for the common man

2. Ask the students to utilize what they know about well known personalities in determining their special bias in statements they make:

	Biased	Unbiased	Reason
A United Auto Workers Union leader says that the automotive manufacturers can afford a substantial raise to their employees.	_____	_____	_____
A former president's wife says that her husband was one of the ten great men in the history of the United States.	_____	_____	_____
A well-known movie actress says that gentlemen prefer blondes.	_____	_____	_____

3. Teach the students to use the reference sources, such as "Who's Who in

America," and "Men in Science," to discover if the authors they are
reading may have any special bias.

4. Ask a local newspaperman to discuss how a newspaper tries to keep
   bias out of the news.
5. Select headlines from the newspapers and news magazines. Ask the
   students to identify those that do not express opinion or contain bias.
6. Ask the students to list arguments for and against something (helping
   with dishes, long hair and beards, homework). Then ask them to combine both lists into a paragraph. They should be cautioned to keep all
   personal opinions, judgments, inferences, and conclusions out of the
   paragraph.

Determining the Reliability of Information Read

A critical reader must constantly be aware of the reliability of the information he reads. The source of the information as well as the date of the information are important considerations in determining the reliability. Sample exercises
follow.

1. Teach the importance of the date of publication for an accurate and
   complete treatment of different subjects.
   (a) Crime in the United States (1927)
   (b) Boundaries of Europe (1947)
   (c) The Use of Plastics (1964)
   (d) Juvenile Delinquency (1963)
2. Teach students to use library references to check reliability.
3. Have students examine the logic behind statements:
   (a) Mother is a great cook and bakes bread every Saturday.
   (b) He eats hamburgers every day, so he must love hamburgers.
   (c) He must be well informed because he reads three newspapers a day.
4. Ask the students to compare the treatment of a controversial point in
   more than one textbook, newspaper, magazine, or pamphlet.

Drawing Conclusions and Making Inferences

The critical reader can be characterized as one who not only can read for
literal meaning but also can infer meaning from the printed page and draw
relevant conclusions. Current magazines and newspapers can supply the content
for exercises such as the following:

1. Ask the students to identify the kind of person to whom certain advertisements are probably geared:
   (a) A man with a tattooed arm smoking a cigarette
   (b) A beautiful girl reclining on top of a sports car
   (c) The picture of the Rock of Gibraltar in an advertisement
2. Give students practice in interpreting the meaning of cartoons from
   current newspapers and magazines.

SUMMARY

Critical reading is the act of evaluating reading material based on some norm which relates to the content of a printed page to determine its pertinent values. Critical reading is a constructive process and its practice is not limited to the gifted student.

Critical reading is necessary to get more out of the material read and to make judgments based on available facts—not emotions, prejudices, and opinions. A "good" critical reader has accurate perception, whereas one who is not a "good" critical reader may be gullible.

Both directly and indirectly, teaching can enhance the critical reading process which should be introduced in the earliest grades, provided it has the assistance of proper materials. A child must be permitted to question and interpret material he reads, not merely recite skills he has memorized.

Five major obstacles to the teaching of critical reading skills are: use of the single textbook; the halo effect of the printed word; a desire to avoid controversy, especially in the classroom; the emphasis on conformity, particularly among adolescents; and emotional involvement and response of individual students.

Distinguishing fact from opinion, detecting bias and prejudice, determining the reliability of information read, and drawing conclusions and making inferences are four exercises presented to help students develop skills in critical reading.

REFERENCES

Aaron, I. E. "Developing Reading Competencies Through Social Studies and Literature," *Reading as an Intellectual Activity*, IRA Conference Proceedings, VII (1963), pp. 107-112.

Artley, A. S. "Critical Reading in the Content Area," *Critical Reading: An Introduction*, National Council of Teachers of English (1959), pp. 14-22.

Austin, Mary. *The First R*. New York: The Macmillan Company, 1963.

Caskey, Helen. "Developing Power in Critical Reading," *Journal of Educational Research*, XXIX (1963), pp. 51-53.

Clements, H. M. "Inferences and Reading Instruction," *Claremont Reading Conference Yearbook*, XXVII (1964), pp. 144-156.

Ennis, Robert H. "A Concept of Critical Thinking," *Harvard Educational Review*, XXXII (Winter 1962), p. 81.

Gordon, Lillian G. "Promoting Critical Thinking," *Reading and Inquiry*, X (1965), pp. 119-121.

Gray, William. "How Well Do Adults Read," *Adult Reading*, Fifty-fifth Yearbook, Part II, National Society for the Study of Education (1956), p. 39.

Huus, Helen. "Critical and Creative Reading," *Reading and Inquiry*, J. Allen Figurel (ed). IRA Proceedings of the Annual Convention, Newark, Delaware (1965), p. 115.

Marksheffel, Ned D. *Better Reading in the Secondary School.* New York: The Ronald Press Company, 1966.

Piercy, Dorothy. "Using the Newspaper to Develop Reading Skills," *Reading Improvement,* II (1964).

Rogers, Bernice. *Directed and Undirected Reading Responses of High School Students.* Unpublished doctoral dissertation. Department of Education, University of Chicago, 1960.

Russell, D. H. *Children's Thinking.* Boston: Ginn and Company, 1956.

Russell, D. H. "The Prerequisite of Knowing How to Read Critically," *Reading Teacher,* XV (1961), pp. 162-171.

Sheldon, W. D. "Role of Critical Thought in Developing the Independent Reader," *Developing the Independent Reader Through Reading.* Nineteenth Annual Reading Conference Proceedings, University of Georgia, 1958.

Smith, H.P., and E. Dechant. *Psychology in Teaching Reading.* Englewood Cliffs, N.J.: Prentice Hall, Inc., 1961.

Smith, Nila. "The Good Reader Thinks Critically," *Reading Teacher,* XV (1961), pp. 172-181.

Stauffer, R. G. "Reading and the Educated Guess," *Changing Concepts of Reading Instruction,* VI. IRA Proceedings of the Annual Conference, 1961, pp. 173-177.

Williams, Gertrude. "Provisions for Critical Reading in the Basal Readers," *Critical Reading: An Introduction.* National Council of Teachers of English, 1959, pp. 29-37.

Wolf, Willavene. "The Logical Dimensions of Critical Reading," *Reading and Inquiry,* X, IRA Proceedings of the Annual Conference, 1965.

ADDITIONAL READINGS

Dale, Edgar. "The Critical Reader," *The Newsletter.* Columbus, Ohio: Ohio State University, Vol. 30, No. 4 (January 1965).

Denberg, Robert, and Charles Jones. "Critical Reading in a Developmental Reading Course," *Journal of Reading,* X (March 1967), pp. 399-403.

Durr, William K. "Building Initial Critical Reading Abilities," *Vistas in Reading,* XI, Part I. IRA Proceedings, 1966, pp. 55-58.

Howards, Melvin. "Ways and Means of Improving Critical Reading Skills," *Reading and Inquiry,* X. IRA Proceedings, 1965, pp. 124-127.

Quaintance, Brother William J. "Critical Reading—As If There's Any Other Kind," *The Reading Teacher,* XX (October 1966), pp. 49-53.

Schell, Leo M. "Distinguishing Fact from Opinion," *Journal of Reading,* XI (October 1967), pp. 5-9.

REQUIRED READING FROM BOOK OF READINGS

VI. Developing Comprehension and Interpretation Skills
    Factors in Critical Reading—William Eller and Judith Goldman Wolf.

chapter 5

Vocabulary Development and Word-Recognition Skills

Any successful reading program at the secondary school level must include considerable attention to the development of vocabulary and word-recognition skills. In a developmental reading program at this level, the basic objective is to refine those skills initially introduced at the elementary school level.

Regardless of the particular methods and materials used, most reading programs at the elementary school level emphasize many different word-recognition and vocabulary skills. Elementary school teachers seem to accept the linguistic concept that words are arbitrary symbols having no intrinsic meaning. Words take on meaning only to the extent that people can bring meaning to them, understand their relationships to other words, and make sense out of the combinations. Without this ability to translate, there can be no effective communication and thoughts cannot be expressed. These understandings and the skills involved receive considerable attention in the early school years, and secondary school teachers must carry on these responsibilities.

VOCABULARY DEVELOPMENT

Types of Vocabularies

Before discussing specific techniques that can be used to develop the reading vocabularies of secondary school students, it is important to realize that at least five different types of vocabularies are involved in the communication act among people. Although the reading vocabulary is the major focus of attention in this chapter, secondary school teachers should be aware of all the different types and should assume responsibility for their development.

The *nonverbal vocabulary* is by far the largest vocabulary, although scholars are not sure exactly how large. Many of the understandings that people have are the result not of the spoken word but of gestures, facial expressions, and body movements. These may help to convey the meaning of words and even give more meaning than words do by themselves. Studies of underprivileged students indicate that this type of communication is the primary means of communication for them and takes on the aspects of a language itself. For some students with other limited vocabularies, this nonverbal communication is a vital factor in understanding and is receiving increased amounts of attention by linguists and educators.

The *listening vocabulary* is the second largest vocabulary and, like the nonverbal, is an extremely important means of acquiring information for the culurally deprived student or the slow learner. One can often understand the meaning of what a person is saying by the emphasis, pitch, and tone of his speech. These speech factors along with nonverbal clues expand understanding to a point far beyond that achieved by any other vocabularies people may have.

As a student grows in his ability to work with words, build concepts, and broaden his understandings, his ability to recognize and understand words in his reading expands rapidly. There are many words that a student will read and understand in the context of certain material but will never use either in speaking or writing. The *reading vocabulary* is limited by the experiences and concepts the reader brings to the material. There is no oral interpretation (except his own), and a reader cannot rely upon gestures and facial expression to help him understand. While reading, the student is in an "isolation booth."

The *speaking vocabulary* is even more limited than those vocabularies previously discussed. Students seem to accept the standards of the peer group and will limit themselves generally to the group's accepted means of expressions. A student will remain at one level only unless he is helped to understand that there are many means of expressing oneself, and that various situations demand different kinds of vocabulary. The means of expression should fit the situation and the thoughts one is trying to express. However, if a student is not put into various situations where he has a chance to use and develop his speaking vocabulary, there is little likelihood that he will see any use for learning things that have no application in his ordinary, everyday life.

Our schools appear to have done a poor job of encouraging students to acquire a rich *spelling vocabulary*. Teachers have emphasized correct spelling to the point where students hesitate to write for fear of misspelling a word. Spelling is, of course, important and should be emphasized, but the most important element is *thought*. After the thought has been expressed is the time to make corrections. If students are required to think with a large vocabulary and then translate their thoughts into their limited spelling vocabulary their thoughts tend to become limited as well.

Methods of Furthering Vocabulary Growth

It is axiomatic that the larger the vocabulary of the student, the more accurately he will understand what he reads. He will also be able to read more rapidly. It is also evident that the extent and depth of his vocabulary have a noticeable effect upon his ability to think and exchange ideas with others.

The number of words in all of the various vocabularies discussed previously will increase proportionately to the opportunities one has to learn and use new words. The all too common school practice of introducing twenty new words per week in list form to students has little meaning unless teachers multiply the students' chances to use each word by at least ten experiences. "New words for new words' sake" outside of a genuine learning situation is ridiculous. Words have meaning only as they help people to express ideas and understand ideas. Words have very little "showcase value."

There are a number of different types of vocabulary development materials available for use at the secondary school level. These materials, usually in a workbook format, contain various word games and exercises designed to provide students practice in using new vocabulary words. Such materials can, if used with discretion, help provide part of the experiences necessary if students are to give new words a place in their vocabularies. However, if the workbook exercises become mere busywork or an easy opportunity for the teacher to acquire a multitude of test grades to average at the end of a ranking period, then one should not be surprised to find that the exercises do not affect students' vocabulary growth.

Thanks to the ever-increasing influence of linguists on language arts programs at all levels, schools are beginning to realize how important it is for students to become acquainted with the English language and all its complexities. In this connection, the study of the origins of words and word changes can develop in students an increasing awareness of the language and can arouse an interest in vocabulary study. Students might even make up words and ask others to tell what they mean (for example: Beethorama, stealology). The book, *Word Origins and Their Romantic Stories* by Wilfred Funk (New York: Funk and Wagnalls, 1954; paperback ed., 1968), is a valuable resource book for teachers who are interested in developing materials of this type.

WORD-RECOGNITION SKILLS

Knowledge of how words are put together is basic to vocabulary development. The able reader has many techniques for attacking words which are unknown. Most adult readers use four basic aids in attacking such unknown words:

Context—the way in which the word is used.

Structure—the construction of the word; root, prefix, suffix, or inflectional ending.

Sound—the sounds of the letter combinations in the word.

Dictionary—the key aid to meaning and pronunciation if the previous three approaches fail.

The experienced reader is able to get the general meaning and the pronunciation of many words that he has never seen nor heard because of his ability to use the word-attack skills. Context clues often provide enough information to enable the reader to understand a sentence even though a particular word in the sentence may be completely unknown. Many other unfamiliar words, when analyzed for structure, often contain elements that are familiar in other words. These elements give the reader clues as to the possible sounds that the combinations of letter can make. A mature reader will try these aids in attempting to pronounce the unknown word on the assumption that if he pronounces it correctly he may well know the general meaning from having heard the word before. If neither context, structure, nor sound clues provide satisfactory help, the dictionary becomes the final source of aid.

Although context, structure, and sound skills will be discussed in the following sections independently, all are used almost simultaneously by the experienced reader. In unlocking words, the structure and sound are so interrelated that one cannot be used profitably without the other.

It is important to realize that the word which a student understands when he hears it aurally may be a complete mystery to him when it appears in print. Students first learn the skills of attacking new words phonetically and structurally in the elementary grades, but there is a clear need to review at every level in the secondary school. All too frequently students reach the junior and senior high school without having mastered the skills. Even if students have acquired some mastery of the skills, as the words they meet become increasingly complex they need help in applying the principles learned with more complex words.

The following is a test of the principles of word-recognition skill development with which secondary teachers should be familiar. Take this test and then check your answers with the key on page 87.

WORD-RECOGNITION TEST

Part 1. True-False Items

Directions: Write a *plus* sign if the statement is true. Write a *zero* if the statement is false. If it is partly true and partly false, consider it as false.

1. A capable reader uses only one technique of attacking unknown words.
2. If word-recognition skills are taught successfully, one may assume that the reader is well equipped for reading.
3. Students should be instructed in skills appropriate to the grade level.
4. A stem of a word is the word form from which another word is made.
5. A consonant digraph consists of two consonant letters blended together so that sounds of the consonants may be heard when the word is pronounced.
6. Consonant blends may be taught in isolation rather than in words to be sure that children know exactly what the blend is.
7. Planned instruction is seldom necessary for teaching the various dictionary skills.
8. Vowel letters in open syllables usually represent the short sounds.
9. Phonics principles should be developed inductively.

10. The adoption of intensive phonic instruction seems to be justified according to research.

11. The job of teaching the word-recognition skills is that of the teachers of the first three grades.

12. Word identification and word recognition are the same aspects of word perception.

13. A child's first stock of sight words is learned by the look-and-say method.

14. There is little consensus among authorities concerning how many sight words should be taught prior to any instruction in phonetic analysis.

15. Evidence from research and classroom experience indicates that a pupil can make a great amount of progress using the look-and-say method.

16. Words similar in shape as *house* and *horse*, and *these* and *there*, *beard* and *board* should be taught by use of configuration clues.

17. The words *her*, *bird*, *burn* when used together can help to explain the schwa sound.

18. Training in using context to recognize words should continue throughout the grades.

19. Phonetic analysis is the most important of the word-recognition techniques.

20. When the student comes across a word in his reading that does not adhere to the general principles of word analysis, the teacher should tell him the word.

21. There are five letters of the alphabet which have no sound of their own.

22. The long and short sound of a vowel refers to duration.

23. A diphthong is a combination of two consonant sounds blended together so that traces of both sounds are retained.

24. If a student cannot attack initial sounds of words or substitute initial sound or find the root word when endings are added, he is deficient in general reading.

25. It is generally recommended that the vowel sounds be taught before the consonant sounds.

26. While context clues may be stressed too much for children, there is little or no danger of overuse of the word-recognition clues of structural analysis or phonetic analysis.

27. In words of two syllables, the first syllable is usually accented.

28. Any two letters representing one speech sound may be called a diphthong.

29. A phonics program which places syllabication before the identification of individual consonant sounds has definite merit.

30. The first structural analysis generally comes in the first grade when children learn to identify words by adding "s," as in *cars*.

31. Overemphasis upon any one technique of word recognition over a long period of time can result in reading disability.

32. The best approach to the teaching of rules or generalizations about phonics is to let them grow out of activities in the basic reading period.

33. Simple contractions are usually taught at first-grade difficulty level.

34. All words contain at least one vowel or vowel sound.

35. In most two-syllable words that end in a consonant followed by *y*, the first syllable is accented and the second unaccented.

36. A digraph is a combination of letters that form one speech sound.

37. The *oi* in *boil* is a diphthong.
38. The words *get*, and *give*, and *gum* illustrate the principle of the hard sound of *g*.
39. Instruction in word analysis and phonics should be integrated with the rest of reading instruction rather than taught as a separate subject in separate periods.
40. A sound phonics program teaches the child the sounds of individual letters and then gives him practice in blending these sounds into words.
41. The *y* in *yes* is a consonant.
42. In words ending in *tion* and *sion*, the accent falls on the last syllable.
43. If two consonants come between two vowels, the word is usually syllabicated between the consonants.
44. If a word ends in *le* preceded by a single consonant, the consonant goes with final syllable.
45. A vowel is called an open sound because it is made with open throat, mouth, teeth, and lips.
46. Structural analysis is the process of teaching the child to look for "little words" in big words.
47. Structural and phonetic analysis should be taught together.
48. A closed syllable usually contains a short sound.
49. The *o* in *lemon* and the *u* in *circus* are represented by ə.
50. Pronunciation units are prefixes, roots, and suffixes.
51. In the analysis of words, structural analysis should precede phonetic analysis because the child must first identify familiar parts including phonetic elements, before he can blend them in pronouncing a new word.
52. An open syllable ends in a consonant.
53. Systematic lessons in the use of the dictionary as an aid to word analysis and word meaning should begin in the middle grades.
54. The *ow* in *howl* is a digraph.
55. Helping the child to recognize the new word *sand* because of its similarity to the known word *band* is a use of word form analysis.
56. Vowels are more stable in their sounds than are consonants.
57. The sound of an *a* followed by *l* or *w* is controlled by the *l* or *w*.
58. The prefixes *de*, *be*, *re*, and *a* are usually accented.
59. In attempting to unlock a new word the child should be taught to analyze it visually before he attempts to sound out particular elements.
60. The *a* in *car* has a short vowel sound.
61. A root is that part of a word which has no prefix, suffix, or variant ending.
62. *A*, *e*, *i*, *o*, *u*, and sometimes *y*, and *w* are vowels.
63. It is recommended that phonics be taught in a separate period.
64. There is complete agreement among educated people in the United States on the pronunciation of any English word.

Part 2. Multiple-Choice Items

Directions: Write the number corresponding to the best answer among the stated possibilities.

65. The most rapid technique for unlocking new words is the use of
    1. context clues
    2. configuration
    3. phonetic analysis
    4. syllabication
66. Children need to learn the alphabet in order to
    1. begin reading
    2. tell the name of letters that make sounds
    3. begin work in phonics
    4. arrange words alphabetically
67. The vowel sound in the word *hit* is represented in most dictionaries by a:
    1. breve
    2. macron
    3. circumflex
    4. schwa
68. Three of the following words contain consonant digraphs and one contains a consonant blend. The word containing a consonant blend is
    1. sing
    2. write
    3. there
    4. tree
69. In a short word ending with *e*, the *e*, is usually silent and the preceding vowel is
    1. short
    2. modified
    3. long
    4. silent
70. Which from among the following is *not* a factor in structural analysis?
    1. noting basic word in derivatives and variant word forms
    2. interpreting diacritical marks
    3. identifying prefixes and suffixes
    4. identifying familiar elements in larger words
71. The ability to distinguish likenesses and differences among printed words and letters is
    1. visual acuity
    2. peripheral vision
    3. fusion coordination
    4. visual discrimination
72. In teaching phonetic analysis principles the first step one should take is to
    1. establish a visual understanding of the elements
    2. establish visual-auditory understanding of the elements
    3. demonstrate the existence of the principle through showing several examples containing it
    4. establishing auditory perception of the elements
73. Inability to recognize words like *and*, and *down*, *that*, *find*, and *here* indicates
    1. lack of basic sight vocabulary

      2. inability to "sound out" phonic elements
      3. inability to use context clues
      4. inability to use structural analysis clues

74. When two vowels appear side by side in an accented syllable the first is usually long and the second is usually
      1. stressed
      2. short
      3. long
      4. silent

75. In phonetic analysis of words, which word attack method would be taught first in the following:
      1. using visual clues to vowel sound
      2. using visual clues to syllabication and vowel sound
      3. using consonant substitution
      4. using visual clues to accent

76. Phonics serves the reader adequately when it enables him to
      1. pronounce any word he contacts in his reading
      2. comes so close to the word's identity that with the help of the context he can guess the word
      3. pronounce words read without hesitation
      4. succeed in identifying a new word even though he loses contact with the author of the sentence while he works out the word

77-80. In teaching a child to attack a three syllable word, such as *carpenter*, in what order would you ask the following questions? If you think #1 is the first question you would ask, put a #1 in the blank 77. If you think it would be the fourth question asked, you would put #4 in blank 77.
      1. How many syllables does this word have?
      2. Where do you think the first syllable ends?
      3. How many vowel sounds do you hear?
      4. How many vowel sounds do you see?

81. A child meets the word "baseball" in his reading. He has previously known the word "base" and the word "ball." His best attack on the word initially is to use
      1. configuration clues
      2. phonetic analysis
      3. structural analysis
      4. dictionary

82. In most cases of word recognition when the child meets a rather complicated unknown word, he uses
      1. not one but a variety of attacks on the word if it appears necessary
      2. only the dictionary approach to word recognition
      3. context clues first and then phonetic analysis
      4. configuration clues first

Context Clues

    The context of reading material is utilized in arriving at the meaning for many words unfamiliar to the reader in their written forms. The efficient reader uses context clues constantly in the material he reads. There are, however, some limitations to the use of context clues of which teachers need to be aware:

1. If the reading material is too difficult for the student, he will not be able to use the context clues to help him arrive at the meaning of any unfamiliar word. To take an extreme example, if a reader was faced with material that contained twenty-five unknown words in one hundred running words, any context clues would be of little or no value to him.

2. If the reading material is outside of a reader's background of experience, the context may not only be of little use, but may be misleading.

In order to make students continually aware of the possible use of context clues, teachers should write on the board sentences from textbooks they are using. Each sentence should contain one unknown word. Then the teacher should ask the students to discuss what the possible meanings can be for the word in order for the sentence to make sense. The objective is to make the student context aware.

Some reading authorities have attempted to classify the specific types of context clues that are present in written materials. The following are some of the types of context clues that such authorities have identified and which students may encounter as they read:

1. *Experience.* In the experience clue situation, the word is predictable from the students' everyday experience with life. Example: Don't put those dirty feet on the chair. Do you want to *sully* the new furniture?

2. *Comparison or Contrast.* In the comparison or contrast situation, the word is like or opposite to another word. Example: "A thick, rare piece of steak with scrambled eggs and black coffee makes a masculine breakfast that puts to shame *epicene* toast and tea."

3. *Synonym or Definition.* In a synonym clue situation, an appositive structure is often the clue. Example: "The *vendetta*, a violent blood feud, often involved an entire village or clan."

4. *Familiar Language Expression.* This clue uses the students' everyday language associations. Example: "The policeman gave him artificial *respiration* immediately after he was taken from the icy water."

5. *Summary.* In a summary clue situation, the unknown word summarizes a series of ideas. Example: "In a club where you are expected to dress for supper and speak in hushed tones, where politeness is expected, you are to *comport* youself with good manners."

6. *Mood or Situation.* In this clue situation, the word fits into a mood or situation already established. Example: "As he sank deeper and deeper into sleep with the soft sound of a piano playing in the distance, he was completely *relaxed*."

Actually, teachers must be careful not to overemphasize these or any other specific types of context clues. Evidence now available indicates that there is no guarantee that if a reader recognizes a particular pattern or type of clue present in the material he will be able to use the clue successfully to unlock an unknown word. Specific types of aids can serve as illustrations to the students, but ultimately the goal is to get students to become aware of context and its possibility as an aid in unlocking unknown words. Students must realize that in many situations, the clues may be too vague or there may be no clue present.

Structural Clues

In this approach to recognition of an unknown word, the reader attacks the word by looking for familiar pronunciation units or meaning units. Pronunciation units are syllables; meaning units are prefixes, suffixes, and words (root words) to which units have been added.

Words of more than one syllable are difficult to analyze by "sounding out" the separate letters. Students need to be shown how to unlock unknown polysyllabic words by noting the general structure and breaking them into the fewest parts necessary to their solution. There are four types of polysyllabic words:

1. The simplest type of structure to analyze is the compound word that is made up of two known words joined together, such as *commonwealth, matchmaker.*

2. The second type is a word that contains a recognizable stem to which a prefix or suffix has been added. *Insurmountable, deoxygenize* and *unsystematic* are examples of this type.

3. The third type is words that may be analyzed into familiar pronounceable units. *Calcify, strangulate, pugnacious,* and *subterfuge* are examples of this type.

4. The fourth type is words that contain so many nonphonetic parts that unless the word is identified through context, the student cannot be sure of its pronunciation without consulting a dictionary.

Prefixes and Suffixes. A prefix is a meaning unit that is attached to the beginning of a root word to change its meaning. A suffix is a meaning unit attached to the end of a root word to change its meaning. Frequently, in teaching prefixes and suffixes, there is a tendency for teachers to teach them in isolation rather than in a real word. This approach has limited value, since in some words what appears to be a prefix or a suffix may in reality be a part of this root-word itself. In the word *undulate* for example, the *un-*, although it is a syllable in the word, it is not a meaning unit. A student who has been taught that *un-* means "not" when it appears in the beginning of a word would be grossly misled. The same would also be true of teaching suffixes. Therefore in teaching words that have a prefix or suffix added the student should be taught the specific change brought about in that word.

Stauffer (1942) in his study of the 1930 edition of Thorndike's *The Teacher's Word Book of 20,000 Words* found that fifteen prefixes made up

82 percent of the total number of prefixes found in the list. The most frequently occurring prefixes were: *com-* (with), *re-* (back), *ad-* (to), *un-* (not), *in-* (into), *in-* (not), *dis-* (apart), *ex-* (out), *de-* (from), *en-* (in), *pro-* (in front of), *pre-* (before), *sub-* (under), *be-* (by), *at-* (from).

Suffixes usually have several meanings and therefore should not be taught as having specific meaning in a word, since confusion in the meaning of a word may result. The most common suffixes are *ness, -y, -er, -ment, -ive, -our, -less, -ly* and *-ure.*

Syllabication. Principles of syllabication are developed as a means of attaching sounds to small pronounceable units within a polysyllabic word. In the secondary school this is a very necessary series of skills, since the student will frequently come in contact with a word that is in his listening and speaking vocabulary but not in his reading vocabulary.

The task of the secondary school student is to visually analyze the word in order to break it down into smaller units. In order to do this he first looks for any prefixes, suffixes, or inflected endings that have been added to the word. He then finds the root word and if necessary breaks this down into pronounceable units. For the mature reader then, the analysis is first visual and then sounding out the units. In the majority of cases the sounding out will be based upon his familiarity with these same units in other words.

Principles of syllabication should be taught as generalizations not as rules to be followed. The following principles should be taught and reviewed as the student comes in contact with new vocabularies within the various content areas.

1. A syllable must contain a vowel sound.
2. When a single vowel in the first syllable of a two-syllable word is followed by a double consonant, the first syllable ends with the first consonant. Example: *ac-cent.*
3. When the first vowel of a two-syllable word is followed by two consonants (except blends and digraphs), the first syllable ends with the first consonant. Example: *fac-tor.*
4. When the first vowel of a two-syllable word is followed by a single consonant, the consonant usually goes with the second syllable. Example: *pla-cate.*
5. When a two-syllable word ends in *le* preceded by a consonant, the consonant goes with the *le* to form the second syllable. Example: *no-ble.*
6. Prefixes and suffixes form separate syllables.
7. When a word ends in *ed* preceded by *d* or *t*, the *ed* forms a separate syllable.

The above generalizations are only guidelines to aid the student. There are too many exceptions to the rules as students read in various content areas. The whole purpose of the skill is to get the student close enough to the correct pronunciation so that he can make an adjustment if the word is in his speaking or listening vocabulary. If the word is unknown to him, the mere pronunciation is of little or no value.

Sound

Sound or phonetic analysis involves the association of sound and printed symbols. In order to use this type of analysis the student must have the ability to hear the sounds in words (auditory discrimination) and the ability to see the phonic elements in words (visual discrimination).

Since the English language is in part phonetically regular, the student should learn some of the applications of the phonics generalizations. Teachers need to be cautioned however, that the generalizations are of value only in conjunction with the other word-analysis skills. They are of very limited value if used as the only tool.

The secondary school teacher should be aware of the following basic principles to see that the student is applying them in his reading.

1. Most consonants represent only one sound.
2. Three consonants (*c, q, x*) have no speech sound of their own.
3. A consonant digraph consists of two consonant letters representing one speech sound. Some of the commonly taught digraphs are: *ch* as in *church* and *chicken*, *ph* as in *phone*, and *th* as in *thick*.
4. A consonant blend consists of two or three consonant sounds blended together rapidly. Examples: *bl, br, fl, sm, str*, and *thr*.

The vowel principles that the effective reader uses include the following.

1. Each vowel letter (*a, e, i, o, u* and sometimes *y*) represents more than one sound.
2. When the vowel is the final letter in a syllable, the vowel usually has the long sound (say its name). This is called the "open syllable" principle.
3. When the vowel is not the last letter in a syllable, the vowel usually has the short sound. This is called the "closed syllable" principle.
4. When there are two vowels in a word, one of which is final *e*, the vowel before the final *e* is usually long and the *e* is silent. This is called the "final *e*" principle.
5. When a vowel is followed by the *r*, the vowel is neither long nor short, but controlled by the *r*. This is called the "r controller."
6. When the letter *a* is followed by *l, u*, or *w*, the sound is neither long nor short but usually takes the sound of *a*, as in *haul*.
7. The vowel digraph is a combination of two vowel letters representing one sound. Example: *oa* (goat), *ea* (heat), *ie* (yield), and *oe* (hoe).
8. The vowel diphthong is made up of two vowel sounds blended together so that a trace of both sounds is retained. Example: *oi*-(oil), *ou* (out) and *oy* (boy).

It is important for the teacher to realize that many of the generalizations learned concerning silent consonants and adjacent vowels have more exceptions in the secondary school than they have in elementary. This is true because of the increased vocabulary and various derivations of the technical words which do not fit the generalizations. For this reason each teacher must take the time to aid the student with the analysis of the vocabulary unique to his subject.

The Dictionary

Effective use of the dictionary involves the following skills.
1. Alphabetizing
2. Using guide words
3. Using keys to pronunciation
4. Using diacritical markings
5. Using pronunciation spelling
6. Using accent marks
7. Knowing how to divide words correctly so that prefixes and suffixes can be identified
8. Using word-origin comments
9. Using parts of speech

Locating a word in the dictionary begins with a knowledge of the alphabet. Not only must the student know the order of the alphabet, but to use the dictionary efficiently he should know which letters immediately precede and which letters follow each other. He must be taught in which quarter of the dictionary the letters are found so that he can find a word rapidly.

The student must also know what guide words are and how to use them. The guide word that appears at the top of the *first* column of the page is the *first* word on the page, whereas that at the top of the *second* column is the *last* word on the page.

The entry words are words that are defined in the body of the dictionary. Sometimes a difficulty may arise in making a decision as to what the entry word is. The student must decide what the entry word is when the word has a prefix and/or suffix or a word variant (a root word with variant or inflectional ending).

Another group of skills which the student must have are those dealing with the phonic respelling of the word and the use of the key words. Each of the various dictionaries published today has its own unique way of indicating the pronunciation of words. The teacher, because of this difference, must be extremely careful to teach the techniques of using the dictionary and not a pronunciation key. The student must be taught to look at the phonic respelling and to refer to the key pronunciation words at the bottom of the page. He must isolate the sounds he needs, pronounce each syllable, note the accent, and pronounce the whole word.

The same word may have several meanings in the dictionary entry. The student is faced with the problem of selecting the appropriate meaning for the word being studied. The student should never be asked to write all the meanings for a word. Looking for the meaning has no value unless the word has been encountered in a specific context. The following is an example of the type of exercise that might be used.

PRONUNCIATION: DIACRITICAL MARKS[*]

Because the dictionary can't talk, special symbols are used to show in print the sounds of English. Dots, dashes, and other signs called **diacritical marks** are often used with vowel letters to show how they are pronounced. In addition, a special symbol called the **schwa** (ə) is used to represent the vowel sound often found in an unaccented syllable. Every dictionary has a pronunciation key (usually at the bottom of each right-hand page) which tells you what each mark or symbol means by showing it in a word that you already know how to pronounce. A key of this kind is shown below. Notice that in this key the short vowel sounds and the vowel combinations have no special marks.

hat, āge, cãre, fär; let, bē, tèrm; it, īce; hot, gō, ôrder; oil, out; cup, pùt, rüle, ūse; ch, child; ng, long; th, thin; (ŦH), then; zh, measure; e represents **a** in about, **e** in taken, **i** in April, **o** in lemon, **u** in circus.

Exercise 2

Use the key above. Decide which of the two pronunciations given at the right completes the sentence. Both represent English words, but only one stands for a word which makes sense in the sentence. Write **A** or **B** in the blank to show which is the correct pronunciation.

		A	B
1.	The soldier acted with much _____ .	kėr´ij	kar´ij
2.	They will _____ him with a gift.	pri zent´	prez´nt
3.	Do you like orange _____?	güs	jüs
4.	He bought some valuable _____ .	an´tiks	an tēks´
5.	I poured water from the _____ .	pik´chər	pich´ər
6.	Please carry this _____ to her.	mə säzh´	mes´ij
7.	He strapped a _____ on the dog.	muz´l	mus´l
8.	He joined the _____ .	ūn´yən	un´yən
9.	What kind of weather do you _____ ?	pri dikt´	pred´ə kit
10.	They found the _____ of a buffalo.	skul	skül
11.	He was very _____ about his work.	sir´ëz	sir´ē əs
12.	Chickens go to _____ .	rüst	rust
13.	How many books do you _____ ?	pos´ē	pə zes´
14.	I met him in his _____ .	ôf´is	ə fens´
15.	A cat is a _____ animal.	für´ē	fėr´ē
16.	The dress is made of cotton _____.	klôth	klōŦH

*From Olive S. Niles et al., *Tactics in Reading I* (Glenview, Ill.: Scott, Foresman and Company, 1961), p. 40. Copyright © 1961 by Scott, Foresman and Company.

Exercise 3

Use the key at the top of the page to pronounce the words at the left. Then match each word with its correct explanation at the right. Write the letter of the explanation in the blank following the word. In each part there are two explanations that you will not use.

Part A

1. klok_____	A.	a piece larger than a tenth
2. ātth_____	B.	something children make a lot of
3. sēz_____	C.	something to eat with
4. īl_____	D.	take hold of quickly
5. noiz_____	E.	weave cloth
6. kar´ij_____	F.	useful if you don't want to be late
7. spün_____	G.	eaten
8. kroun_____	H.	a king wears one
	I.	an old-fashioned way to travel
	J.	a passage between rows of seats

Part B

1. rēth_____	A.	a group of words
2. wof´l_____	B.	a watchman
3. frāz_____	C.	a circle of flowers or leaves
4. sōl´jer_____	D.	take something offered
5. sen´che rē_____	E.	something like a pancake
6. kwôr´ter_____	F.	a wild animal
7. ri sēv´_____	G.	a long period of time
8. pèr´fikt_____	H.	small change
	I.	practice makes it
	J.	a person in uniform

KEY FOR WORD-RECOGNITION TEST

Part I. True-False Items

1. False	13. False	25. False
2. False	14. True	26. False
3. False	15. False	27. True
4. True	16. False	28. True
5. False	17. True	29. False
6. False	18. True	30. True
7. False	19. False	31. True
8. False	20. False	32. True
9. False	21. True	33. True
10. False	22. False	34. True
11. False	23. False	35. True
12. False	24. True	36. True

37. True	47. True	56. False
38. True	48. True	57. True
39. True	49. True	58. False
40. False	50. True	59. True
41. True	51. True	60. False
42. False	52. False	61. True
43. True	53. True	62. True
44. True	54. False	63. False
45. True	55. True	64. False
46. False		

Part II. Multiple Choice

65. 1	71. 4	77. 4
66. 4	72. 4	78. 3
67. 4	73. 1	79. 1
68. 4	74. 4	80. 2
69. 3	75. 3	81. 3
70. 2	76. 2	82. 1

SUMMARY

In a high school developmental reading program, students basically must learn to refine vocabulary and word-recognition skills introduced in the elementary school.

There are five types of vocabularies: *nonverbal*, consisting of gestures, facial expressions, or body movements; *listening*, based on tone, pitch and emphasis of the spoken word; *reading*, based on experiences and concepts a student brings to the written material; *speaking*, various types depend upon the particular setting; and *spelling* vocabulary.

The more extensive a student's vocabulary the more he can read, the faster he can read, the better he can think and verbalize his ideas to others. New vocabulary words introduced to a student are of no value to him unless he has an opportunity to use them frequently. Workbooks, if used properly, are a good method of learning new vocabulary, as is the study of word origins.

To attack and decipher the meaning of unknown words, four basic aids are used: *context* (way in which the word is used), *structure* (construction of words of more than one syllable), *sound* (sound of letter combinations in words using both auditory and visual discrimination), and the *dictionary* (the key aid if the former three methods fail). With these aids an experienced reader is able to successfully attack unknown words.

REFERENCE

Stauffer, Russell G. "A Study of Prefixes in the Thorndike List to Establish a List of Prefixes That Should Be Taught in the Elementary School," *Journal of Educational Research*, XXXV (February 1942), pp. 453-458.

ADDITIONAL READINGS

Curry, Robert L. "Teaching the Decoding Skills," in Lawrence E. Hafner (ed.), *Improving Reading in Secondary Schools*. New York: The Macmillan Company, 1967, pp. 84 - 93.

Edwards, Thomas J. "The Language-Experience Attack on Cultural Deprivation," *The Reading Teacher,* XVIII (April 1965), pp. 546-551, 556.

Gagon, Glen S. "Modern Research and Word Perception," *Education,* LXXXVI (April 1966), pp. 464-472.

Lefevre, Carl A. "Contributions of Linguistics," *Instructor* (March 1965), pp. 77, 103 - 105.

REQUIRED READINGS FROM BOOK OF READINGS

V. Developing Vocabulary and Word Recognition Skills

Developing Vocabulary: Another Look at the Problem—Lee. C. Deighton.

Teaching Word Recognition for Better Vocabulary Development—Arthur V. Olson.

Teaching Essential Reading Skills - Vocabulary—Earle E. Crawford.

chapter 6

Rate of Reading

Since about 1955 considerable interest has been generated in various types of speed reading programs. Indeed, some people have unfortunately equated the need for developmental reading programs at the secondary school level with the need for programs to improve students' speed of reading. The result has been rather narrowly conceived reading programs with an emphasis on speed to the neglect of various vocabulary, comprehension and critical reading skills.

Actually the emphasis upon speed is not new to our culture. The demands made upon students to assimilate rapidly the ever-increasing body of knowledge is a formidable task put before most students. It is because of these demands that the schools have logically indicated an interest in the problem of increasing students' rates of reading. Considerable controversy exists, however, in regard not only to how increased speed may be attained but also as to its desirability and effect.

CAUSES OF SLOW READING

A large number of secondary school students have very slow rates of reading. The causes of slow reading may generally be found within three categories.

The first general category has to do with the developmental level of the student. A child begins formal reading instruction with his oral and silent reading speed developing at approximately the same rate. As he progresses through the elementary grades, both oral and silent speed increase at about the same rate until approximately grade 4. After grade 4, the rate of silent reading increases at a much faster rate. The table below shows a comparison or oral and silent reading rates for grades 1 - 6 that indicates the trend described.

If a junior or senior high school student is at an elementary developmental level in his reading, it is reasonable to expect that his rate of silent reading will be slower than expected of a student at his grade level. Students should be helped to increase and adjust their developmental level. The teacher should seldom, if ever, provide practice in increasing the rate of silent reading if the student is functioning at sixth-grade developmental level or below.

Rate in Words Per Minute (Durrell, 1958)*

Grade	1	2	3	4	5	6
Oral	45	80	110	135	150	170
Silent	45	78	125	156	180	210

*From Donald D. Durrell, *Improving Reading Instruction* (New York: Harcourt Brace Jovanovich, Inc., 1956), p. 174. Reprinted with permission of the publisher.

The second major source of difficulty to explain a slow rate of reading may be found within the habits and psychological make-up of the student himself. Any one of the following factors could interfere with the development of adequate silent reading speed.

1. The student has the habit of moving his lips, tongue, or larynx while reading silently. If a student has subvocalization it means that, although he is reading silently, he is in effect reading orally. His silent reading speed is the same as his oral reading speed.

2. The student does not read frequently enough to gain any speed.

3. The student has been taught during his early reading instruction to analyze every word with which he comes in contact.

4. The student's background of experience is so limited that he is unable to read rapidly.

5. The student has a limited vocabulary, both in breadth and depth, making any reading slow.

6. The student has developed such poor study habits that he is unable to concentrate on reading material for even a limited period of time.

A third source of difficulty in improving rate may be within the make-up of the reading material. If the material contains too many unknown words or difficult concepts, the student will have an almost impossible task in understanding what he reads. He will also tend to read slowly when the material is uninteresting to him. In instances where the style or language structure is different than most material read by the student, difficulties in communication will be found.

The reader's approach to the reading may also seriously influence his rate of reading. Poor study habits or inability to adjust the rate of reading to the purpose for reading may make relatively simple reading assignments seem lengthy and involved. It is obvious to most experienced teachers who observe classroom behavior with an educated eye that poor study skills along with poorly defined purposes for reading are the chief causes of slow reading. All of the causes of slow rate of reading can be cured and students can improve if appropriate reading instruction is given.

METHODS OF IMPROVING RATE

The best possible way of improving rate is to provide an abundance of easy reading material of high interest. No student can improve and sustain an improved rate of reading without reading frequently. Often teachers believe that rate of reading will improve if the poor reader follows along in his text as the good reader reads orally. This assumption is not only incorrect but a harmful. The teacher in this situation has no control over the learning and is forcing the poor reader into a silent reading speed that is the same as the oral reading speed.

If the rate of reading is to be improved the student needs to have supervised practice and training in some specific techniques for increasing rate. The SQ3R study method described in Chapter 3 is one highly profitable technique for reading. Later as the student improves his ability this technique can be broadened to skimming for key words and topic sentences.

Improvement of rate of reading may also be achieved by using a wide variety of devices. The devices can be classified into four categories: (1) pacers, (2) tachistoscopes, (3) controlled readers, and (4) skimmers and scanners. A brief discussion of each category follows.

Reading pacers are designed to control reading rate without imposing a set or pattern of phrasing. A shutter gradually covers a page from top to bottom at a speed which can be regulated by the individual.

The tachistoscope is a device which presents timed exposures of pictures, numbers, and letters. Students learn to pay careful attention to detail, to perceive in a left-to-right fashion, and to remember more of what they see. Exposure time can range from 1/100 second to as long as 1 1/2 seconds.

Controlled reading is accomplished by having reading material printed on specially prepared rolls of films, or on special filmstrips. There are a variety of shutter arrangements for presenting the material. One device has a shutter that exposes one third of a line at a time; others present one phrase at a time, and the filmstrip technique involves a slot which moves across the page uncovering words and then covering them again to keep the reader from regressing. Some of the devices have more flexibility than others in terms of speed control, and some have a more extensive library of materials.

The skimming and scanning devices are constant-speed devices which aid the already competent reader to move from all-inclusive reading, in which every line of print is read, to selective reading, in which the reader looks for more significant facts and then stops to read them. These devices should not exercise control or direct the reader. One device employs a single bead of light which moves at a constant speed down the centerfold of the text.

Specific examples of each of the four major types of speed-reading devices follow. The purposes of each device and the training program connected with the device is included.

1. Pacers

SRA Reading Accelerator, Science Research Associates, Inc., 259 East Erie Street, Chicago, Ill.

Description

The reading accelerator is a reading pacer device. It is portable, lightweight, and entirely mechanical. The accelerator has a shutter, a dial control for speed setting and a wide range of speed settings (30-3,000 words per minute). The shutter moves at a consistent pace down the page forcing the individual to keep ahead and at the same time covers the preceding line so that the reader cannot make the regressions that he makes in normal reading. There are three *SRA Better Reading Books* designed to accompany this device.

Purpose

The accelerator is designed to help correct word by word reading, vocalizing, and unnecessary eye regressions. It encourages good phrasing, effective eye movements, and increased span of perception. Because the person using the accelerator cannot look back, he develops those patterns which result in better speed of reading and comprehension.

Program

The accelerator has many applications. It can be sued for individualized training within the classroom, reading laboratory, or for free reading. It is suitable for all types of books, newspapers, or magazines. There is no grade level assigned. After each session on the accelerator, rate and comprehension should be checked without using the accelerator. The *SRA Better Reading Books* were designed for this. This unpaced check has three purposes:

(1) To give immediate practice in applying accelerator habits in a normal situation.
(2) To make sure that comprehension remains high as rate is increased.
(3) To provide a sound method for determining rate setting for the next accelerator session.

Rateometer, Audio-Visual Research, 1509 8th Street S.E., Waseca, Minn.

Descriptions

The Rateometer is a pacing device. It weighs less than three pounds and is easy to handle, carry, and store. There are three models available.

Model A. The standard range model which can be set from 70 to 2,500 words per minute. This model serves all ages and levels except for special needs.

Model B. Speed range is 20 to 500 words per minute. It is used for very slow or remedial readers.

Model C. Speed range is 140 to 5,000 words per minute. This model is used for special college and adult reading programs.

Purpose
The Rateometer was designed to help all persons to improve their reading
speed and to improve comprehension.

Program
There is no definite program designed to accompany the Rateometer. It can
be used with all levels of materials and with all types of publications. It is
an individual device and not for group purposes. The literature accompanying the Rateometer states: "Surveys show that Rateometer practice sessions
vary from 20 to 60 minutes with a majority at 30 minutes."
A typical session would be as follows: First 10 minutes—the T-bar is set a
speed slightly beyond reader's normal rate to provide a challenge. Second
10 minutes—rate is increased 25, 50, or 100% to provide a visual and mental challenge to read phrases instead of words or syllables, to move eyes
smoothly and rythmically line by line, and to extract ideas more quickly.
Third 10 minutes—rate is returned to same as the first 10 minutes, then
moved left to find a higher reading speed.

2. Tachistoscopes
Tach-X Tachistoscope 500, Educational Developmental Laboratories, Huntington, N.Y.

Description
The Tach-X is a 35-mm filmstrip projector equipped with a timing
mechanism that provides exposure speeds of $1/100$ second to 1 ½ seconds.
The Tach-X flashes pictures, numbers, letters, words, or phrases on the
screen for a brief time. The students say or write what they saw; then the
material is focused for another look and the student checks his work.
Filmstrips are available for kindergarten through adult levels. Each set of
filmstrips is accompanied by a description of the materials and a list of
suggested activities. A write-on kit is available with filmstrips printed with
blank spots which the teacher can fill in.

Purpose
The Tach-X training helps the beginning reader build visual discrimination
skills and to stabilize a sight vocabulary. For the older student, it helps to
sharpen his powers of visual perception and retention. The timed exposures
help the student learn how to pay careful attention to details, to see in the
left-to-right sequence, and later to transfer their seeing skills to meaningful
content. Words and phrases flashed can serve as a basis for spelling exercises, word analysis, vocabulary building, and other activities.

Program
One Tach-X can serve from eight to sixteen teachers in a building. This will
depend on the scheduling. In addition to the programs for the Tach-X, a
write-on kit is available for the teachers who want to try out an unusual
approach or special content. There are programs designed for kindergarten
through adult levels. At the secondary, college, and adult levels the Tach-X
can be used to extend vocabulary and retain accuracy of perception. There
are three sets of filmstrips with 25 to 36 films in each. There are two plans

for scheduling and either may be used. Plan A incorporates word phrase drills in twenty two-part sessions of 30 to 35 minutes each. The first part involves nonverbal training and the second part is devoted to word recognition drills or vocabulary building exercises.

Keystone Tachistoscope, Keystone View Company, Meadville, Pa.

Description

The Keystone Tachistoscope is an overhead projector which has a flash meter attached. The flash meter is a timing device of the multiblade type with metal blades which provide speeds from 1 second to $1/100$ second. This device can only be used on the Keystone overhead projector. The lever opens the timing device regardless of setting of speed control to provide for easy viewing of the image at all times.

Purpose

Speed of perception is increased so that students perceive more at each eye-fixation. Quick and accurate perception of words, phrases, and sentences is developed. The span of recognition is increased so that pupils read phrases rather than words.

Program

One set of Tachistoslide units is available for elementary schools, which may consist of the primary grades, as one unit of phrase and sentence reading is for the first level, which is assumed to be for the early grades. Other sets are available for intermediate, secondary, and adult classes. This device may be used with quite a large group as the material is flashed on a screen.

3. Controlled Readers

Controlled Reader, Educational Developmental Laboratories, Huntington, N.Y.

Description

The controlled reader is a 35-mm filmstrip projector equipped with a speed control (0 to 1,000 words per minute) and a left-to-right scanning mechanism. The instrument is equipped with a means of starting and stopping the exposure slot which permits the teacher to use the machine in readiness and oral reading. The left-to-right slot should be used to bring trainees up to speeds of approximately 500 words per minute, then the free-reading slot should be used. The free-reading slot is designed for acceleration only and should not be used until the reading attack is sufficiently developed. Filmstrips are available for levels from readiness to adult level. The general content of these filmstrips is persons, animals or objects; locale or setting; type of plot; motivating agent; and degree of realism. Each set of story filmstrips is accompanied by a copy of questions and story books for the teacher to use.

Purpose

The controlled reader purports to develop the functional and interpretive skills in the reading process. The funcitonal skills developed are:

1. Coordination and mobility—developed by the left-to-right moving slot.

2. Directional attack—improved as the moving slot directs the reader's eye's in a constant left-to-right fashion and decreases the fixations and regressions.

Developed simultaneously with the functional skills are the interpretive skills:

1. Orderly perception
2. Heightened attention and concentration
3. Faster thinking and more rapid reading
4. Ability to organize thoughts
5. Better comprehension

The basic purpose of the controlled reader is to improve the reader's functional effeciency and comprehension by modifying his reading attack and perceptual organization through left-to-right control.

Program

The controlled reader can be used effectively for small group instruction. There is a temptation for teachers to use it with the entire class but this should not be done except during the "get-acquainted stage" in which the students are becoming familiar with the training. During this period the teacher will find it advantageous to use easy materials so that all students can comprehend with ease.

For best results, the students should be grouped according to their reading proficiency, placing emphasis on vocabulary and experience background, in grades one and two and on rate, in higher grades.

Many factors should be considered in giving controlled reading training. A discussion of these follows.

1. Grouping
2. Scheduling
   (a) minimum sessions recommended

   | grade 1-3 | 50 | Junior, Senior High | 30 |
   | grade 4-6 | 40 | College | 20 |

3. Training-developing functional and interpretive skills.
4. Content

   Students should begin reading one or two levels below grade level. When comprehension falls below 70 percent content should be dropped to a lower level.
5. Rate

   Graduating from the guided to the free reading slot. This is done usually after a person attains a speed of 500 - 600 wpm.

4. Skimmers and Scanners

   EDL Skimmer, Educational Developmental Laboratories, Huntington, N.Y.

   Description

   The Skimmer is a rate motivator and timing monitor which has a bead of light which travels down the center fold of the book at a constant rate of 800 - 1,000 wpm. The Skimmer has a timing dial which provides a measure of completion timing for scanning.

Purpose
The skimmer is designed to help the competent reader move from inclusive reading to selective reading in that the reader looks for important points and stops to read them inclusively. The skimmer helps the reader to attend perceptually and organizationally at the highest possible level.

Program
Students work with the skimmer individually for approximately 30 minutes each day.

VALUE OF MACHINES IN DEVELOPING READING RATE

Since the early 1940's there has been an increased emphasis on mechanical devices to increase students' rates of reading. The experimentation done during World War II to increase the quick recognition of enemy aircraft and warships was so successful that it was assumed the same techniques could be used to improve the speed of reading.

The research that is available on the use of machines indicates that they are no more effective in increasing rate than any other method. The devices can be used with some effectiveness as motivational devices, but studies show that even when used for this purpose, the motivation is lessened once the novelty of the machine dies. If the machines will provide some needed motivation for the reading program, and if they can be purchased without hurting the rest of the program, the teacher should not hesitate to use them. The machines can complement the total reading program if they are utilized wisely.

The critics of machines to improve rate of reading often state as one of their arguments the problem of transfering the gain in speed to the act of reading a book. Some manufacturers have tried to overcome this criticism by using the book as the material on which the machine is used. In one machine, for example, the machine is placed over the book and the student reads through a piece of glass while a shutter moves down over the page at a predetermined speed.

Most of the machines used for increasing rate of reading do not insure the transfer of increased rate by training. If transfer is to occur the teacher must take care to teach for the transfer. This can be done by giving the student practice in the skill being taught through regular reading materials until he has mastered the skill. Then and only then should the student be encouraged to apply this skill in a speeded situation. After the speeded work the student should do further application in regular school material, trying to apply the skill while maintaining speed. Training procedures must provide for the transfer of the skills if the machines are to be of any value.

FLEXIBILITY IN READING RATE

Many newspapers throughout the United States have carried advertisements or articles claiming that speed training can produce rates of reading of several thousand words per minute. The problem seems to be one of definition of the meaning for reading. Reading is usually meant to involve the act of reading most of the words on the printed page. If this is part of the definition of reading, then it is impossible to read faster than 800 or 900 words per minute. Anything that is done beyond this rate refers only to skimming, scanning, or other rapid reading techniques.

Actually, the major objective in a secondary school reading program with regards to reading rate is not simply to develop one fast rate of reading for all students. Rather, the key principle to get across to students is flexibility of reading rate. There are several speeds of reading, and the appropriate one depends upon the material to be read and the purpose for reading. Students should be given a variety of material and reading purposes and learn to adjust their rates accordingly.

SUMMARY

Since about 1955 the emphasis in developmental reading programs in high school has been on speed, almost to the exclusion of other skills. This emphasis is an outcome of the increasingly strenuous demands placed on students in regards to the amount of material they are required to cover while in high school.

Generally speaking, there are four major causes of slow reading: (1) developmental level below normal, (2) habits and psychological make-up, (3) reading material, and (4) approach to reading or poor study habits.

In order to improve his reading rate, a student must be exposed to supervised practice and training in specific "rapid reading" techniques. He must be provided with an adundance of high-interest reading material, and he must read frequently.

Pacers, tachistoscopes, controlled readers, and skimmers and scanners are some of the devices that are employed in a developmental reading program. Machines have been used but research has shown that they are generally no more effective than other methods.

Flexibility in reading rate is an extremely important aspect of "speed reading," and the appropriate rate of reading is dependent upon the material read and the purpose for reading.

ADDITIONAL READINGS

Adams, R. Buchanan. "Reading Comprehension and Reading Speed: A Discussion of Research," *Reading as an Intellectual Activity*, VIII. IRA Proceedings, 1963, pp. 241 - 243.

Berger, Allen. "Controversial Issues Pertaining to Reading Rate," in George B. Schick and Merrill M. May (eds.), *Seventeenth Yearbook of the National Reading Conference*. Milwaukee, Wis.: National Reading Conference, 1968.

Braam, Leonard S., and Allen Berger. "Effectiveness of Four Methods of Increasing Reading Rate, Comprehension, and Flexibility," *Journal of Reading*, XI (February 1968), pp. 346 - 352.

Cason, E. B. "Mechanical Methods for Increasing the Speed of Reading," *Teachers College Contributions to Education*, No. 878, pp. ix - 80.

Rankin, Earl F., Jr. "A New Method of Measuring Reading Improvement," *Reading and Inquiry*, X. IRA Proceedings, 1965, p. 207.

REQUIRED READINGS FROM BOOKS OF READINGS

VII. Developing Reading Rate

Uses and Limitations of Speed of Reading Programs in Schools—Miles A. Tinker.

Reading Rate is Multilevel—Don H. Parker.

Skimming in Reading: A Fine Art for Modern Needs—Helen S. Grayum.

chapter 7

Reading in the Content Areas

As students progress through the secondary school, they face the increasingly difficult problem of bringing special reading skills to the content subject-matter fields. The reading skills learned in the elementary grades offer no guarantee of equally successful skills in history, science, English, or any other field. In fact, reading in the subject-matter areas makes different demands upon these skills than those used in reading a newspaper, magazine, or novel. Students should use the fundamental reading skills already learned, but in addition they must learn new and special skills.

Attention must be paid to the special reading abilities required in subject-matter areas or students will fail to achieve as they should. Reading instruction in any of the subjects must become an integral part of the teaching program. The job cannot be left for someone else on the school staff. There is no question that failure to teach the necessary reading skills is failure to teach the subject matter well.

THE CONTENT-AREA TEACHER'S ATTITUDE AND ROLE

It is not unusual for teachers in the secondary school to be completely indifferent to the ranges of reading ability in their classrooms. In a recent study conducted with 585 junior and senior high school teachers, Olson (1968) found that only 10 percent of the teachers made any provision for using other reading materials with students who were unable to read the regular text. The principals supervising these same teachers said that less than 7 percent provided textbooks or other reading materials. With this type of practice occurring in secondary schools, it is easy to see why the dropout rate among students is so high.

One may wonder about the reason for this odd attitude on the part of some teachers. An oversimplified yet reasonable answer would be that the philosophy which permeates secondary schools is not in harmony with the philosophy of society. The European schools, which this country's secondary schools copied, can maintain standards because of the basic philosophy of their system. Students in this country, however, are compelled to attend school until they

Reading in the Content Areas 101

reach a certain chronological age, after which school attendance is no longer compulsory. Under this system, rigid standards by which all students are judged, cannot be maintained. The teacher who says, "If he can't do the work he shouldn't be here," is transposing a philosophy from one system to a situation where it has little or no meaning and indeed contradicts the basic philosophy of that system. Standards are appropriate if the product being produced can be controlled. There is no quality control in this educational system, and the idea of maintaining standards for specific pupil performance is therefore unrealistic.

Teaching the Content and Reading

The content-area teacher's primary job is to help students master the particular content of the subject. Reading is one means by which learning is reinforced and extended, and thus the teacher must be sure that the student can effectively apply the reading skills to particular reading material. The content-area teacher is a teacher of reading to the extent that he is aware of the varying abilities of his students, provides for these differences when assigning materials, and teaches students the skills necessary for the mastery of the content of his teaching area.

Every content-area teacher should engage in the following classroom practices.

1. Make certain that the text materials are suited in difficulty to the reading levels of the students.
2. At the beginning of the school year, take adaquate time to introduce the text and discuss how to use it effectively.
3. Teach the specialized vocabulary and new concepts to the students before they begin to read the material in the textbook.
4. Take time to teach the special reading skills necessary in the subject area.
5. Make the assignments clearly and concisely so that the student will know what he is reading for, and how to go about the reading.
6. Help the poor reader to develop adequate reading skills to the extent of the teaching capabilities of the teacher.
7. Group students within the classroom for differentiated instruction.

There need not be a conflict between teaching the content of the subject and teaching the skills needed to acquire that content. Any classroom teacher who provides for the instructional needs of the students is at the same time teaching the student how to read the particular content more effectively. The application of the reading skills also has to be done through reading matter. In each case, the reading matter of the content material would be the reading material.

At least five major responsibilities face the content teacher who would help give his students direction in reading the instructional material. These five responsibilities may be summarized as follows:

1. *Teaching the specialized vocabulary.* Each teacher needs to take the time to teach the vocabulary that is unique to the content. The new words should be used in verbal context and presented on the board before the student is asked to read them in the textbook.

2. *Building the background for understanding the material.* Many of the content-area reading materials are heavily loaded with concepts. The teacher should take time to develop these concepts through use of discussion and visual aids before the student reads the material. It is a poor practice to try to correct misconceptions after the student has read the material if the concept were developed fully and then the student read to reinforce.

3. *Students need to be taught how to read effectively.* The teacher needs to be sure that the student is taught how to read the material in order to get the information the teacher wants. If the aim of the reading is to get the main idea, then one type of reading is needed; if inferential thinking is the aim, another type of direction must be given. If the teacher cannot help the student to apply the correct skills in order to comprehend the material then there is no reason for complaint when the student fails to understand. If there is a "best way" to read the material the teacher should make an effort to teach it.

4. *Reading special symbols of the subject.* In almost every subject there are symbols and abbreviations which need to be taught to the student. Many of these occur in the less "academic" subjects such as home economics or shop and drafting, which are often considered the easy reading areas.

5. *Reading maps, graphs, charts, and other types of aids.* Special attention needs to be given to these areas by teachers who use these as an integral part of the learning.

EFFECTIVE READING IN ENGLISH

Today a greater number of teachers are recognizing the need for reading instruction in the secondary school. Many realize this need is not because of poor teaching in the elementary school but because the subjects studied require a use of reading skills at higher and more refined levels. Before any content-area teacher can begin to improve his students' levels of reading ability he must be aware of the required skills and have some knowledge of the means by which they may be developed. In this section and for the rest of the chapter various content areas, together with the reading skills important for each, will be discussed.

If one of the primary objectives in English is to help students learn to read, to enjoy many kinds of literature, and to understand what they are reading, then they must be offered the opportunity to explore. They must have the chance to read the deep and the light, the good and the bad, the factual and the narrative type of material. If they are not given these opportunities, they will not grow in understanding and appreciation because they will be unable to compare or choose according to their likes and dislikes.

The materials that are used to develop the reading skills in English need to be administered with judgment. It is far better for a student to read something of poor literary quality that he understands and likes than to force him to read material of "better quality" that the teacher likes. It is painfully obvious that appreciation does not come from exposure. The student must be led slowly and with understanding. As the skills of understanding, figurative language, responding with emotional reactions, inferring meaning, and the like are developed, the student can be exposed to material of more literary merit. In making a judgment on the merits of any reading material, these statements should be considered:

1. The material may be a poor choice for him because it is at a much lower level than he is capable of reading and appreciating. If this is true, the material is a poor choice and he should be guided to better reading with a similar approach.

2. The material may be of poor quality, but is at his present level of understanding, appreciation and ability. In this case, the student needs to know that the teacher accepts what he is reading. The teacher needs to work on understandings, background, appreciation, and skills.

In order to read with understanding and appreciation, the students must have the following skills. All of these skills can be taught at various levels of ability, but not in the same way nor with the same depth.

Comprehension: The student should

1. Be able to find the main idea of a paragraph when it is stated in the beginning, middle, end, or is inferred.
2. Be able to read in order to pick out details.
3. Be able to interpret tables, charts, and diagrams.
4. Be able to interpret cartoons.
5. Be able to comprehend material written in sequence and recognize the organization of material.
    (a) Recognize the relationships of time, place, analogies, and cause-and-effect.
    (b) Recognize the sequence of plot, argument and character development.
    (c) Recognize the patterns of organization: time, contrast, main idea, climax.
    (d) Be able to outline material.
    (e) Be able to recall the author's pattern of organization.
6. Be able to read creatively in order to predict events, recognize mood, visualize, interpret figurative language, distinguish fact from opinion, generalize, and judge character.

Vocabulary: The student should

1. Have a knowledge of phonetic and structural principles that he can apply.

2. Be able to use context clues in unlocking the meaning of a new word.
3. Be able to select the correct meaning for words which have several different meanings.
4. Have a knowledge of the meaning for common prefixes, suffixes, roots, and their relationship to the whole word.
5. Be able to understand dialect.

Location Skills: The student should

1. Be able to find words quickly and efficiently in a dictionary or glossary.
2. Be able to use a table of contents and index effectively.
3. Be able to use the card catalogue.
4. Be able to find and select reference materials.

Speed: The student should

1. Be able to adjust the speed of his reading according to the type of material he is reading, his purpose for reading, and his previous knowledge of the material.

Oral Reading: The student should

1. Be able to read with correct phrasing.
2. Be able to read so as to interpret the author's meaning to the audience.
3. Be able to read at a speed according to the dictates of the material.
4. Be able to use punctuation signals as a means of interpretation.

Some other skills which are also of importance are

1. Interpreting the clues that reveal the personality of the characters.
2. Inferring setting and anticipating events from clues.
3. Reading to visualize.
4. Interpreting shades of meaning.
5. Recognizing the mood of a selection and changes in mood.
6. Following the development of a plot, subplot, and secondary details.
7. Recognizing the theme.
8. Reacting to the material.
9. Learning to evaluate the literary worth of material.
10. Recognizing the features of the short story.
11. Recognizing the features of the novel.
12. Recognizing the features of poetry.
13. Recognizing the features of the play.
14. Recognizing the features of the essay and biography.
15. Conveying interpretation through oral reading.

The mature reader makes inferences and other reactions to his reading while he is in the act of reading, not after he completes the material. The problems he encounters in his reading are solved almost immediately upon meeting them. Of primary importance, therefore, must be the task of helping students to interpret the clues as they are met. The teacher needs to prepare the student to meet the problems in his reading and then put him into a situation where he can apply the skills.

In teaching any of the skills in English the steps are not very definite and there is a great deal of overlapping. An attempt at a progression can be made, however, based upon experience in the teaching of the skills.

The teacher should attempt to teach only one skill at a time or at the most two or three related skills. Every selection which a student reads will contain a number of skills, but the teacher must concentrate on the skill or skills to be featured as the focal point of the lesson.

The reading difficulties present in English classroom materials are perhaps best understood by looking at the different literary genres. Each genre by the very nature of its form presents a unique problem for the student.

The Short Story

The short story is difficult to read because of the telescoped effect. Everything is omitted that is not absolutely necessary. Much of the background must be inferred from a few facts, and many incidents are undeveloped or unexplained. The hurried quality of the short story makes it necessary for the teacher to build a good background of experience for the concepts to be encountered so that the students can restore the imagery that has been left out.

The singleness of effect produced by the short story makes it necessary for the teacher to help students see the dominant intent of the story at an early stage in its development. This can be done by relying on the inference skills as they have been developed and by recognizing the nature of the story from hints in the author's style.

The Novel

The novel is different from the short story not only in length but also in the unhurried pace. It includes more characters and often tells the story of several persons and their relationship by interweaving several subplots with the main plot. It also develops character at great length by means of "scenes" or confrontations, usually with much dialog.

Trying to keep small subplots in mind while the author digresses the reader into another plot often makes the novel difficult to read. The reader who does not follow the trends in the story will soon be confused, will no longer try to understand what he is reading, and will lose interest. It is because of these characteristics that occasional reviews with all students are helpful, especially when the reading is resumed after the delay of a day or two.

Usually the novel can be read with greater speed because the reader is not required to supply so much from his own imagination. The language is more direct than that in the short story and it does not make telescope events important to the plot development.

Poetry

A poem must be understood before it can be appreciated. In order to understand poetry the student must pass through a hierarchy of types of poems. The simplest type of verse is the jingle, whose appeal lies almost entirely in its rhythm. Next, the humorous poem may contain elements of rhyme, but it is the humor that is of primary importance. Next are ballads or short narrative poems, although the language and the concepts may add to their difficulty. Lyric poems are usually not concerned with a story, but try to arouse a mood. They require considerable inferential ability and employ metaphor, simile, and imagery in their technical structure.

Poetry is best understood when heard by someone who reads it well. The student should be exposed to poetry but only to poetry he can understand and appreciate.

One of the comments often heard by teachers is that their students do not understand the abstractions of language in poetry. The comment is true when discussing particular poems and specific students, but the blanket statement that students cannot understand the abstractions of language is not true. Students are able to understand abstractions that are familiar to them.

An example of students' ability in dealing with poetic form and abstract language can be found in their work with haiku. Haiku is a poem in three lines of five, then seven, then five syllables. Following are some examples of an average ninth-grade class' efforts in writing haiku. After reading these poems, it is difficult to believe teachers when they say, "They don't understand poetry."

Radio is low;
No one will hear it playing
Under my pillow.

The sounding of Life
is only a respite from
the Silence of Death.

Love blooms and blossoms
Love stabs, stings, and hurts; but Love
true love, never dies.

Run, stop, turn, look, plump!
Now you've got the ball, so run.
Fake, stop, go, TOUCHDOWN.

Reach for the ceiling.
Just put your hands in the sky.
This is a hold-up.

They are cold, so cold
people without warmth and love
in their little world.

Waves along the shore
rush with sounds of rustling skirts
seagulls far away.

Love cannot be heard.
It can't be seen or described
—only felt by you.

The Drama

Of all the forms of literature, drama is the most difficult to read. Students of low ability should seldom be asked to *read* a drama, since it requires skills very seldom acquired at the level needed for appreciation by the poor reader. The drama is reduced to a bare minimum of essentials. The details regarding the appearance of the characters, the background for the action, and the world offstage are all left to the reader's imagination. The reader has to make innumerable inferences from the most subtle clues. Not only must he visualize the action and scene, but he must also utilize audile ability. He must obtain the auditory images of the characters so that he can understand the emotional verbal communication taking place.

Teaching the reading of drama is probably the most difficult task the English teacher must face. It requires accurate evaluation of the ability of the student to understand and a great deal of mastery on the part of the teacher.

READING IN MATHEMATICS

With the emphasis upon mathematics, it is unlikely that even the poor student in the secondary school will graduate with less than two or three years of work in this area. Because every student is expected to take some math work, whether it be general, business, shop, or college math, there are some reading skills that must be taught. Some of these skills are not taught in other content areas because they have no application or very limited application outside of mathematics. One of the major problems is the minimum number of words with the maximum amount of information. There is more information packed into a single sentence in mathematics than in any form of communication. The sentences utilize symbols rather than words. Another problem is that of a specialized vocabulary. The terms used in mathematics may be doubly confusing to the student because many of the words have common everyday meanings. There are several terms that can mean the same thing, and there are mathematical symbols as well as word symbols.

The difficulties which students experience in reading problems indicate that the teacher may have to provide help in one or more of the following areas:

1. *Understanding the Vocabulary.* In mathematics the student is exposed

very early in his school life to technical and unique vocabulary. The words he is asked to learn are not easy. In many cases, in order to really understand, the student must have a concept of a process. In the word *product,* for example, the student not only needs to change the common meaning for the word into the specific meaning in mathematics, but also has to understand how the word *product* is used in relationship to a process.

In the development of understanding and the ability to communicate in mathematics, it is vitally important that the vocabulary be understood and used precisely. The most logical thing for a teacher to do is to check the students' understanding of the commonly used terms and plan for reteaching those that are giving difficulty. This should be done before new vocabulary and concepts are introduced. The teacher can aid in the initial teaching and reteaching by using the vocabulary often, explaining through diagrams, interchanging terms where possible, and giving the students opportunities to use the vocabulary.

The old adage, "One picture is worth a thousand words," has much meaning in mathematics. The ability to visualize the problem and see relationships is of major importance. In the geometry problem, "If lines *DF* and *BC* meet so that $\angle 1 = \angle 2$, what is the relationship of lines *DF* to *BC?*," the student must be able to form a picture in his mind or he will be unable to make an accurate

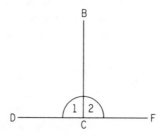

relationship. Once the words are visualized, it is easy to see that line *DF* and *BC* are at right angles to each other, making $\angle 1 = \angle 2$ ($\angle 1 = 90°$). Visual aids are important for making the problem more tangible, and should be used by the teacher as well as the student in developing concepts.

2. *Distinguishing Between Relevant and Irrelevant Facts.* In every mathematics problem there are words and phrases which are of primary importance in helping the student to read and understand the problem. The students must have some skill in weighing details. Without this ability, little can be expected.

3. *Visualizing Clearly.* The problem of visualizing as one reads has been, in recent years, an area of much discussion and little information. It is not known why some students visualize what they read and others do not, nor is it known with any degree of certainty how to develop the skill. Probably the best a teacher can do is to dramatize the problems as vividly as possible and to develop early problem study around the manipulation of concrete objects. For many students this will be the only way they will be able to operate, regardless of their

grade level. Students who fall within the normal range of intelligence, and certainly those who are in the low normal, need this kind of concreteness.

4. *Relating a Phrase to Other Phrases.* In mathematic problems the phrase is of primary importance since it usually contains a fact necessary for the solving of the problem. It is also important that the relationship between the phrases be grasped. In the problem: If Bob has *5 apples* and gave *1 to you* and *2 to Mary*, how many does he have *left for himself?* The relationship of the phrases is obvious.

5. *Translating a Work Statement into Computation.* After the reading of the problem, the student must take the word symbols he has read and translate them into mathematical symbols. In order to do this the student must be able to visualize, understand the vocabulary and translate.

6. *Following a Sequence of Operation.* After the problem has been comprehended and translated, the student must decide upon the plan of operation for finding the answer or answers. It is in this area that students need a great deal of guidance.

Techniques in Teaching the Reading of Mathematics

One useful technique in helping students read mathematics material more effectively is to give them a scheme or plan to follow in reading and solving mathematics problems. The following steps should be presented to students as a guide.

1. Read the entire problem slowly and carefully.
2. Read the problem again. Pay special attention to the sentence in the problem which asks or tells you what to find out. Decide what it asks you or tells you to do.
3. Read again to find out what facts are given that will help to solve the problem.
4. Decide what process to use. If there is more than one step involved, what should be done first, second, third, and so on.
5. With a good understanding of the problem in mind, try to estimate your answer.
6. Set your figures down on paper and make your computations carefully.
7. Compare your answer with the estimate. See if it makes sense.
8. Check your computation.

The teacher may find it beneficial to discuss the vocabulary and meaning of the problem with the class as a whole and then let the students do steps 1-5 in small groups for all of the problems assigned. After all of the problems are discussed, the students should do steps 6-8 individually. Class discussion and further evaluation by the class with the teacher's help is the final step.

Other activities that might be used to foster the skills and abilities needed in mathematics reading:

1. Encourage the students to keep 3 X 5 cards on which they have written

words, symbols, or formulas, with an explanation on the opposite side. These cards can be used for study and review.

2. Give the students a problem written in mathematical symbols and ask them to put it into a word problem. The reverse of this may also be done.
3. Have the students make graphs and charts.
4. Make visual aids to help in understanding difficult concepts.
5. Help the students to make a practical problem out of some mathematical concepts.
6. Reword the problems that are likely to give some students difficulty.
7. Use an easier text for those students having difficulty. Sometimes short sentences are easier to understand than long involved ones.
8. Give the students practice in visualizing by taking the problem segment by segment. This is particularly applicable to geometry.

READING IN SCIENCE

The complaint of science teachers is often that "the pupils cannot read." This reference to the inability of certain students to read has resulted many times in looking up the individual records of these students only to find that the reading ability as scored on a standard reading test is relatively high.

There is probably less reading in science than there is in any other content field in the elementary school. The students entering the junior high school, therefore, may not be very familiar with the kind of reading required in this field. Many of the basic skills apply to all subjects, but the skills must be directed to getting information from scientific materials.

The skills listed below are fundamental for effective reading in science:

1. Ability to change the rate of reading according to the purpose.
2. Ability to select and locate and use information from various sources.
3. Ability to learn and use the science vocabulary of the subject.
4. Ability to use and understand scientific symbols and formulas.
5. Ability to use graphs, charts, maps, scales, and diagrams to get information.
6. Ability to read for main idea and supporting detail.
7. Ability to organize material.
8. Ability to recognize and follow the sequence of steps in following directions.
9. Ability to evaluate the value of the material.
10. Ability to use the problem-solving technique:
    (a) Formulate the hypothesis
    (b) Collect the data
    (c) Organize the data

(d) Form a conclusion

(e) Test the conclusion

11. Ability to apply the information in helping to understand everyday problems.

The problem of vocabulary is probably one of the primary difficulties in reading science materials. There are several reasons for this: (1) The vocabulary in science is more exact, specialized, and extensive than in any other field. (2) Many commonly used words have a different and/or more exact meaning in science. For some students this will cause more difficulty than if they had to learn a totally new term. Some examples of words requiring scientific meanings are: *boil, carrier, cell, colony, culture.* (3) Many scientific words are derived from Greek and Latin words that are completely foreign to the student. The word analysis skills learned in previous grades will probably be of little or no help in pronunciation. The student will have to make new applications of the skills and formulate new generalizations to help him. (4) One word is often applied to a complicated concept or process. Some examples are: *sterilize, magnetism, photosynthesis, electrolysis, maturation.*

In order to reduce vocabulary difficulties to a minimum, it would be helpful to introduce only a few new words at a time. To further reduce confusion, there should be a readiness period where the meanings and processes are discussed when the term is introduced. Another technique is to encourage the students to use a card system for learning technical terms. The cards can be handled easily, can be carried and kept for study any time during the day when free time is available. They can be categorized into an "I don't know" pile and an "I know" pile. Sometimes a pretest on the vocabulary of a new unit will help the teacher to determine the terms that will cause the most difficulty and those known by the majority of the students. As another technique, the teacher should spend some time on teaching the meanings of important suffixes and prefixes found in scientific terminology. After learning some of the important root words, suffixes, and prefixes a good way to practice this knowledge is to try to unlock the meanings of words coming up in the unit. Another approach would be to coin new terms for imaginary compounds, devices, or laws.

Because it is an important teaching-learning tool, the science textbook needs to be examined closely for possible problems or difficulties. According to Mallinson (1964), research done on the reading difficulties of science textbooks has brought to light the following generalizations:

1. The reading levels of many textbooks in science are too advanced for the ability level of the students.

2. Differences between levels of reading difficulty of the easiest and hardest texts in all areas of sciences are significant.

3. In some texts whose average level of reading difficulty seems satisfactory, there are passages that would be difficult even for some students reading two or three years above grade level.

4. Many texts contain nontechnical words that could be replaced with easier synonyms.
5. Too many scientific terms are not defined when introduced.
6. Earlier passages tend to be more difficult than later passages.

Techniques in Teaching the Reading of Science

The following are some ways in which students may be helped to learn the reading skills for science while, at the same time, learning content. Some of the suggestions given for reading in other content subjects may be adapted to science:

1. Provide a section of the classroom where attractive pamphlets, magazines, and books can be displayed. Quantities of excellent materials can be obtained free or inexpensively from industrial firms and government agencies. The materials usually provide a wide range of subject matter as well as reading difficulty. The American Association for the Advancement of Science and the National Science Foundation both publish material of considerable value for teaching.
2. Underline, number or write down the steps in a process.
3. Try to write the findings of an experiment in one sentence.
4. In material where there are many facts, try to determine the most important ones by the aids given by the author. Some of these aids are: listing of important terms, use of italics, amount of space given to discussion of any one fact, pictures, or diagrams.
5. Have the students explain the practical use of what they have learned.

READING IN SOCIAL STUDIES

Reading in social studies demands many of the general skills needed for all areas, but it also demands some special skills. The student must learn a new vocabulary and how to use maps, charts, diagrams, and graphs. He needs to read critically and interpret relationships, especially cause-and-effect.

The skill of perceiving relationships is of primary importance in social studies. Without it a student would find it impossible to integrate ideas or to summarize and organize. If a student has a weakness in this area, one or all of the following problems will be evident. The student will be (a) unable to answer questions that ask *why* something happened, (b) unable to make a simple outline, (c) unable to relate facts from various sources into a meaningful whole, or (d) unable to summarize.

Every major event in history is made up of a series of causes and effects. The effects of one event may cause another which results in a chain reaction. If social studies is to be understood, the student must grasp this relationship.

Although all of the material in a social studies book is not concerned with cause-and-effect relationships, generally this pattern is prominent. A preview of the headings or titles in a chapter will often give an indication of cause-and-effect. The headings "Fertile Soil for Democratic ideas," "The Irritations of Mercantilism," "The colonies at war: 1775 - 1783" and finally, "Significance of the American Revolution" clearly indicate a cause-and-effect relationship. Questions that emphasize this type of relationship are necessary for the development of the ability.

Unless helped to do otherwise students also have a tendency to treat all the ideas in social studies material as equally important or at least try to remember as many of them as possible without discriminating among them on any basis whatever. In reading to remember, students should develop the ability to

1. Select those ideas that should be remembered for a given purpose.
2. Improve the quality of a single reading of material.
3. Make and use questions of one's own to help remember ideas for a given purpose.
4. Put an idea in one's own words without changing the meaning of the written material.

The possession of information and ideas is necessary for real thinking in social studies, but to allow students to accept facts as facts without discrimination is poor teaching. Skill in critical thinking of social studies material involves certain subskills in which students should have practice in a variety of situations. These subskills should be applied not only to written material used by students but also to the solution of social problems that arise both in school and out.

Teachers will think that many of these critical thinking skills are too mature to attempt with the students they teach. That is true if one considers full development of competency in each of the skills. On the other hand, a beginning can be made with each one of them in the light of the situations where children meet the opportunities to use them. Students should develop the ability to

1. Base opinions on data.
2. Recognize when there is insufficient information to answer a question.
3. Recognize conflicting viewpoints.
4. Draw a conclusion.
5. Stay within limits of information in reaching conclusions.
6. Justify conclusions.
7. Sense when the author is stating opinions and when he is sticking to facts.
8. Understand degrees of probability.
9. Weigh the reliability of different statements.
10. Cultivate a cautious, but not suspicious, attitude. (How do you know? Who says it? How does he know?)
11. Make simple comparisons and contrasts.
12. Select material with respect to relevance.
13. Sense cause-and-effect relationships.

READING IN OTHER CONTENT AREAS

The content areas discussed earlier in the chapter are not the only subjects taught within the curriculum of the school. After reading how to develop some of the skills listed under the other areas, however, it may suffice to list the skills in other content areas in hope that the creative teacher will be able to use appropriate teaching techniques from the information already given.

Reading and Industrial Arts

The effective reader is able to
1. Identify tools by their labels in context.
2. Identify objects and detail from various illustration formats: blueprints, schematic, two-dimensional, artist-conception, exploded-view, templates.
3. Identify and interpret graphic symbols—dimensions, soil, concrete, wood, window, axis, and the like.
4. Locate resources and information relative to problems, tools, and materials.
5. Select materials and equipment rapidly from labels.
6. Read and follow directions from context, flow charts, diagrams.
7. Plan procedures from details in context and illustrations.
8. Locate, select, and use reference manuals.
9. Sort and arrange equipment and materials according to context.
10. Locate information by special indexing systems: manufacturer, system usage, sectional.
11. Evaluate manufacturer's claims.
12. Evaluate procedures suggested, designs, and illustrations for accuracy and completeness.
13. Predict results from procedures of materials suggested and/or used.
14. Evaluate difficulty from directions and apply to own ability.
15. Define, explain, illustrate specialized vocabulary: *warp, woof, pearl, steep, simmer, organza.*
16. Interpret meanings and implications of descriptive phrases: *polished, shrink-resistant, enriched, fortified.*

Reading and Music

The effective reader is able to
1. Identify, recognize, demonstrate, and explain specialized vocabulary: *opera, libretto, symphony, fugue.*
2. Identify, recognize, explain meanings of symbol orientation.
3. Interpret intended moods and purposes of composer from notations, signature, lyrics, tempo, description, and critiques.
4. Relate the mood effects of text with mood effects of the sound.

5. Relate total music effect to own experiences.
6. Identify, recognize, and relate identification terms to instruments and instrument parts.
7. Follow directions in several formats: music score, context, manuals, stage directions.
8. Recall words and notation.

Reading and Art

The effective reader is able to
1. Identify, recognize, pronounce, and interpret foreign words.
2. Recognize and interpret implied moods and meanings from descriptive passages.
3. Relate meanings to historical and social referent of artist.
4. Relate mood effects of descriptive material to art work.
5. Identify and comprehend technical terms of various crafts: pottery, sculpture, paint, architecture, geometry.
6. Identify value or emotional terms in descriptive context and detect their effect upon self.

Reading and Physical Education

The effective reader is able to
1. Identify, recognize, and interpret abbreviations and symbols.
2. Interpret special meanings for common words.
3. Define, identify, and illustrate equipment, procedures, and physiology from terms in context.
4. Follow directions presented in various formats: context, listing, flow charts, diagrams, photographs.
5. Identify detail and procedures from various formats.
6. Locate resources and information relative to problems, procedures, sports, and physiology.
7. Interpret from diagrams, charts, and photographs.
8. Evaluate by comparing performance with description or directions.
9. Recall procedures and regulations (memorize).
10. Interpret implied theory (strategy) from procedural instructions.
11. Predict outcomes from directions and self ability.
12. Visualize performance from directions, or spatial relationships from illustrations.
13. Relate spatially and sequentially.

Reading and Health

The effective reader is able to
1. Identify, recognize and interpret abbreviations and symbols.

2. Identify, recognize, and interpret special vocabulary of physiology, nutrition, pathology, social medicine.
3. Define, identify, explain, and illustrate equipment, processes, materials, physiology from discrete terms in context.
4. Follow directions.
5. Relate symptomatically and cause-and-effect relationship.
6. Analyze and diagnose problems from data.
7. Relate data by grouping.
8. Identify, recognize, and interpret foreign terms.
9. Visualize procedures, appearances.
10. Predict outcomes.

SUMMARY

It is the major task of the content-area teacher to help students master the content of a particular subject. This teacher is a teacher of reading to the extent that he is aware of the various abilities of his students, provides for these differences when assigning materials, and teaches his students the skills necessary to grasp the content of his subject matter. A high dropout rate in high school may be partly attributable to the inability of content-area teachers to gear the reading level of the subject matter to the reading level of all of the students.

The content-area teacher has five major responsibilities: teaching specialized vocabulary; building background for understanding; teaching how to read effectively; teaching special symbols particular to the subject; and teaching how to read maps, graphs, and charts. The teaching of content compliments the teaching of reading and vice versa, and the "Directed Lesson," used frequently in the elementary schools, is an excellent way in which to integrate the teaching of reading with the teaching of content.

English: To read and enjoy literature, a student must not be forced to read "quality" literature, but rather permitted to progress from material which is easy to read and enjoyable to that which is more difficult, "better" literature. Appreciation does not come from exposure; it comes from being led slowly with understanding.

Math: Two major factors must be taken into account in the reading of mathematical material: a minimum amount of words are used to express a maximum amount of information and a specialized vocabulary is involved.

Science: Students entering junior and/or senior high school have not been exposed to much science reading and they must learn to adapt their rate of reading to grasp the word meanings and details necessary for understanding scientific material.

Social Studies: In the area of social studies, students must develop and refine three major skills: critical reading, discrimination, and interpretation, especially cause-and-effect relationships.

Specialized reading skills are also necessary in the areas of industrial arts, music, art, physical education, and health.

REFERENCES

Mallinson, George G. "Reading and the Teaching of Science," *School Science and Mathematics*, LXIV (February 1964), pp. 148 - 153.

Olson, Arthur V. "Attitude of High School Content Area Teachers Toward the Teaching of Reading," in George Schick (ed.), *Multidisciplinary Aspects of College-Adult Reading*, Seventeenth Yearbook of the National Reading Conference, 1968, pp. 162 - 166.

ADDITIONAL READINGS

Carlin, Jerome. "A Pattern for Teaching Literature," *English Journal*, LV (March 1966), pp. 291 - 297.

Ekwall, E. K. "Science Teacher's Role in Reading," *Science Teacher*, XXXIV (September 1967), pp. 31 - 32.

Michaels, Melvin L. "Subject Reading Improvement: A Neglected Teaching Responsibility," *Journal of Reading* (October 1965).

Palmer, John R. "The Problem of Understanding History," *The Educational Forum*, XXX (March 1966), pp. 287 - 294.

Simmons, John S. "Teaching Levels of Literary Understanding," *English Journal*, LIV (February 1965), pp. 101 - 102, 107, 139.

Smiley, Marjorie B. "Gateway English: Teaching English to Disadvantaged Students," *English Journal*, LIV (April 1965), pp. 265 - 274.

REQUIRED READINGS FROM BOOK OF READINGS

VIII. Developing Reading Skills in the Content Areas

Developing Reading Skills in the Content Areas—Ruth Strang.

Attitude of High School Content Area Teachers Toward the Teaching of Reading—Arthur V. Olson.

Reading: In and Out of the English Curriculum—Margaret J. Early.

The Reading of Fiction—Edward J. Gordon.

The Reading of Literature: Poetry as an Example—John S. Simmons.

Reading—Helen Huus.

Reading and the Teaching of Science—George G. Mallinson.

Research on Problems in Reading Science—J. Bryce Lockwood.

Measuring the Readability of High School Health Texts—Aubrey C. McTaggart.

Reading in Mathematics—I. E. Aaron.

Reading and Mathematics—Russell J. Call and Neal A. Wiggin.

Reading Improvement in the Industrial Arts Class—Malcolm Heyman and Richard Holland.

Solving Reading Problems in Vocational Subjects—Isidore N. Levine.

chapter 8

The Directed Lesson

The preceding chapters in this text have dealt with the various skills thought to be crucial at the secondary school level, and considerable emphasis has been placed on the responsibility of subject-matter teachers to develop these skills in their respective classes. In order for the teaching of the various reading skills to be properly integrated with the teaching of content, the subject-matter specialist needs a definite organization pattern for all his lessons.

The directed-lesson concept, which is an established part of the teaching of reading in the elementary grades, is one possible answer to this organization problem and is presented in considerable detail in the pages to follow. In addition, certain related topics such as the use of questions to promote reading comprehension will be presented.

The directed lesson, as normally used in the elementary school reading program, consists of the following parts:

1. Preparation for reading
   (a) Providing necessary background
   (b) Presenting new vocabulary
   (c) Establishing purposes for reading
2. Directed reading and discussion
3. Extending skills and abilities
4. Enrichment and follow-up activities

Each of these four phases will be delineated further in the sections that follow with the emphasis on modifying the concept to make it highly applicable to the content-area teacher interested in incorporating reading instruction with her content.

PREPARATION FOR READING

Providing Necessary Background

The first phase of the directed lesson is involved with three aspects of preparing a student for what he is about to read. One aspect is concerned with providing any necessary background of experience so that the eventual reading and understanding of the material will be enhanced. What the nature and

118

amount of this background experience should be, and the form in which it should be presented, depends on the material to be read and the objectives for including the material in the curriculum.

For example, an English teacher might, for certain poems, present as a preparatory experience considerable biographical material about the poets. Many teachers would maintain that poems such as "To Helen" and "Annabel Lee" are better understood and appreciated if the students are acquainted with the life of Edgar Allan Poe and, in particular, his rather tragic romantic life.

On the other hand, it would be reasonable to assume that one need not know much about the life of Robert Nathan to understand and appreciate the poem "Dunkirk." What *would* be relevant background material for this poem? Certainly, some historical material about World War II and the importance of Dunkirk would be in order.

The teacher must decide for each selection or assignment what would be relevant background material to present to his students. Of course, the effective teacher is the one who first assesses what the students already know about the material, because in some cases the students may have the necessary background. In a junior high science class there may well be boys whose knowledge of automobile engines surpasses anything the teacher might provide.

Teachers should not forget that the kind of background material presented is also highly dependent on the objectives for using the reading material. For example, suppose an English teacher is about to begin her annual unit on Shakespeare's *Julius Caesar*. Her teaching plan will be to assign the play to be read by scenes and acts, and then there will be daily class discussions over the material. Her stated objectives for teaching the play have primarily to do with students understanding of the play's theme play as well as their developing an appreciation of the universality of the theme, even in today's world. Secondarily, she hopes to develop in her students an appreciation of the power and eloquence of Shakespeare's language.

The question is: How does she introduce this unit so that the proper background is provided? Suppose she goes ahead and spends two or three class periods on an elaborate and detailed discussion of the Globe Theater and how plays were performed in Shakespeare's time, complete with a model of the theater. Is this a defensible use of the time?

Perhaps the inclusion of the material can be justified by the teacher on the grounds that she simply wants students to know about the Globe Theater and play production for its own sake. But the use of the material she chose could hardly be justified as providing the necessary background for an understanding and appreciation of the play, as her own objectives for teaching the play reflect.

In other words, a teacher should ask herself certain questions before giving out assignments: Why am I asking students to read this selection? What do I intend to stress in any discussion of the material? What do my students already know about the subject which I can bring out in a discussion before actually assigning the material to be read? What gaps need to be filled in their experiential backgrounds before I ask them to encounter this new material?

Presenting New Vocabulary

The second task for the content teacher in the preparation phase of the directed lesson is to present the new, and/or crucial vocabulary for the assigned reading material. The teacher must look over the material to be assigned, determine what words should be stressed because they are keys to understanding the content, and then decide the various ways in which she will introduce the words to the students.

The material in Chapter 5 in this text can be used as a guideline for determining different means of vocabulary introduction. As an example, a new word for a given lesson is made up of prefixes, suffixes, and roots which the teacher feels the students already know; then she might simply display the word and ask them to unlock it by structural analysis.

As another example, she may choose to use a new word in a phrase or sentence, perhaps the very sentence in which the word appears in the assigned text, and ask her students to use context clues to determine the meaning of the word. (An illustration of how a teacher introduced words to students through asking them to use contextual analysis is given in the second example of a directed lesson at the end of this chapter.) Or the teacher may display still another new word and ask her students to use a dictionary or the glossary in their textbooks to determine both pronunciation and meaning.

It seems only reasonable to follow this practice of helping students with the new and difficult vocabulary in an assignment prior to their having to read it. Too often, teachers will ask students to read and discuss the material without any prereading vocabulary assistance, merely because the new vocabulary is given at the end of a chapter in the textbook. They wait until after the material is discussed and then tell students about the new terminology. In effect such teachers seem to say to the student: "Here, read this assignment and after you've struggled with it and failed to discuss it intelligently, I'll tell you about the vocabulary you should have known before you read it." It is good to note in this regard that in increasing numbers of newer textbooks the list of key vocabulary items is now being placed at the beginning of chapters.

For those who feel more comfortable with a practice when there is supportive research evidence, two recent studies have appeared in the literature which support this prereading vocabulary assistance approach. Smith and Burns (1970) conducted a study involving ninth-graders reading the poem "The Ballad of Father Gilligan" by William Butler Yeats. The students were divided into four groups by the type and amount of prereading assistance given. Two of the four groups are of special interest here. One group was given background information about ballads in general, this particular ballad, and the poet, then read the poem silently. The other group was given the same background information but was also helped by having the key words and word groups visibly indicated and were told to read silently with careful attention to these words. The second group, given the additional vocabulary assistance, scored significantly higher on an interpretation test.

Arnold Rehmann (1968) reported a similar study, using U.S. history material with seventh-graders. The students were divided into four experimental groups with three of the groups receiving varying amounts of background information and guiding study questions. However, the fourth group, which received this assistance but also was given specific vocabulary aids with marginal notes explaining the vocabulary concepts, scored significantly higher on comprehension tests.

Establishing Purposes for Reading

The third task in the preparation phase of the directed lesson is the establishment of purposes for which students are to read the assigned material. The assumption is that other things being equal, the student who has some definite purposes for reading a selection will read it with greater understanding than the student with no direction other than a command to get the job done. These purposes usually take the form of questions for which the student reads to find answers.

In other words, the feeling is that simply telling students "to read Chapter 22 for tomorrow" is not enough. The teacher should give the students some direction to guide their reading and study. What should be the type of purposes given? The simple and most direct answer is that teachers should offer purposes that truly reflect what they consider to be the most important parts of the material. Hopefully, the purposes which the students are given to guide their reading are both an accurate reflection of what the teacher expects to discuss in class and what she wishes the students to remember for any subsequent evaluation.

To put it another way, there should be a consistency present in all aspects of instruction. The college professor who is reported to have said he was a "triple threat" in that he asked his students to read one topic, talked in class about a second topic, and tested over still a third is more the rule than the exception.

Too often it appears that teachers are afraid of "spoon feeding" their students. They seem to fear that if they help students before reading and if this prereading assistance reflects their eventual discussion and coverage of the material, then their students might do too well on any subsequent tests. As a result, there would no longer be any easy way to assign grades, since *all* students would be learning. (Perish the thought!)

Others may say that by the time they are in secondary school, students should be expected to establish their own purposes for reading. Such people must have had little contact with large numbers of undergraduate and even graduate students in colleges and universities who have great difficulty in surveying textbook material and thereby fail to develop clear-cut purposes for reading.

Teachers at the secondary school level can, unfortunately expect some disappointments in initial attempts to use purposes to guide students' reading. One of the present authors recently helped direct a small action research project conducted by a high school social studies teacher which brought out this point.

This social studies teacher had decided to find out if his students would profit from his giving them definite purposes for reading. A selection was chosen from an economics textbook which his classes were not using. The selection chosen covered three major topics in a systematic, highly organized manner. The topics were: (1) the criteria for a "good" tax as developed by experts; (2) the major advantages of the property tax; (3) the major disadvantages or weaknesses of the property tax.

The teacher then randomly assigned all of his tenth-grade students to four different groups. The four groups all read the same selection and took the same test but were given different purposes for reading. The test over the material consisted of three questions: What are the criteria for a "good" tax? What are the major advantages of the property tax? What are the major disadvantages of the property tax?

One group of students was given these three test questions as prereading purposes. A second group was given only two of these three questions as purposes; and a third group was given only one of these three test questions as a prereading purpose. The fourth group was given no prereading help and was simply told to read the selection.

Common sense would dictate that the first group, the students actually given the entire test as prereading purposes, should preform best on the test. However, results showed no significant differences on any of the three questions, or on the test as a whole, for any of the four groups.

Fortunately the social studies teacher did not stop at this point. In spite of his disappointment over the results of the experiment, he did begin in his regular assignments to give clear-cut and consistent purposes for reading the material. He discussed only what he told the students to look for, and any tests he gave covered this same material. He found that after about six such attempts, the efforts began to bear fruit. He reported better class discussions and much higher scores on tests over the material.

Although one cannot be absolutely sure of the reasons behind these findings, a possible or at least logical explanation is that it took time for the students to build up their trust and confidence in the teacher. It might be that the students initially paid little attention to the teacher's prereading assistance because they had learned from bitter experience that it did not pay off. They had encountered too many teachers in the past who gave them purposes for reading but then expected them to learn and retain large amounts of material not covered by the purposes.

They had perhaps been asked to read a selection for the purpose of evaluating the strengths and weaknesses of Andrew Jackson as President of the United States but had then been held accountable for such details as the date of his birth, the name of his wife's first husband, and the number of men lost at the Battle of New Orleans.

The message seems clear. If a teacher feels that Rachel Jackson's first husband's name is an important part of American history and the selection he is asking the students to read contains this information, then, he should direct students in the prereading phase to look for it.

It has been emphasized in this discussion that these prereading purposes should be specific and clearly stated. The reason for this is that some teachers faced with the task of wanting to cover a great many points in a given chapter may try to develop a prereading purpose or two which would cover anything in the material. The unfortunate result may well be a purpose that is so vague it tells the student nothing.

A delicate balance must be maintained so that the purposes given do not just deal with trivia yet are not too general. To avoid giving an unmanageable number of purposes for which students are to read, teachers may have to cut down the amount of material assigned at a given time.

Before leaving this first phase of the directed lesson, it should be emphasized that teachers must be realistic about the power of these three steps in prereading assistance. Doing an effective job of all three tasks will still not overcome the problem of the high school student who is reading at a third-grade level but is asked to read and study material written at a tenth-grade level. This assistance can be of considerable help, however, to the corrective or developmental reader. If a teacher feels that she would have to spend two or three class periods just to fill in the gaps in her students' experimental backgrounds and to present the vocabulary they will not know in the assignment, then she should seriously consider a change in reading material.

DIRECTED READING AND DISCUSSION

The second phase of the directed lesson is designed to allow the teacher to cover the important content in the reading material. The student provided direction through the purposes given him by the teacher reads the assignment and then usually is asked to participate in a teacher-led discussion of the material. The traditional tool of the teacher in this phase has been the problem. Methods books for years have stressed the value of teachers making judicious use of questions and discussion techniques rather than the exclusive use of lecture methods.

In recent years a number of research studies have been directed toward a look at the interrogating practices of teachers at various grade levels and in several different subject matter fields. Two such studies have been specifically directed toward the teaching of reading, both conducted at the elementary school level (Bartolome, 1969; Guszak, 1967).

Most of these studies reach similar conclusions. Teachers appear to ask a great number of questions. Most of the questions teachers ask call for the recall of specific facts and details. Thus, although the teachers may espouse rather lofty goals and objectives, her questions require students to operate at quite low levels of cognition. Studies have also indicated that many teachers do not really use discussion techniques but simply ask one student one question, then another student another question, and so on, with little discussion among students.

It appears that teachers at the secondary school level should take a look at their own questioning practices in light of their goals and objectives for their subject matter. It is going to be hard to realize the goal of developing critical thinkers and readers if one does not ask students penetrating questions requiring thought and critical analysis.

Presented below is a taxonomy developed by Dr. Thomas Barrett of the University of Wisconsin (Clymer, 1968) which can be used as a guide for developing questions by teachers concerned with their own practices. The same taxonomy can also be used in developing purposes for reading which call for different levels of cognition.

Teachers attempting to use the Barrett Taxonomy should realize that there is an implied hierarchy of difficulty present. In other words, is is assumed that questions at the Appreciation Level will be more difficult for students than questions at the Reorganization Level. However, one can forsee certain questions at lower levels being more difficult to answer than a relatively simple question at a higher level. It should also be realized that there is considerable overlap present in the Barrett Taxonomy, making precise placement of a question very difficult.

THE BARRET TAXONOMY COGNITIVE AND AFFECTIVE
DIMENSIONS OF READING COMPREHENSION

1.0 LITERAL COMPREHENSION. Focuses on ideas and information *explicity* stated in selection itself.

1.1 *Recognition*. Requires student to locate or identify ideas or information explicitly stated in selection itself or in exercises which use the explicit ideas and information presented in the selection.

1.11 *Recognition of Details*. Required to locate or identify facts such as the names of characters, time of story, place of story.

1.12 *Recognition of Main Ideas*. Required to locate or identify an explicit statement in or from a selection which is a main idea of a paragraph or a larger portion of the selection.

1.13 *Recognition of a Sequence*. Required to locate or identify the order of incidents or actions explicitly stated in selection.

1.14 *Recognition of Comparison.* Requested to locate or identify likenesses and differences in characters, times, and places that are explicitly stated in the selection.

1.15 *Recognition of Cause-and-Effect Relationships.* Locate or identify the explicitly stated reasons for certain happenings or actions in the selection.

1.16 *Recognition of Character Traits.* Locate or identify explicit statements about a character which helps to point up the type of person he is.

1.20 *Recall.* Requires student to produce from memory ideas and information explicitly stated in selection.

1.21 *Recall of Details.* Produces from memory facts such as name of characters, time or place of action.

1.22 *Recall of Main Ideas.* Required to state a main idea of a paragraph or a larger portion of the selection from memory, when main idea is explicitly stated in selection.

1.23 *Recall of a Sequence.* Asked to provide from memory the order of incidents or actions explicitly stated in the selection.

1.24 *Recall of Comparisons.* Call up from memory the likenesses and differences in characters, times, and places that are explicitly stated in the selection.

1.25 *Recall of Cause-and-Effect Relationships.* Provides from memory explicitly stated reasons for certain happenings or actions in the selection.

1.26 *Recall of Character Traits.* Asked to recall explicit statements about characters which illustrate type of persons they are.

2.0   REORGANIZATION. Requires student to analyze, synthesize and/or organize ideas or information explicitly stated in the selection. To produce desired thought product, reader may utilize statements of author verbatim, or paraphrase or translate author's statements.

2.1   *Classifying.* Required to place people, things, places and/or events into categories.

2.2   *Outlining.* Required to organize selection into outline form using direct statements or paraphrased statements from the selection.

2.3   *Summarizing.* Asked to condense selection using direct or paraphrased statements from the selection.

2.4   *Synthesizing.* Asked to consolidate explicit ideas or information from more than one source.

3.0   INFERENTIAL COMPREHENSION. Demonstrated when student uses the ideas and information explicitly stated in a selection, his intuition, and his personal experience as a basis for conjectures and hypotheses. Inferences drawn may be either convergent or divergent in nature and student may or may not be asked to verbalize the rationale underlying his inferences. In general then, inferential comprehension is stimulated by purposes for reading and teachers' questions, which demand thinking and imagination going beyond the printed page.

3.1   *Inferring Supporting Details.* Asked to conjecture about additional facts the author might have included in the selection which would have made it more informative, interesting, or appealing.

3.2   *Inferring Main Ideas.* Required to provide the main idea, general signifi-
      cance, theme, or moral which is not explicitly stated in the selection.

3.3   *Inferring Sequence.* May be requested to conjecture as to what action or
      incident might have taken place between two explicitly stated actions or
      incidents, or he may be requested to hypothesize about what would hap-
      pen next if the selection had not ended as it did but had been extended.

3.4   *Inferring Comparisons.* Student required to infer likenesses and differ-
      ences in characters, times, or places. Such inferential comparisons revolve
      around ideas such as: "here and there," "then and now," "he and she,"
      and "she and she."

3.5   *Inferring Cause-and-Effect Relationships.* Required to hypothesize about
      the motivations of characters and their interactions with time and place.
      He may also be required to conjecture as to what caused the author to
      include certain ideas, words, characterizations, and actions in his writing.

3.6   *Inferring Character Traits.* Asked to hypothesize about the nature of
      characters on the basis of explicit clues presented in the selection.

3.7   *Predicting Outcomes.* Requested to read an initial portion of the selec-
      tions and on the basis of this reading he is required to conjecture about
      the outcome of the selection.

3.8   *Interpreting Figurative Language.* Asked to infer literal meanings from
      the author's figurative use of language.

4.0   EVALUATION. Purposes for reading and teacher's questions require stu-
      dent responses which indicate that he has made an evaluative judgment by
      comparing ideas presented in the selection with external criteria provided
      by the teacher, other authorities, or other written sources, or with internal
      criteria provided by the reader's experiences, knowledges, or values. In
      essence, evaluation deals with judgment and focuses on qualities of ac-
      curacy, acceptability, desirability, worth, or probability of occurrence.

4.1   *Judgments of Reality or Fantasy.* Could this really happen? Judgment
      based on experience.

4.2   *Judgments of Fact or Opinion.* Does author provide adequate support for
      his conclusions? Is author attempting to sway your thinking? Questions
      like these require student to analyze and evaluate the writing on the basis
      of the knowledge he has on the subject as well as to analyze and evaluate
      the intent of the author.

4.3   *Judgments of Adequacy and Validity.* Is information presented here in
      keeping with what you have read on the subject in other sources? Ques-
      tions here call for reader to compare written sources of information, with
      an eye toward agreement and disagreement or completeness and incom-
      pleteness.

4.4   *Judgments of Appropriateness.* What part of the story best describes the
      main character? Such questions require the reader to make a judgment
      about the relative adequacy of different parts of the selection to answer
      the question.

4.5   *Judgments of Worth, Desirability, and Acceptability.* Was the character
      right or wrong in what he did? Was his behavior good or bad? Questions of
      this nature call for judgments based on the reader's moral code or his
      value system.

5.0   APPRECIATION. Involves all the other dimensions, as it deals with the psychological and aesthetic impact of the selection on the reader. Appreciation calls for the student to be emotionally and aesthetically sensitive to the work and to have a reaction to the worth of its psychological and artistic elements. Includes both the knowledge of and the emotional response to literary techniques, forms, styles and structures.

5.1   *Emotional Response to the Content.* Asked to verbalize his feelings about the selection in terms of interest, excitement, boredom, fear, hate, amusement. Concerned with the emotional impact of the total work on the reader.

5.2   *Identification with Characters or Incidents.* Teacher's questions will elicit responses which demonstrate reader's sensitivity to, sympathy for, and empathy with characters and happenings portrayed by the author.

5.3   *Reactions to the Author's Use of Language.* Required to respond to author's craftsmanship in terms of the semantic dimensions of the selection—namely, connotations and denotations of words.

5.4   *Imagery.* Reader required to verbalize his feelings with regard to the author's artistic ability to paint word pictures which cause the reader to visualize, smell, taste, hear, or feel.

Below are some examples of questions for each of the five levels of the Barrett Taxonomy. These questions were developed by secondary school English and reading teachers and are intended for use with the short story, "The Dragon" by Ray Bradbury at the ninth-grade level.

Level I. *Literal Comprehension*
1. Who was trying to kill the dragon?
2. The knights know exactly where the dragon always passed. Where was it?
3. Where does the story take place?

Level II. *Reorganization*
1. What are the two main stages of the story?
2. From what is said as the story opens about the scene—the moor, the night, the fire, and the men—describe it as if you were describing a painting being unveiled before you.
3. Describe the dragon, using the clues and details supplied by the knights in the first part of the story.

Level III. *Inferential Comprehension*
1. Compare and contrast the feelings of the knights and the train crew toward the moor.
2. Is the train likely to pass through the moor in the tenth century again? Why or why not?
3. What comment is Bradbury making about human nature and progress at all points in history?

Level IV. *Evaluation*
1. Based on other stories you have read, do the men in the first part of the story act as knights should?
2. Compare what Bradbury is saying in this story about progress to what he said in the story you read last year, "The Flying Machine."
3. What is your reaction to the train crew's decision not to stop the train after they realized they had hit the knights? Was their decision right or wrong?

Level V. *Appreciation*
1. How does Bradbury's choice of words in describing the dragon's fate effectively achieve a double purpose?
2. How would you have felt and how do you think the two knights felt while they were on the moor waiting for the dragon?
3. Bradbury has organized this story so that there is a change in perspective towards the end of the story, from the knights suddenly without warning to the men on the train. Did you like this dramatic technique, and why do you think the author chose it?

EXTENDING SKILLS AND ABILITIES

The third phase of the directed lesson is concerned with the teaching of any important reading skills needed in this and future lessons. The instruction may either take the form of a review of previously introduced skills or the presentation of a new skill. In other words, this is the place where the actual direct teaching of reading in the various content fields should take place.

The possible reading skills that need attention by the various subject-matter teachers are discussed in Chapter 3 through 7 of this textbook. Teachers must study the material they are asking their students to read carefully to identify the skills to highlight in this portion of the directed lesson.

For example, suppose it is early in the school year and the students have just read in their social studies textbooks a chapter in which a map is used to clarify certain concepts. This is the time for the teacher to develop a skill lesson in map reading, for she knows the students will be asked to use maps as a study aid throughout the year.

A science teacher should do the same thing when his students encounter a section in the textbook where a technical process is explained through the use of a diagram. Students need to be shown how to make the most effective use of the accompanying diagram both in their initial reading and in future review sessions.

This reading instruction will not always deal solely with comprehension and interpretation. A given section of material in a science textbook might contain several excellent examples of situations where the meaning of a word can be determined by the use of context clues. These examples could serve *as* the basis for some further instruction in the use of context as a vocabulary aid.

In all instances it should be stressed that the ideal material to use in this reading instruction is the material from the textbooks the students are using so that the maximum opportunity for transfer is present. Additional supplementary material such as workbook exercises can be used for reinforcement purposes, but the focus should be on the regular classroom textbooks.

ENRICHMENT AND FOLLOW-UP ACTIVITIES

This last phase of the directed lesson should not be thought of as any less important than the others. The obvious purpose of any enrichment activities and projects is to reinforce and expand the skills and concepts introduced in earlier portions of the lesson. Such activities can also, if planned carefully, serve as the background experiences needed by students to deal with subsequent reading assignments.

The possibilities for meaningful enrichment activities are endless and are limited only by the resourcefulness of the teacher. Unfortunately, there are some attitudes that detract from the power of this phase. One such attitude is that skills are most important and if one is pressed for time, then enrichment activities must take a back seat to the third phase of the directed lesson.

It has been reported that this unfortunate neglect of this fourth phase is all too prevalent in elementary school classes where use is made of the directed-lesson concept. The time is usually in the spring of the year, and the place is usually a school where there is an unwritten rule that third-grade teachers must complete all the work in the books that have 3's on them. The teacher feels something has to give, and what usually gives is the enrichment phase. The result is that many skills and concepts are introduced but there is not sufficient time for students to use those skills in meaningful situations. The necessary reinforcement does not occur, and thus the skills are actually not acquired by the students.

Another attitude that hinders the realization of the potential of this phase of the directed lesson is that some teachers believe such enrichment activities are to be pursued only with the so-called high achiever or gifted student. In actual fact, if *any* student is reading material that is basically of interest to him and which is generally within his grasp, then relevant enrichment experiences can be provided for him.

SAMPLE DIRECTED LESSONS

Two examples of modified directed lesson plans follow. Neither follows the scheme of the directed lesson exactly as has been presented previously, but both show the structure and organization needed.

The first is a plan for teaching the poem, "The Cremation of Sam McGee," by Robert W. Service. This selection, found in *Literature and Life* (Boston: Houghton Mifflin Company, 1958), could be used at the ninth-grade level.*

The second example is a modified directed lesson designed for use with a section of Chapter 4 in *Understanding Our Economy* (Boston: Houghton Mifflin Company, 1969). This textbook was designed for use in any basic high school economics course.†

DIRECTED LESSON 1

"The Cremation of Sam McGee"

A. Building readiness for the story

Before letting the students open their books to the selection, the teacher should build readiness and try to motivate them to want to read the poem. She may talk about the name of the poem, "The Cremation of Sam McGee." She should introduce some of the words which may cause difficulty either in pronunciation or in understanding the appropriate meaning intended by the author. Some of the words which may be listed are *cremation, mushing, parka, code, loathe, grub, derelict,* and *trice*. These words may be written on the chalkboard and pronounced and definitions given. Next, the teacher should introduce the author, Robert W. Service. He was born in England in 1874 but grew up in Scotland and moved to Canada in 1897. Although he spent the latter forty years of his life in France, his early years in the Yukon (1897 - 1912) where he worked as a bank employee and civil servant, were the most productive of his writing career. He wrote verses about the gold miners, prospectors, and trappers he met while traveling in the Klondike.

B. Directed silent reading

Ask the students to turn to page 69 and read silently the title and the author's name. Have them read the short paragraph at the bottom of the page. This contains additional information about the author. Refer to the sketch at the top of the page and discuss the humor depicted by the artist. Have students read the tinted section titled *Before You Read*. This section sets the stage by describing the locale of the poem and by introducing the main character, Sam McGee. *Setting up reading purpose:* "Read the entire poem to find out what fantastic development occurred."

C. Comprehension check and skill building

Get the students to respond orally to the following questions:
   1. What fantastic development occurred?
   2. Did you believe the author throughout the poem? Why? Why not?
   3. What is internal rhyme? Skim and find examples of internal rhyme.
   4. How does this add interest?

*Lesson plan reprinted with permission of Dr. Hazel Simpson, Associate Professor, University of Georgia.

†Lesson plan reprinted with permission of Mrs. Susan Carter, Cobb County School District, Georgia.

5. How does Service make you feel the cold?

6. What line provides a hint concerning the unbelievable ending of the poem?

Many types of exercises may be prepared by the teacher. She should be concerned with those skills for which the students show a need. The type of material read should be considered in preparing the exercises. Several types of comprehension skills may be developed after having read this particular section.

Examples of the different types of exercises are as follows.

Recalling Facts

1. Who wrote "The Cremation of Sam McGee?"

2. Where did the action take place?

3. Why did McGee believe he would die on this trip?

4. What promise did Cap make McGee?

5. What was the name of the derelict?

6. Why did Cap take a hike while McGee was being cremated?

Finding and Understanding Main Ideas

Find and write the one sentence in each paragraph that contains the central thought of that paragraph.

Sequence of Events

Ask a student to retell the story.

Understanding Details

Directions: Circle "T" if a statement is true; circle "F" if a statement is false.

T F   1. Sam McGee was cremated along the shores of the Yukon River.

T F   2. Cap was from Tennessee.

T F   3. It was Christmas Day when the last trip was made.

T F   4. Sam McGee told Cap he thought he would die this trip.

T F   5. Sam died three days later.

T F   6. It was the code of the trail to keep a promise.

T F   7. Cap used pieces of lumber found on the shore for the cremation of McGee.

T F   8. The ending of the story was sad.

D. Word-recognition skill building

Write the following words on the board: *cremation, parka, code, loathe, grub, derelict,* and *trice.* Have the students write a short definition for each word and use it in a sentence.

E. Rereading for another purpose

The teacher or a student may read orally for the purpose of getting the students to catch the beauty of the rhythm. The feeling of the two characters should be emphasized to bring out the humor of the dialogue.

The class may read together orally so they can enjoy the rhythm.

F. Follow-up activities

It may be suggested to the students that Service wrote other poems and stories. They may wish to read some of these and compare rhyme and dialects used to tell the story.

The life of Robert W. Service may be read and discussed.

Reports may be written concerning the history of the gold-rush days in the Yukon River area, the life of the sourdough, or life in the mining towns.

DIRECTED LESSON 2

"The Role of Cooperatives in Our Economy"

Preparation for Reading

Background of Experience. To establish background for this lesson, capitalize on the fact that the parents of several students work at the large aircraft manufacturing plant in town. Begin the discussion by giving the students an opportunity to tell what they know about the operations of the employees' credit union at the plant. The discussion should be guided to help the students realize that the credit union exists to help its members by loaning them money and by encouraging them to save. Semiannually, earnings are paid to each member according to the amount of money he has deposited in the credit union. The credit union is a special type of business that students will learn about in this lesson.

Vocabulary. This lesson provides an excellent opportunity for teaching vocabulary through context clues. Accordingly handle the majority of the words by using context clues. If possible, prepare a transparency before the class period for each of the vocabulary words with its exemplary sentence from the lesson. Should there be no overhead projector available, use the chalkboard. There are several technical terms which are the most important to present before assigning the lesson. An understanding of the more technical terms is necessary if the students are to get any meaning out of their reading. Encourage the students to look up other words that they do not know that hamper their understanding of the material.

1. *cooperative—*"A cooperative is a jointly owned business organization operated for the benefit of its members." Ask a student to define the word *cooperative* after reading the sentence. After the students understand the meaning of *cooperative*; ask if the credit union can be classified as a *cooperative.* "What characteristics of the credit union, which we discussed earlier, distinguish it as a cooperative?"

2. *patrons—*"Members are also patrons, persons who utilize the services offered by the cooperative." Ask the meaning of *patron* according to this sentence. Be sure that the students recognize that the dash indicates that the word *patron* is being explained. After the students have developed an understanding of the word *patron*, discuss with them what a *member-patron* would be.

3. *net income—*"The money the company had earned after all expenses were paid (net income) was $50,000." In discussing this term with the students, it may be necessary to discuss the term *gross income.* The students should recognize that the words *net income,* in parentheses, are giving a concise term for the explanation given in the first part of the sentence. Then tell

the students that the word *savings* in this article is used to mean the same as *net income.*

4. *refunds*—"The deposits usually take the form of refunds, or payments based on the net income of the cooperative." In helping the students to get the meaning of *refunds* from the exemplary sentence, point out that the conjunction *or* shows that the meaning of the first portion of the sentence is being restated. "Because the savings are distributed on the basis of patronage, they are usually called *patronage dividends* or *refunds*."

   The discussion of this sentence will be guided so that the students understand that *patronage, dividends,* and *refunds* have the same meaning in the article. Again, the word *or* shows that the idea is being stated in another term.

5. *corporations*—"Like regular stock companies (corporations), cooperatives must be chartered under the laws of the state in which they are organized." Lead the students to see that again punctuation is important in determining the meaning of the word. The term *corporations,* in parentheses, after "regular stock companies" is giving a name to that phrase. Do not introduce the word *dividends* as a separate word, but lead the students into a short discussion of *corporations* to see that they understand the term. Be sure that they understand that *dividends* are profits paid to stockholders as refunds are paid to patrons of a cooperative. (If the occasion permits, the term *dividends* may be discussed when refunds are discussed. It would depend on the class and the way that the discussion develops.)

Purposes. Mimeograph two different sets of purposes. Set I will be for the students who are of limited ability and Set II will be for the students of higher ability. The students will not be required to write the answers to the questions given but *will* be asked to keep the mimeographed sheet of purposes.

Set I

   "Read the section in your textbook, 'The Role of Cooperatives in Our Economy,' with the following purposes in mind. These are the most important things for you to understand from your reading."
1. The characteristics of a cooperative
2. The three basic principles on which cooperatives operate
3. The four types of cooperatives

Set II

   "Read the section in your textbook, 'The Role of Cooperatives in Our Economy,' with the following purposes in mind. These are the most important ideas for you to understand from your reading."
1. An understanding of the three basic principles on which cooperatives operate
2. The four types of cooperatives and their purposes
3. Advantages and disadvantages of cooperatives
4. Differences and similarities of cooperatives and corporations

Directed Reading

   "Your assignment for tonight is to read the section in your textbook 'The Role of Cooperatives in Our Economy.' Read over the list of purposes that you have been given carefully before you begin your reading. Keep these purposes in mind as you read. When you have finished your reading try to tell yourself the information which would be needed to explain fully each of the purposes. If you cannot remember the material, reread any section of the lesson that you do not understand thoroughly."

Discussion

The following is a list of the questions to be asked. The discussion should involve the entire class. It is hoped that the students who were given the Set I of purposes will benefit from the discussion and will understand from the discussion the more difficult information which they may not have understood from their reading. The questions denoted by an asterisk(*) are the ones that should be directed to a student who was given Set I of purposes. This will enable these students to contribute to the discussion. The ones that are not marked will probably have to be directed to a student who was given Set II of purposes but will not be restricted to those students.

Questions for Discussion:
* 1. Describe a cooperative.
* 2. What are the three basic principles on which a cooperative operates?
  3. Explain what is meant by the principle of "democratic control."
  4. Explain what is meant by the principle of "limited returns from capital." Why is there a limited return?
  5. Explain what is meant by the principle of "fair distribution of savings."
* 6. What are the four types of cooperatives?
  7. Give the purpose of a "purchasing cooperative." What types of goods are purchased by this type of cooperative?
  8. What is the purpose of a "marketing cooperative?" In what areas have these been successful?
  9. What is the purpose of a "servicing cooperative?" What is an example of the types of services it may render?
 10. What is the purpose of an "industrial cooperative?" In what areas have these been successful?
*11. What type of cooperative is the credit union that we talked about yesterday?
 12. How are cooperatives and corporations alike? How are they different? (List answers on board in two columns and ask students to copy them.)
 13. What are the advantages of a cooperative? the disadvantages?
 14. From your reading and our discussion, would you say that cooperatives and corporations are formed for the same or different purposes? If different, how do the purposes differ?

EXTENDING SKILLS

This lesson provides good material for helping the students to learn to make notes in outline form on their reading assignments. Give to the same group which had Set I of purposes the outline which has been entitled Outline I, and for the group which had Set II of purposes the outline which is entitled Outline II. (When the outlines are given to the students, they do not carry the designations I and II.) The students will be instructed to use their textbooks to complete the outlines which are partially filled in. Move around the room and give help to the individual students as they need it while doing this exercise. The students will be asked to do this outline in their notebooks where they can keep it as a study guide for this lesson. To check the completed outlines, meet with each group separately while the other group is working on preparation material for the next lesson. (The outlines for this section follow.) This is assuming one has previously worked with the students on outlining, explaining topics, subtopics, indentions, and the like.

When the time comes to give a test over this material it will probably be necessary to prepare two different tests. There is some material that the lower group may not be able to master even after the class discussion. Their test should be made somewhat easier if this be the case.

OUTLINE I

This exercise is designed to help you to organize the ideas presented in this lesson about cooperatives. It is hoped that this organization of ideas will help you to remember the information more easily. This practice should also help you to learn to organize material as you are reading it on your own.

Directions: With the help of your textbook, complete the following outline. Choose the missing topics and subtopics from the list at the bottom of the page.

The Role of Cooperatives in Our Economy

I. Characteristics of a cooperative
   A. Jointly owned business
   B.
   C.
   D. Benefits in form of refunds
   E.
II.
   A.
   B. Limited returns from capital
   C.
III.
   A.
   B. Marketing cooperatives
   C.
   D.
IV. Success of cooperatives in United States
   A.
   B. Cooperatives successful today, especially in agricultural areas
   C.

Purchasing cooperatives   Fair distribution of savings
Democratic control   Early success limited in the
Members are patrons   United States
Fundamental principles   Major types of cooperatives
Industrial cooperatives   Operated for benefit of mem-
Industrial cooperatives least   bers
   successful   Servicing cooperatives

OUTLINE II

This exercise is designed to help you to organize the ideas presented in this lesson about cooperatives. It is hoped that this organization of ideas will help you in remembering the information. It is also hoped that through this additional practice in outlining you will be able to better organize information when studying your assignment.

Directions: Complete the following outline by choosing the missing topics and subtopics from the list at the bottom of the page. Use your textbook to help you. You will also have to supply the title for the outline on the space provided. (The title is not in the list at the bottom.)

 I. Characteristics of a cooperative
    A. Jointly owned business organization
    B.
    C.
    D. Benefits in form of refunds
    E. Chartered under laws of state in which organized
 II. Fundamental Principles
    A. Democratic control
        1.
        2. Member-patrons determine nature of service and policies
    B.
        1.
        2. Capital needed to expand business
    C. Fair distribution of savings
        1. Savings distributed on basis of patronage
        2.
III.
    A. Purchasing cooperative
        1.
        2. Example of items: seed, fertilizer
    B.
        1. Purpose to sell produce for members
        2.
    C. Service cooperatives
        1.
        2.

D.
   1. Purpose for worker-members to cooperate in large-scale industries
   2.
IV. Success of cooperatives in the United States
   A.
   B.
   C. Cooperatives successful today, especially in agricultural areas.

Limited returns from capital
Products sold as cheaply as possible
Purpose to provide goods at low prices
Example—credit union; supplying electricity
Marketing cooperatives
Savings sometimes used to expand business
Example—Dairy products industries

Industrial cooperatives least successful
Operated for benefit of members
Example—mining; manufacturing
Industrial cooperatives
Members are patrons
Types of cooperatives
Voting—"one member, one vote"
Purpose—perform service
Limited early success

SUMMARY

Content-area teachers do have a responsibility and an obligation to help develop the reading competencies of their students in the subject-matter fields. So that neither the content itself nor the instruction in reading will be neglected, the content teacher must structure and organize the instruction effectively. The directed lesson has been presented as a possible structure from which to operate. If it appears that so much of what has been referred to in this chapter as good reading instruction is just good teaching, so be it! The label is not the important concern; the students and their learning are.

REFERENCES

Bartholome, Paz I. "Teachers' Objectives and Questions in Primary Reading," *Reading Teacher*, XXIII (October 1969), pp. 27–33.

Clymer, Theodore. "What is 'Reading'? Some Current Concepts," *Innovation and Change in Reading Instruction. 67th Yearbook of the National Society for the Study of Education* (1968), pp. 7–29.

Guszak, Frank. "Teacher Questioning and Reading," *Reading Teacher*, XXI (December 1967), pp. 227–234.

Rehmann, Arnold M. "Guided Reading at the Seventh Grade Level—An Experimental Study." Unpublished doctoral dissertation, University of Minnesota, 1968.

Smith, Richard J., and Thomas Burns. "The Effects of Different Instructional Practices on Student Enjoyment and Interpretation of a Ballad," *Journal of Reading*, XIII (February 1970), pp. 345–354.

ADDITIONAL READINGS

Davis, O. L., Jr., and F. P. Hunkins. "Textbook Questions: What Thinking Processes Do They Foster?" *Peabody Journal of Education*, XLIII (March 1966), pp. 285–292.

Grant, Eugene B., and Marcia Hall. "The Effect of a Thought-Directing Question on Reading Comprehension at Differing Levels of Difficulty," *Forging Ahead on Reading*. Proceedings of the Twelfth Annual Convention of the International Reading Association (1968), pp. 498–501.

Smith, Richard J., and Clinton R. Barter. "The Effects of Reading for Two Particular Purposes," *Journal of Reading*, XII (November 1968), pp. 134–138, 174–176.

Smith, Richard J., and Karl D. Hesse. "The Effects of Prereading Assistance on the Comprehension and Attitudes of Good and Poor Readers," *Research in the Teaching of English*, II (Fall 1969), pp. 166–177.

chapter 9

Guidelines for Instruction

The classroom factors confronting every teacher are complex. In many secondary schools, although the classes are homogeneous according to achievement level, there is still a very large spread in ability. Unfortunately in our schools the concept of providing for individual differences has become equated with dividing students into ability groups and then assuming that the groups can be taught as a single individual. The practice is not uncommon; it is endorsed not only by the overwhelming majority of administrators, but also by most teachers. Where this practice of meeting individual needs is adopted with little or no corresponding adjustment in instructional techniques, or where the system is so rigid that flexibility and mobility are impossible, the organizational pattern serves no realistic educational purpose.

There are a number of reasons why more provisions are not made for individual differences within the secondary schools.

1. Class size
2. Scheduling of five to six 50-minute periods
3. Lack of continuity in instruction
4. Classification of students on a grade basis
5. Rigid classification of materials on a grade basis

Schools can be organized in a variety of ways to overcome these problems, but until some imaginative administration is employed teachers must function within the limitations. The problem is not hopeless however. There are many things a classroom teacher can do to improve the learning environment.

REASONS FOR LACK OF ATTENTION TO INDIVIDUAL DIFFERENCES

Class Size

Class size is never a barrier to good instruction, it is merely an excuse. Every teacher can determine the instructional level of the students in the classroom and thus provide instruction at their level. Regardless of the class size, students can be grouped so that they are reading at their ability level. The alternative to not doing this is to put reading material into the hands of the students with the realization that they will not be able to read the material.

Materials, whether magazines, newspapers, books or other reading matter, can be used for instructional purposes. "Useful instructional materials" does not necessarily mean the text provided for the class by the administration. Nor does the teacher have to immediately provide different instructional materials for the student in every period during the day.

It would be only prudent to start with the class that has the greatest need. As the teacher works with a particular class in differentiating the reading material he will find that applications can be made to other classes without extending his preparation time. It is unrealistic to expect that all needs be met at the same time. Realistically a teacher can provide for differentiated instruction if the goals are planned for over a one- or two-year period. The key to solving the problem is that a start must be made—not later, but now.

Scheduling

The scheduling of classes for fifty-minute periods is a travesty on education. To expect that instruction which is viable can take place within the confines of a rigid bell schedule is a contradiction of all we know about the psychology of learning. It would be far better for the learning environment if teachers were to organize classes into larger blocks combining two or more closely allied areas—i. e., social science and English. This type of organization would extend the period of instruction and allow for more individualizing.

Continuity

The lack of continuity in the instructional program is one of the reasons why teachers find it so easy to reflect the feeling that a skill deficiency in some students is the responsibility of someone else. It also helps to explain why some deficiencies go unnoticed by teachers. If teachers in English, mathematics, and social science, as well as in other areas, were able to have constant association with a given group of students over a two- or three-year period, perhaps some of our educational problems would be minimized.

There are expressed problems attributed to the idea of continuity of instruction based upon student-teacher association. One factor frequently mentioned is personality conflict; another is poor quality of instruction. It is interesting that both these arguments are based upon individual considerations rather than the welfare of the group. In each argument we are talking about only a small number of cases.

Classification of Students

A public school system that makes it mandatory for all students to attend school until age 16 cannot realistically set arbitrary standards and expect that all students will meet the standards. Realistic standards must be established for students of varying abilities and background. Secondary school teachers who believe that the students who come to them should have specified levels of academic achievement are not realistic about the philosophy of our public school system and thus find themselves in constant conflict with the system. Perhaps some of our school problems, both at the secondary and college level, are the result of the naive concept we have concerning education that constantly places the school, the student, and the society in conflict. The philosophy may be wrong; it may not even be viable.

Classification of Materials

Because of the wide range of ability levels within our schools, it is impossible to designate a book as being at either the eighth grade, sophomore, or senior-grade level. In light of all that has been said previously, materials cannot be designated for a grade when the grade has no meaning in identification of achievement. We should be astute enough to recognize that a wide range of material is needed to meet the needs of a diversified student body that exists, not arbitrary standards that do not.

The concept of individual differences is as old as education itself. Most educators express their weariness with discussing individualizing instruction by commenting that it only makes common sense. It is unfortunate that the discussions that have taken place and the books that have been written about the concept have made so little change in classroom practice. If indeed the concept is only common sense, it is obvious that the application of common sense in the classroom is rare.

CLASSROOM PRACTICES

Every secondary school teacher needs to be aware of some basic classroom procedures that will foster the development of reading skills. There is much that the teacher can do to insure that the procedures of instruction employed in the classroom are in line with what we know to be good sound practices.

The following is a checklist* of some practices that are recommended in teaching effectively the reading skills in the secondary school. Indicate by circling the response which *best* indicates how *you* apply the practices in your classes.

1 = almost always	3 = sometimes	5 = never
2 = most of the time	4 = seldom	

1. Text material used is suited in difficulty to the reading levels of the students.   1 2 3 4 5
2. Students are encouraged through assignments to read widely in related materials.   1 2 3 4 5

*Developed by Dr. Ira Aaron, Professor, University of Georgia.

1 = almost always   3 = sometimes   5 = never
2 = most of the time 4 = seldom

3. At the beginning of the school year, adequate time is taken to introduce the text(s) and discuss how they may be used effectively.   1 2 3 4 5

4. I am aware of the special vocabulary and concepts introduced in the various units.   1 2 3 4 5

5. Adequate attention is given to vocabulary and concept development.   1 2 3 4 5

6. Provisions are made for checking on extent to which important vocabulary and concepts are learned, and reteaching is done where needed.   1 2 3 4 5

7. I know the special reading skills required for teaching my subject.   1 2 3 4 5

8. I teach the special reading skills required in my subject. 1 2 3 4 5

9. My course content is broader in scope than a single textbook.   1 2 3 4 5

10. Assignments are made clearly and concisely.   1 2 3 4 5

11. I teach the students how to use the appropriate reference skills needed for my subject.   1 2 3 4 5

12. Adequate reference materials are available.   1 2 3 4 5

13. Related informational books and other materials are available for students who read below grade level.   1 2 3 4 5

14. Related informational books and other materials are available for students who read above grade level.   1 2 3 4 5

15. I take advantage of opportunities that may arise to encourage students to read recreational as well as informational reading material.   1 2 3 4 5

16. I help the poor reader to develop adequate reading skills.   1 2 3 4 5

17. Readings from various textbooks are provided for those who cannot read the regular assigned materials.   1 2 3 4 5

18. I group students within the classroom for differentiated instruction.   1 2 3 4 5

19. I know the reading level of the textbook(s) I assign in class.   1 2 3 4 5

20. I know the reading ability of the students from standardized tests, other evaluative materials, and/or cumulative records.   1 2 3 4 5

Look over the practices you have just checked and come to some evaluation as to how effective a job you have done in your teaching. The twenty statements are not far-out, impossible tasks for any teacher. They can be performed by all teachers—at least sometimes.

There are other practices that the authors have observed in classrooms (and in some cases have engaged in themselves) which also should be discussed.

ORAL READING

Some of the practices we use in our classrooms are not the result of instructions we have been given in a methods course, but are rather a repetition of our own educational experiences. Some of these practices are good but some are horrible. An example of a "horrible" practice is the use of oral reading in a classroom.

It is not unusual to find a teacher following the practice of having poor, inadequate readers reading orally from textbooks that are too difficult for them. The reason given for the practice is that it gives the teacher an opportunity to help the student and to provide a needed educational experience. If this were actually true it could be a worthwhile experience, but in most cases the teacher can only pronounce the unknown words for the student, because he does not have knowledge to aid the student in unlocking the meaning.

Oral reading *is* useful if it is used for any or all of the following purposes.

1. *Oral reading is for communicating information.*

   If the purpose of the oral reading is to communicate information to the class, it should be read by the best readers in the class, with the other students listening—not "reading along."

2. *Oral reading is for enjoyment.*

   In some courses, particularly English, the object may be to read a story orally, in which case the material should be read by the best readers.

3. *Oral reading may be done for the purpose of identifying reading problems or to determine the readability of the material by a particular student.*

   If the oral reading has this purpose, it should be on a one-to-one basis with the teacher. Oral reading that is done to determine problems assumes that the teacher has evidence that a problem does exist and evaluation should be performed in a manner that reduces the embarrassment of the student to a minimum.

During the adolescent years students are extremely conscious of peer status and in the main do not like to be singled out to perform a task in which they know they perform poorly. Forcing a student to read orally when he and the teacher both know that he will do it poorly is courting a disciplinary problem. Most students and adults will take any evasive action necessary to avoid appearing foolish, especially before people important to their self-esteem.

A not uncommon practice is the "barber-shop approach," in which the teacher goes down the aisles asking each student in turn to read a paragraph or two.

Let's take a look at the barber-shop approach and see what really happens to the student and teacher in the process.

1. If the student is at all perceptive he soon will know whether you are a one-, two-, or three-paragraph teacher. Once he has this information he will start counting the number of students in front of him, the number

of paragraphs, and as a result be several pages beyond where a given student is presently reading.

2. Frequently the result of this educational disaster is that the teacher calls on the "inattentive" student in the middle of the room, knowing full well that he has lost the place where the last reader left off. The class is thrown into a panic and the student is punished for doing what any sane person would have done if placed in a similar situation.

3. The assumption is incorrect that if a student follows along in the text, reading silently as another student reads orally, he is being reinforced by associating the written symbol with the spoken word. The teacher has no control over what word the student is looking at when the word is read orally. It could just as reasonably be an incorrect association as a correct one.

4. The assumption is also incorrect that the student isn't paying attention because he is several pages ahead of the oral reading. The student is paying attention to what is going on. The problem is that several factors are operating at once and he selects the avenue of action that is most important to his well-being.

5. If you as a teacher have learned somewhere along the line in your educational career that when a student isn't following along in the book, he isn't paying attention and if you call on someone in the middle of the room you create a chaos. At this point the teacher has made a serious error about how students learn to read.

Another reason for not having students follow along in a text is the effect it has upon silent reading speed. If students are forced to read silently at the average oral reading speed (170 wpm) they are being given practice in slow silent reading. Since slowness of silent reading seems to be a factor noted by many secondary teachers, this factor alone should make "following along" an unwise practice.

ATTITUDES TOWARD READING

Adolescents who cannot read find it difficult to function in the school setting because of the reading demands placed on them. One difficulty of a poor reader is that he looks and feels like a misfit in the school environment. The results of a study by Penty (1956), based upon a population of almost 600 tenth-grade students located in the lower fourth of their class in a reading test indicates that almost half dropped out of school before graduation.

According to Penty, the poor readers who dropped out showed evidence of low self-esteem as a characteristic associated with their reading difficulties, as compared with those who graduated. Many who graduated also had feelings of inferiority, were disgusted with themselves, were ashamed of their performance in class, or frequently wanted to leave school. Of the total population reported, 73 percent of the dropouts and 23 percent of those who graduated expressed the feelings described.

Penty's interpretation of the study is that the influence of the classroom teacher, the acceptance of the students as to the way they were, and a willingness to help them to face their weaknesses and develop their ability were very important determining factors. The assurance of the professional friendship of the teacher and the understanding of their peers were critical factors in the lives of many of the students who stayed on to graduate.

The teacher is the key in developing a positive attitude toward reading. The teacher who doesn't care, who doesn't know how, or is unwilling to meet the needs of students is not doing his educational job. It is only through the positive attitudes and practices used by the teacher in the classroom that students are assured that education is "right" for them.

Some specialists feel that a major contributing cause of reading difficulties is the apathy or lack of concern of many students. High school students who have never seen any practical value in reading are not highly motivated to learn to read well. The materials and content used seem dull, insipid, and irrelevant to the adolescent. No connection is made between reading instruction and "real life."

If one doubts these conditions exist he should talk to some adult illiterates. Interviews conducted with undereducated adults reveal that they feel a major reason for their failure to learn to read while they were in school is that it did not seem to be important. When these adults muster up the courage and strength to return to school, they do so with very practical interests and needs, and the reading program should fill these needs.

This situation can be readily corrected for high school students. Teachers can, given the opportunity, develop very meaningful content and exercises which not only help students learn to read better, but deal with practical and meaningful concerns.

Following are three examples of teacher-made lessons prepared in a graduate reading-methods class and designed for use with either adult or adolescent illiterates. In each case the teacher identified a reading task or set of content she felt to be important in keeping with the needs and interests of the population. For each of the lessons there is first an introduction where a rationale is built for the choice of the content, followed by the actual content and exercises.

The three lessons are presented just as they were originally prepared by the teachers and are not meant to represent finished products. What the lessons do show is the ingenuity and talents of three teachers, and the fact that it can be done. Too often, very competent teachers do not use their own abilities but spend their time in the endless search for the "perfect workbook."

LESSON PLAN NUMBER 1*

Road Signs

Rationale

This lesson is designed to acquaint adults and adolescents of driving age or near driving age with the task of reading road signs. This is an important task because most adults and adolescents do (or will) drive at some time in their life, and it is important for their own safety as well as for the protection of others to be able to read and understand the information conveyed by road signs. The purpose of this lesson is to help students learn to recognize and read road signs and to understand the rationale or meaning behind them.

Ten signs have been chosen for this lesson. At the beginning of the lesson the teacher will go over each sign with the class, helping them with vocabulary and explaining the meaning of each sign. After that the students should be able to work alone with little or no help from the teacher, but he must pay attention to the directions for each exercise and follow them. Following directions is one of the skills which hopefully will be strengthened through this exercise, though more emphasis will be given to other skills.

In the first exercise, choosing the proper sign requires that the students be able to read and understand the meaning of each sign, and further requires that they exercise the power of discrimination (or, in some cases, elimination) in deciding which sign would be the best answer in light of the situation given. Requiring them to reproduce the sign and the information on it gives them experience in reading and writing it, thereby creating a deeper, more lasting impression.

Most of the words in this lesson are already part of the student's speaking vocabulary. They know the meaning of the words and use them in convertion, but they can't recognize them in print. The problem then is to help the students figure out a way to pronounce the words. For this reason, I have chosen syllabication as the specific reading skill to be emphasized.

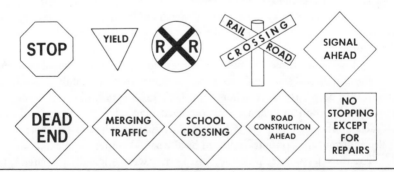

FROM THE GROUP OF SIGNS FOR EACH QUESTION, CHOOSE THE ONE THAT *BEST* ANSWERS THE QUESTION. COPY THIS SIGN AND THE INFORMATION ON IT IN THE SPACE PROVIDED.

*Reprinted by permission of Mrs. Judith McQuagge Henderson.

Ned is driving down the street. He sees several children walking home. All the children are carrying books. Which sign might Ned see here?	DEAD END SCHOOL CROSSING ROAD CONSTRUCTION AHEAD	
Ned is driving on a dirt road that crosses a main road. What sign is he likely to find at the place where the two roads meet?	DEAD END R R STOP	
Ned is coming close to a traffic light. What sign is he likely to see here?	SIGNAL AHEAD DEAD END RAIL CROSSING ROAD	
What kind of sign would Ned find right next to a railroad track?	NO STOPPING EXCEPT FOR REPAIRS YIELD RAIL CROSSING ROAD	
What kind of sign would warn Ned that a railroad crossing is ahead?	STOP MERGING TRAFFIC R R	
Ned has just seen a sign that tells him he must give the right of way to the other driver. Which sign has he seen?	DEAD END SIGNAL AHEAD YIELD	
What kind of sign might Ned see at the point where cars are coming onto the highway from a side street?	R R NO STOPPING EXCEPT FOR REPAIRS MERGING TRAFFIC	
The road Ned is driving on comes to a sudden end. What sign might he see here?	MERGING TRAFFIC DEAD END SIGNAL AHEAD	
Up ahead of him, Ned sees men working on the road. What sign is he likely to see here?	R R SCHOOL CROSSING ROAD CONSTRUCTION AHEAD	

| What sign might Ned see on a highway where traffic moves very fast? | STOP | DEAD END | NO STOPPING EXCEPT FOR REPAIRS | |

DIVIDING WORDS INTO SYLLABLES HELPS US TO LEARN TO PRO-
NOUNCE THEM. THE FIRST RULE FOR DIVIDING WORDS INTO SYL-
LABLES IS THIS:

RULE 1: When two consonants come between two vowels, divide the word between the two consonants.

EXAMPLES:

pencil _pen/cil_   certain _cer/tain_
larder _lar/der_   obtain _ob/tain_

USING THE RULE YOU HAVE LEARNED, DIVIDE THESE WORDS INTO
SYLLABLES:

1. stopping _____   6. enter _____
2. narrow _____   7. letter _____
3. signal _____   8. sudden _____
4. railroad _____   9. correct _____
5. traffic _____   10. distance _____

FROM THE READING MATERIAL, FIND FIVE (5) WORDS *NOT* ON THE
LIST ABOVE) WHICH FOLLOW THIS RULE FOR DIVIDING WORDS INTO
SYLLABLES. WRITE THESE WORDS IN THE BLANKS BELOW AND DRAW
A LINE BETWEEN THE TWO SYLLABLES.

1. _____   4. _____
2. _____   5. _____
3. _____

LESSON PLAN NUMBER 2*

Dress Patterns

Rationale
  I. Content
     While sewing is not a crucial task in the sense that it is necessary in
     order to get along well, it could be categorized as a crucial task for the
     illiterate, because of his generally low financial level. Through use of
     her sewing skill, a woman can dress herself and her family adequately

*Reprinted by permission of Miss Irene McMillan.

for a much smaller sum than she would have to spend in buying ready-made clothing. Sewing can also be a useful skill for a woman in decorating her home, as in making curtains. Because sewing has immediate, useful application, a woman may find this material interesting and stimulating content for reading instruction. Ideally, a woman would receive reading and sewing instruction concurrently, with the classes coordinated. This approach would capitalize on the maximum motivation for reading which the desire to learn sewing skills would contribute.

II. Reading Skills

There are two reading skills developed in this lesson.

1. Reading a chart
2. Following directions

The first skill, reading a chart, is developed through the use of a size chart from a pattern book. The size chart is given along with a story telling how a woman used the chart, which explains how to read the chart. Then the student applies this information in finding her own pattern size.

The second skill, following directions, is developed along with reading a chart in the exercise in which the student finds her own pattern size. Step-by-step directions are given, which the student follows in using the chart.

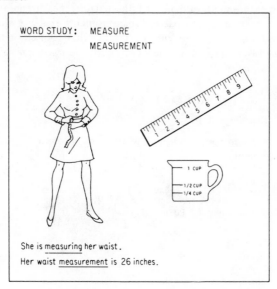

WORD STUDY: MEASURE
               MEASUREMENT

She is measuring her waist.
Her waist measurement is 26 inches.

Mary Buys a Sewing Pattern

Mary is learning to sew. She needs a dress pattern to take to class. She looked through the pattern book at a store and found a dress she liked, but she did not know what size pattern she needed. The sales clerk told her to use the chart in the back of the book. This is the size chart that Mary used.

Size Chart—Misses

	8	10	12	14	16	18
Bust	31½	32½	(34)	36	38	40
Waist	23	24	(25½)	27	29	31
Hip	33½	34½	(36)	38	40	42
Back Waist Length. .	15¾	16	(16½)	16½	16¾	17

Mary looked at the picture that showed how to measure for the pattern. *Look at this picture below.* She had measured before she went to the store, so she knew her bust, waist, and hip measurements, and back waist length. Now Mary could use this chart. Here are her measurements.

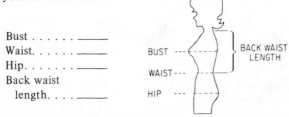

Bust 34
Waist. 26
Hip 36½
Back waist
    length . . 16¼

Mary's measurements did not fit the pattern measurements exactly. The circles on the chart show the pattern measurements that are closest to Mary's measurements. *Look at these on the chart.* Mary then looked on the chart at the first line labeled *Size* and found her size. *Look on the chart* and find Mary's pattern size. Yes, she wears size 12.

What Size Pattern Do You Wear?

Let's find out. Use these steps:

1. Write your measurements below. Use the tape measure if you do not know your measurements.

Bust . . . . . . _____
Waist. . . . . . _____
Hip. . . . . . . _____
Back waist
    length. . . . _____

2. On the size chart below, circle the measurement for *bust* that is closest to your measurement.
3. Circle the measurement that is closest to your measurement for *waist*.
4. Circle your *hip* measurement.
5. Circle your *back waist length*.

Size Chart—Misses

Size	8	10	12	14	16	18
Bust	31½	32½	34	36	38	40
Waist.	23	24	25½	27	29	31
Hip.	33½	34½	36	38	40	42
Back waist length. .	15¾	16	16¼	16½	16¾	17

6. Look at the first row of the chart labeled *Size*. What size pattern do you wear? _____

This SIZE CHART is like the Misses' Size Chart in a pattern book. *You can use any size chart in a pattern book in exactly the same way.* Look at the size charts in the back of the pattern books in the class room. Notice that there is a size chart for Toddlers, Boys, Girls, and Men. There are also two other charts for women, in addition to Misses' sizes. What are these two pattern types?   1. _____
      2. _____

NEXT LESSON: Using Children's Size Charts.

LESSON PLAN NUMBER 3*

Drug Labels

Rationale

I have known supposedly educated people who took patent medicines without reading the label. This is why I chose to work with those labels. Hoping to impress on the adults not only new words but a real danger, I wanted to make them aware that they should read the label of every bottle before deciding to buy or use the product.

I'm assuming that the lesson just before this one was word study of the spelling, meaning, syllable and phonic type. This entire unit will be about labels. This first lesson is patent medicine and the next one would be prescription labels. The third one would bring in more difficult words that might appear. The fourth will be word study, using words they have had in the unit thus far plus related words.

The situations for choosing the proper medicine will require comparison and contrast of the labels in order to make a safe choice. The questions about strong and weak medicine will require ability to deduce which is which from the warning given.

The little story should enable the student to see the effects of taking a randomly chosen medicine without checking either dosage or warning. The text is fifth- or sixth-grade level according to the Dale-Chall test of readability. This is the way I would begin this Unit.

In Unit 3 we will be dealing with safety in using medicine. We won't be dealing with this today, but what is a *prescription*? (Get answers from the class

*Reprinted by Permission of Mrs. Barbara Shirey.

and generally follow any lead they bring up. Then say the following.) Yes, a prescription medicine is one the doctor says you must get after he has told you what is wrong with you. What would you do if you had an upset stomach but did not feel it was serious enough to go to the doctor? (Class will probably say that they would go to the drugstore to buy something. Again, follow any lead they present so they control the discussion.) I think we all would do the same thing—go to the drugstore and buy something to ease the pain.

This is what we are going to be concerned with today. Reading the labels on the medicine at the drugstore is something we should do very carefully. Do you know what PATENT means? Do you know what someone means when they say that something is so good it is PATENTED? (If no response to this question, then explain.) If someone makes a new machine like a can opener, then he gets it listed in an office in Washington that is set up for this purpose. It keeps anyone else from selling a machine that is really nothing but a copy. Now, what do you think that PATENT medicine is? (Write PATENT on the board. If no discussion of this, then follow right along.) The drug people do the same thing that the man with the machine did. They PATENT (underline the word on the board) their particular medicine. Now they call the medicine that we buy without a doctor's prescription a "patent medicine." (Write PATENT again and add MEDICINE.) Many of these MEDICINES are good and can help us get well. But we need to know which ones to take and how much to take.

That is where we start today, with two very important words on most labels. (Write DOSAGE on the board.) This means how much of the medicine to take each time, and how often to take it. DOSAGE gives us the same information on a patent LABEL (write LABEL on the board) that is on a doctor's prescription LABEL. Another word is (write on board) WARNING. WARNING tells us what we should do or not do while taking the drug, how long we can safely take it, who should not take it at all. The WARNING (underline on board) can save your life.

All of you know the word ILL (write on board). What does it mean? O.K., now if I add "NESS" to it, what do I have? (Add NESS on board.) Yes, that is correct. You may feel ILL and your particular ILLNESS is the flu. Keep that in mind because you see that word also.

Now turn in your workbook to pages 31-32 and look at the labels. Then begin to work.

Labels

When people get sick they can sometimes take patent medicine. This is medicine you can buy without seeing a doctor. There are many medicines you can buy in the drugstore to help a cold. In deciding which one to buy there are two major words on most labels—DOSAGE and WARNING. Dosage tells how often to take it and how much to take of the medicine. The warning tells you what not to do while taking it. It also tells people with certain illnesses not to take it.

A

Norun

Dosage: Adults, 2 every 4 hours; children 6 – 12, 1 every 4 hours; under 6 consult your doctor.

Warning: You may get sleepy. Do not operate machinery or drive while taking. Use only as directed by doctor if you have high blood pressure or low sugar. Do not take longer than 10 days.

B

Sinease

Dosage: Adults, 2 twice daily; children under 12, 1 twice a day; under 6 consult your doctor.

Warning: Do not drive or operate machinery while taking. Do not take if pulse becomes fast, if skin rash or sight blurring occurs. Do not take longer than 5 days.

C

Headease

Dosage: Adults, 1 tablet daily; children under 12 only as directed by your doctor.

Warning: Use only as directed by doctor if you have heart trouble, or are taking medicine for nervous disorders.

D

Cleartab A

Dosage: Adults, 2 tablets every 6 hours; children 1 tablet every 6 hours.

Warning: Do not take if stomach pain occurs. Use only as directed by your doctor if you have ulcers.

I. Choose the medicine you would buy in these cases given these four label choices.

___ 1. You have a son who is 5 years old. He has had a cold for a week.

___ 2. Your wife has a cold. She has serious high blood pressure.

___ 3. Your ulcer is acting up again. You must buy something for this cold before driving to work.

___ 4. You had a slight heart attack last year. You buy something for your cold before the bus comes to take you home.

___ 5. You are out of Label 3 since the bottle only had a five-day supply of tablets. You still have a cold and this itching from the rash is awful.

II. Which medicine would you not buy in these situations for a cold?

___ 1. You are a carpenter with high blood pressure and are on a lunch break.

___ 2. You have a ten-year-old daughter. You are going to take her some medicine when you go home.

___ 3. You have just gotten out of the hospital a week ago. Your ulcer is much better.

___ 4. You have a history of heart trouble.

___ 5. Your wife is taking pills to help calm her down. Those kids drive her up the wall.

III. After reading the labels, which medicine seems not to be very strong? Why do you think that it is not?

IV. Which one do you think is the strongest medicine? Why?

V. Read this story carefully and then answer the two questions about it.

Mrs. Martin doesn't feel well today. Although she has taken a cold medicine for seven days, she still has a cold. So she sent her fifteen-year-old son, James, to the drugstore to get her something else to take. She told him, "Just get me anything to clear my head."

James went into the drugstore and saw five medicines in the cold cure section. He selected one for $1.75, since he had only $2 to buy it with.

When he got home, Mrs. Martin quickly took two of the pills. She took two more in the afternoon. By evening she was feeling worse and had a rash on her face and neck.

1. What possibly could be the problem with Mrs. Martin?
2. List things that were done in the story that should not have been done.

IMPORTANCE OF READING

Every teacher has to ask himself these questions: how much reading, what kind of reading, for what purpose is the reading being done, and what is realistic to expect. Reading is important in our society but the matter of how much skill does any student need to have is a good question for discussion.

Our schools have been traditionally organized with the assumption that in order to be a productive member of society the citizen must be able to read. Postman (1970) has expressed the idea that perhaps the emphasis upon reading, as a prerequisite for success in school to the exclusion of all other media for learning, "is a way of keeping nonconforming youth—blacks, the politically disaffected, and the economically disadvantaged, among others—in their place. By taking this tack, the schools have become a major force for political conservatism at a time when everything else in the culture screams for rapid reorientation and change."

It is true that in a highly complex society a person needs to be able to read if he is to function within the society. The student must be able to read for information in order to meet the demands society places upon him. It is true that society is changing and that perhaps other media will and should receive more emphasis within the learning environment, but this does not mean that reading is obsolete as a means of communication. The need is for a more realistic view of the purposes and use of reading rather than its expulsion from the curriculum.

An educational practice that does need examination is the type of material we ask students to read as they are acquiring skills and appreciation. Postman (1970) states the problem well, although with a definite bias.

> One of the standard beliefs about the reading process is that it is more or less neutral. Reading, the argument goes, is just a skill. What people read is their own business, and the reading teacher merely helps to increase a student's options. If one wants to read about America, one may

read de Toqueville or *The Daily News*; if one wants to read literature, one may go to Melville or Jacqueline Susann. In theory, this argument is compelling. In practice it is pure romantic nonsense. *The New York Daily News* is the most widely read newspaper in America. Most of our students will go to the grave not having read, of their own choosing, a paragraph of de Toqueville or Thoreau, or John Stuart Mill or, if you exclude the Gettysburg Address, even Abraham Lincoln. As between Jacqueline Susann and Herman Melville—well, the less said the better. To put it bluntly, among every 100 students who learn to read, my guess is that no more than one will employ the process toward any of the lofty goals which are customarily held before us. The rest will use the process to increase their knowledge of trivia, to maintain themselves at a relatively low level of emotional maturity, and to keep themselves simplistically uninformed about the social and political turmoil around them.

Postman's views express the feelings of many educators who believe that the vehicles (reading materials) through which we profess to be teaching skills and appreciation are completely unrealistic for the society in which we live and students we teach. To expect all students to read Shakespeare, Hawthorne, Melville, et al. is an educational folly of the greatest magnitude. In teaching students we must constantly keep in mind their ability level, their background of experience, their goals (not ours) and what will be necessary for them to be educated productive citizens. This is not meant to imply that some students should not be exposed to "the classics"; they should. It is only meant to suggest that we need to be more discriminating.

In conclusion, it may be well to keep in mind Marshall McLuhan's concept that all media of communication make claims upon our senses and each elicits a behavioral response. Postman reflects this philosophy in his statement:

> The schools are also still promoting the idea that literacy is the richest source of aesthetic experience. This is in the face of the fact that kids are spending a billion dollars a year on LP records and seeing films. The schools are still promoting the idea that the main source of wisdom is to be found in libraries, from which most schools, incidentally, carefully exclude the most interesting books.

FLEXIBILITY IN LEARNING

Regardless of the existing organizational structure of the school program, the teacher will find that deviation from the traditional formal structure of organization is one of the most effective steps toward improving reading ability. By reducing the use of single textbook and increasing the amount of time for guided study in a multiple of materials a teacher can often reduce the degree of reading problems. If flexible time periods and adequate library facilities are available, this approach will aid not only the poor readers but the average and capable as well. With a variety of reading materials ranging from easy to difficult, all students can be helped to reach their maximum reading capacity. This is a must, since the group most often neglected in the classroom is not only the poor reader but students with a great deal of ability.

An increase in flexibility of methods and materials does not mean rejection of the ideas of similar content for all students. The traditional instructional practice of a single textbook perpetuates the tradition familiar to the public and to most members of the teaching profession, but it does have dangers. What appears to be efficiency in instruction often results in the good student being bored and the slower and less academic student losing interest. Identical content and activities which are common to the group have distinct advantages and should also be a part of the curriculum. What is needed is not a revolution (at least not at the moment) but a gradual modification in classroom strategy. A more effective way of instruction must be found that frees the teacher to work with pupils who are in the greatest need of help and others who are so gifted that they lose interest.

Organizing for instruction in order to attain more flexibility in the classroom and to accommodate individual patterns of learning requires more careful planning than traditional teaching practices. If classes are poorly planned, group work and individual instruction collapse into an educational merry-go-round. A first consideration must be to maintain a standard of order and decorum necessary for instruction. Many elementary teachers have achieved these standards for a number of years with children less mature, more active, and far less aware of the goals of instruction than are secondary school students. The elementary teacher typically plans her instructional activities to have group work, large and small, as well as individual instructional sessions with students. The amount of differentiated group instruction done by the elementary school teacher is not recommended as a standard plan in the traditional secondary school, but here too, the secondary school teacher finds that with attention to efficient planning and realistic goals, flexible organization can prove to be equally possible and effective.

Multiple Materials

If adjustments for varying levels of ability is built into the program, differentiated materials can be used to advantage. The following comments by teachers illustrates how multilevel textbooks can be used.

"At first we thought having different textbooks would be unwieldy. Now we find them intensely practical. Students starting a unit are given guiding questions so that they approach reading with broad questions and problems. Though textbooks of varying difficulty are not strictly parallel, such broad topics as the discovery of the New World, Life in the Colonies, The Making of the Constitution, The Opening of the West, and the Industrial Revolution can be found in almost all the books. Two parallel world history textbooks for tenth-grade use have been published: *Man's Story*, on the tenth-grade level, and *Living World History*, on the eighth-grade level, are similar in content and organization."

"In my junior-high-level American history classes, Moon and Cline's *Story of Our Land and People* (Holt, Rinehart and Winston, 1964) can be handled by most of the less able readers or *Exploring American History* (Globe, 1968) which is written at a fifth-grade level can be used. *History of a Free People* (Macmillan, 1964) challenges the best. For in-between-readers, *Story of the American Nation* (Harcourt Brace Jovanovich, 1962) and *Story of Our Country* (Allyn and Bacon, 1963) do the job."

"In my eighth-grade English class we were investigating the theme about how our experiences led to more mature responsibility. Knowing that all my students couldn't read the same materials, we used the following: *Little Britches* for average readers, *Captain Courageous* for superior readers, *Smuggler's Island* for poor readers, and *Swiss Family Robinson* and *Mountain Laurel* for girls who dislike boys' books. Students who couldn't read any of these read individually books that were also related to the general theme."

The preceding statements illustrate how adjustments have been made by teachers to improve the instructional program. They are not unusual, the same kind of activities can be planned by any teacher who makes the effort.

Differentiated Assignments

Teachers do not always have time to design lessons and units that include a variety of materials. It is sometimes possible to provide for a range of reading abilities within the frame of common assignments. Just as most of what students read elicits various levels of understanding, so also can many assignments of teachers represent directed instruction in relation to the comprehension levels represented by the students. Students with reflective abilities and superior reading skills may be challenged with more difficult problems, while poor readers may at the same time be asked to respond to less complicated questions.

The taxonomy developed by Dr. Thomas Barrett of the University of Wisconsin, discussed in Chapter 8, can be used as a guide for assigning and developing questions. Perceptive observations on the ability of a student to answer certain types of questions will also enable you to evaluate where the student is in his comprehension ability and where your instruction should lead him.

Using the Unit Method

The unit method of teaching offers one effective solution to the problem of pupil variation in ability. It need not be used constantly throughout the entire year, but it does allow for a way of integrating content and providing for differentiated instruction. In any course taught in the secondary school, units may be designed so that they are broad enough to permit a variety of reading resource material to be used. When the instructional program is organized topically or thematically, the teacher is able to organize the program and guide the less able student with less demanding reading material while still meeting the needs of the more able.

SUMMARY

In organizing the classroom for effective reading instruction there are a number of educational practices and basic guidelines which every teacher can follow. The practices currently used in the classroom can be modified with a minimum amount of effort to make the educational environment more productive.

All teachers need to evaluate what their own classroom practices are and the implications of the practices they employ. If instruction is to be effective, the teacher has to make some committment to what practices in oral reading, use of multiple textbooks, and using differentiated assignments are to be adopted in his classroom.

REFERENCES

Penty, Ruth. *Reading Ability and High School Drop-Outs.* New York: Bureau of Publications, Teachers College, Columbia University, 1956.
Postman, Neil. "The Politics of Reading," *Harvard Educational Review*, XL (May 1970), pp. 244-252.

ADDITIONAL READINGS

Austin, Mary, et al. *The Torchlighters: Tomorrow's Teachers of Reading.* Cambridge, Mass.: Harvard University Press, 1961.
Braam, Leonard, and Marilyn Roehm. "Subject-Area Teachers' Familiarity with Reading Skills," *Journal of Developmental Reading*, VII (Spring 1964), pp. 188-196.

chapter 10

The Reading Interests
of Adolescents

There is little argument that a basic objective of any reading program at the secondary school level should be the development and refinement of adolescents' reading interests and tastes. As Paul Witty (1964) has stated, the development of lasting interests in reading should be "the concern of all citizens, since it is generally conceded that effective participation in democratic life requires efficient and wide reading."

The evidence on the actual amount of reading done by adolescents and adults in this country is not particularly encouraging. Gunderson (1964) noted that although books, magazines, and newspapers are available in abundant quantities, the citizens of this country are not wide readers. Students studied in the Project Talent search were not found to be reading as much as would be expected. Gunderson feels the present-day statistics "should cause us to wonder what is wrong with us in our work with students; why do they read so few books? If we temporarily overlook the percentage of retarded readers, the figures still leave much more to be desired."

Poor access to central libraries, or access only to smaller libraries in large cities and rural areas could be one factor in explaining the lack of reading by adolescents and adults. Possibly a more important reason is that too few schools have programs designed to develop further the reading skills of students at the secondary level.

All secondary school teachers should be aware of what research has shown to be the relevant interest areas for adolescent students, and should be knowledgeable concerning several issues involved in the further promoting and refinement of reading interests and tastes. Too often educators have assumed that these matters are of concern only to English teachers, which may be another reason that the evidence regarding the reading habits of adolescents and adults is so discouraging.

ADOLESCENT READING INTERESTS AND TASTES

Before discussing the specific reading interests of adolescents it is important to note that a close relationship appears to exist between adolescent reading habits and their general interests. What are the interest patterns of adolescents that affect their reading interests? Observing teen-agers at their daily activities, one can see that they are interested in sports, automobiles, television, transistor radios, movies, and club and gang activities. Although students' interests may vary somewhat with the geographic location, certain trends seem to be quite normal.

Reading interests, of course, may not necessarily correspond with life interests. A student may be interested in baseball or electronics but not interested in reading about them.

It should be noted that the research regarding adolescent reading interests and tastes is far from complete. At times the data seem to present conflicting information, but the research techniques have been so crude that the results may reflect more technical problems than actual differences in tastes and interests. Some studies have dealt with choices of specific books, some with expressed likes for certain topics, and some with what teachers thought about their students' interests and tastes.

Research Studies of Adolescents' Reading Interests

One exemplary study of reading interests was conducted by Vaughn (1963) with eighth-grade students. The subjects were divided into three intellectual groups: bright, average, and dull. Sex comparisons of tastes and interests were also made.

It was found that bright girls chose books relating to home and school materials, mysteries and adventure, while average girls showed a preference for home-and-school stories, novels and poetry. Dull girls chose home-and-school stories, fairy tales, and detective stories. Brighter boys chose adventure stories, invention and science materials, while the average boys chose detective stories, adventure stories, and history materials. Dull boys chose detective stories, biographies, and fairy tales.

Vaughn noted that in the areas of interests, all boys chose mystery stories, adventure stories, and humorous materials, but for intelligent and average boys, humor was much more important than love interest. Likewise, brighter girls were *not* as interested in love stories as the average and dull girls. The magazines most reported as being read by boys in this study were *Sports Illustrated*, *Science Fiction*, *Hunting and Fishing*, and various types of comic books. For girls, the magazines were *Look*, *Saturday Evening Post*,* and *Reader's Digest*. There was also considerable interest in *Modern Romance* and *True Story* among some groups of girls.

Soares (1963), in studying junior high students, said that they tended to be more realistic in their interests and tastes than younger students. Girls chose stories of problems relating to their age groups and boys chose materials relating

---

*The *Saturday Evening Post* suspended on February 8, 1969.

to sports. Boys liked stories with an explicit moral while girls appeared to like stories with implicit morals. It was also noted that any materials having younger children as the central characters were avoided by the junior high students.

Shores (1964) also conducted a study with high school students and found that they were interested in literature, especially mysteries and science fiction and fictional sports stories. He pointed out that at these age levels, sex differences were quite noticeable and that students were not necessarily interested in reading about things that concerned them in other ways.

The researcher admitted that the picture of the reading habits of the high school student was brief and incomplete. The high school student does appear to be more interested in current events than his grandfather or father. He also has a tendency to want to read more about social studies than science.

Shores maintained that elementary teachers were better able to predict the reading interests of their students than high school teachers. He believed that the subject-matter area specialization of high school teachers tended to blind them to the various other reading interest areas.

After comparing his studies with elementary, junior high and senior high students, Shores concluded that there was a remarkable degree of consistency of reading interests from the fourth through the twelfth grade. At all levels, mysteries and adventure tend to be most prominent in literature reading interests. There was also a consistent trend noted for children in all grades to like biography, social science, science, physical science, and recreation and hobbies, personal problems, and the arts. There was a shift away from cowboys and Westerns, fairy tales, and mythology as the student entered junior high school. Animals tended to be interesting to all level students but more important in the lower grades than in the high school.

Olson and Rosen (1967) investigated the reading interests of Negro and Caucasian ninth-grade students. They found that black students appear to have stronger choices for reading current materials such as newspapers and magazines, and stronger reading interests in such topics as social relations, romance, teenage problems, humor, and occupation areas than whites. The black students tended to rate magazines reflecting male and female interests in their least-liked category, while the white students did not. Caucasian females least liked books related to hobbies and newspaper sports. These researchers recommended that curriculum planning should consider making provisions for differences in interests on the basis of race and sex differences.

Stewart (1964) reported on the reading of magazines by students in junior and senior high school. *Life* and *Saturday Evening Post* were more popular than *American Girl* and *Seventeen* among the girls. The boys chose *Life*, *Saturday Evening Post*, and *Time* more often than they chose *Boy's Life*. The girls were more interested in home and social issues while the boys preferred sports, humor and science topics. Stewart from his data that teen magazines were far less important to teenagers than were adult magazines.

Another study reported data concerning the newspaper and magazine interests of students in grades 9-11. For both boys and girls, *Life, Saturday Evening Post, Reader's Digest, Look* and *Time* rated high in preference. *Seventeen* was the second highest choice for girls but was not of interest to boys. In regard to the newspaper, boys chose the first page as the most interesting. Girls found the society section and advice columns most interesting.

Sex Differences in Adolescents' Reading Interests

One common thread running through most of the investigations of adolescent reading interests is that sex is definitely a dominant force in young people's choices of reading material. Boys and girls have different interests that appear to affect their reading interests, and these differences must be taken into consideration in planning any reading program for secondary schools.

The research findings of Thorndike (1941) indicated that sex may be a slightly less potent factor in influencing young people's reading choices in senior high school than in junior high. The gap between the reading interests of secondary school boys and girls appears to close with increasing age. This does not mean, however, that sex is not influential during the senior high school period. It means that, on the average, approximately four and one-half years' growth is required to produce in a student a change in interest as great as the divergence caused by sex between boys and girls in the same grade. Information gathered from research indicates that among younger children in the elementary school, age is more influential in governing reading choices than it is in the secondary school; while beyond the secondary school, changes in age have progressively less influence on reading preferences. On the other hand, it appears that from the fifth grade, at least, to adulthood, sex is a dominating influence which attains its maximum during the junior high school period.

Data from a survey of literary materials commonly used in schools show that girls enjoy more of the basic literary types than do boys. The one type liked better by boys is the speech, although the difference between boys and girls is not great for the novel, short story, or biography.

Indeed, the difference is so small for the novel and biography as to suggest that these literary forms may be equally enjoyed by boys and girls. The sex of the biography is highly significant in influencing boys' interests whereas girls appear to enjoy biographies about men as well as about women with equal satisfaction.

Teachers should weigh the fact that, in general, essays are not enjoyed by secondary school students. However, it is well to note that humorous essays as a group provide exception to the rule, and that (a) among didactic essays there are few that are liked, and (b) humorous essays often make points as important as those found in more serious and formal types.

Science is primarily a boys' reading field, but even boys prefer most other types over science. Those writings concerning science are more popular when the style is simple and the elements are dramatic.

Does sex influence young people's choices of short stories and poems? Taken as a whole, short stories are almost equally well liked by boys and girls. Within this grouping there is a wide range of tastes. Action, adventure, suspense, animal stories, mystery, humor, and stories about teen-agers are popular classifications with both boys and girls.

A librarian's study of reading interests of high school students as determined by their choices of books checked out of the library showed that boys read more stories of adventure than anything else. General fiction was second in popularity, and animal stories were third.

Boys read more stories of strenuous adventure, sports, and hobbies than girls. Adventure may be designated as two types—grim physical and milder types. Girls prefer the milder adventure story while boys favor the story involving vigorous physical activities. Girls have a greater preference for adventure combined with love as compared to boys' preference for "straight" adventure. This rejection of love as the theme in any type of literature by boys seems to be standard as shown by findings of different studies. While boys rate other sentiments higher, girls place romantic love first.

It is interesting to observe that both boys and girls reject, in general, stories of mood, symbolism, myths, legends, and folk tales, and that stories of humor are approved by both sexes. Here again, however, boys tend to reject such stories when love is an important element.

Boys and girls rank animal stories near the top. Animal stories lose their appeal in grades 11 and 12. The choices of animal stories parallel the choices of adventure stories. Boys choose stories about wild animals. Stories about pets and domestic animals rank high with girls. This further illustrates girls' dislike of stories that involve grim physical struggle or savagery.

Before discussing the effects of sex on choices of poetry, it must be understood that neither boys nor girls like poetry well as a whole. On the other hand, some individual poems are popular and there are several subdivisions in which groups of poems rank high.

The poems are divided into lyric and narrative for consideration. Both boys and girls enjoy narrative poems better than lyric poetry. While girls' approval of lyric poetry approaches their approval of narrative poetry, boys on a comparative basis reject lyric poems decisively in favor of narrative poems.

The divisions classifying poetry are similar to the classifications of short stories. As with short stories, narrative poems are liked as a whole by boys and girls. Boys like poems of grim physical adventure markedly better than do girls. In poems with women as principal characters, girls show greater preference. Again love and sentiment bring about a division in the reaction of boys and girls toward narrative poems.

It has been found that even though lyric poetry is regarded unfavorably, many patriotic and humorous poems of the lyric type are liked as well as some lyrics about home life and animals. Lyric poems about nature, sentiment, reflection, religion, philosophy, and didactism, however, are not liked.

DISCOVERING THE READING INTERESTS OF ADOLESCENTS

Information concerning adolescent reading interest trends in the nation as a whole or in regional areas can be helpful to teachers, but one question still remains. What are the particular interests of a teacher's own students? Many teachers want to know effective ways in which this information can be acquired.

Most of the methods of ascertaining reading interests have been based on students' subjective judgments. The following procedure can be used:

Announce to the pupils that we desire the frank opinion of each pupil without reference to what any other pupil thinks. This information will make it possible for recommended lists to be prepared which will contain reading materials genuinely interesting to the pupils who are to use them. Be careful to impress upon students the importance of giving their own candid opinions.

Ask each pupil to take one-half sheet of paper and prepare it to correspond with the sample enclosed. Half a sheet is suggested because reports will be only half as bulky as would be the case if large sheets were used. Perhaps the easiest way will be for the teacher to sketch the heading of the form on the blackboard.

Name of Pupil _____ (check one) Boy, Girl

Grade _____ Age _____ IQ _____ Date _____

Teacher _____ School _____

Selection and Author	Very Interesting	Fairly Interesting	Un- Interesting

When the pupils have prepared the forms, except blanks for IQ's which should be added by the teacher later, read to the class the titles of selections (poems, essays, short stories, plays, novels, biographies) studied or read by the class this school year. After writing the title, each pupil should mark an X in column 1 if the selection was very interesting to him, in column 2 in fairly interesting, and in column 3 if uninteresting.

After the papers have been collected, teachers should add the pupils' IQ's.

If this information is not available, write I, II, III after the name of each pupil to indicate superior, average, or slow in reading comprehension. Using a questionnaire like this one, teachers will find out information about different aspects of the reading interests of their own students—interests by sex, by grades, or which selections are more interesting to the students.

Olson's Reading Interest Inventory can also be of considerable value to any secondary school teacher. The questionnaire should be duplicated and each student given a copy. The instructions are printed on the inventory, but it will speed up the process and eliminate some confusion if the teacher reads the instructions aloud as the students read the instructions silently. Remember to stress the importance of each student's giving his own opinion and not comparing with his neighbor.

Name _____

School _____

Grade _____

Reading Interest Inventory

Please put a cross (X) in the column which best describes your feeling about reading the following kinds of materials.

	1 Like very very much	2 Like quite a lot	3 Like a little	4 Dislike a lot	5 Dislike quite a lot	6 Dislike very much
1. Reading the newspaper	( )	( )	( )	( )	( )	( )
2. Reading the front page of the newspaper	( )	( )	( )	( )	( )	( )
3. Reading the comics in the newspaper	( )	( )	( )	( )	( )	( )
4. Reading the sports page in the newspaper	( )	( )	( )	( )	( )	( )
5. Reading about world events in the newspaper	( )	( )	( )	( )	( )	( )
6. Reading about things of local interest in the newspaper	( )	( )	( )	( )	( )	( )

	1 Like very very much	2 Like quite a lot	3 Like a little	4 Dislike a lot	5 Dislike quite a lot	6 Dislike very much
7. Reading books	( )	( )	( )	( )	( )	( )
8. Reading books that are about real people	( )	( )	( )	( )	( )	( )
9. Reading books that are funny	( )	( )	( )	( )	( )	( )
10. Reading books that have a lot of adventure in them	( )	( )	( )	( )	( )	( )
11. Reading books about my hobbies	( )	( )	( )	( )	( )	( )
12. Reading books about women	( )	( )	( )	( )	( )	( )
13. Reading books about men	( )	( )	( )	( )	( )	( )
14. Reading books that tell about sex	( )	( )	( )	( )	( )	( )
15. Reading books that tell about the same problems you have	( )	( )	( )	( )	( )	( )
16. Reading about mystery stories	( )	( )	( )	( )	( )	( )
17. Reading poetry	( )	( )	( )	( )	( )	( )
18. Reading books about family life	( )	( )	( )	( )	( )	( )
19. Reading books with some romance in them	( )	( )	( )	( )	( )	( )
20. Reading about sports	( )	( )	( )	( )	( )	( )
21. Reading books about personal appearance	( )	( )	( )	( )	( )	( )
22. Reading books about teenage problems	( )	( )	( )	( )	( )	( )
23. Reading books about jobs	( )	( )	( )	( )	( )	( )
24. Reading books about love	( )	( )	( )	( )	( )	( )

	1 Like very very much	2 Like quite a lot	3 Like a little	4 Dislike a lot	5 Dislike quite a lot	6 Dislike very much
25. Reading books about religion	( )	( )	( )	( )	( )	( )
26. Reading animal stories	( )	( )	( )	( )	( )	( )
27. Reading books that have a great deal of violence in them	( )	( )	( )	( )	( )	( )
28. Reading books about social problems	( )	( )	( )	( )	( )	( )
29. Reading books with many pictures	( )	( )	( )	( )	( )	( )
30. Reading magazines	( )	( )	( )	( )	( )	( )
31. Reading sports magazines	( )	( )	( )	( )	( )	( )
32. Reading hobby magazines	( )	( )	( )	( )	( )	( )
33. Reading romance magazines	( )	( )	( )	( )	( )	( )
34. Reading comic books	( )	( )	( )	( )	( )	( )
35. Reading magazines about clothing and styles	( )	( )	( )	( )	( )	( )
36. Reading magazines about women	( )	( )	( )	( )	( )	( )
37. Reading magazines about men	( )	( )	( )	( )	( )	( )
38. Reading magazines about music	( )	( )	( )	( )	( )	( )
39. Reading detective magazines	( )	( )	( )	( )	( )	( )
40. Reading joke magazines	( )	( )	( )	( )	( )	( )

Other such inventories have been devised. These can give the teacher ideas that he can use in preparing his own plan. Some investigators have asked students to list books which they had read and enjoyed and to state briefly why they enjoyed them. Another method is to have students keep diary records of their voluntary reading over a period of time. A method used by librarians is to keep records of the amount and kind of voluntary reading done by the students in the library and the books that they withdrew. The interview has also been used to study the reading interests of adults and adolescents. It is the best method for understanding an individual's reading interests in relation to other facets of his life.

The questionnaire technique can be varied not only by having the students tell the kind of books and articles they liked most and why, but also by asking them to compose a title and a first paragraph for a book or article that all persons their age would want to read. Another method presents a list of fictitious titles and annotations of books and articles, and asks students to check the titles they would like very much to read, would be indifferent to, or would very much dislike reading.

Significant insights can be obtained from freely written compositions and group discussions on what makes a book interesting or uninteresting. Informal but continuous observation of reading can yield valuable information about reading interests. A teacher has many opportunities to listen carefully to students' remarks about books and articles. This will give him an understanding of their lack of interest in particular materials.

No matter what test the teacher administers, the value of the test will be in how the information is used. The validity of the responses depends upon capturing the students' interests and cooperation, and is increased by anonymity.

AROUSING AND DEVELOPING STUDENTS' READING INTERESTS

The basic principle to follow in arousing interest in reading is to use every possible means to make it enjoyable. Within a classroom the teacher can set aside a corner or section of the room for recreational reading. A table with chairs, or chairs without a table, will make the reading seem special and important. A reading-seeing-listening room for browsing, lounging, listening to music, enjoying art, and reading is profitable in increasing reading enjoyment.

Teen-agers are interested in club activities, and book clubs can fulfill the needs of the adolescent in this respect. Such clubs may be a means of arousing interest in some students who never have a desire to read but are sociable. There are many projects possible with a group like this—discussions of books, exploration of new books, dramatized reading of short plays, setting up exhibits, giving assembly programs on books, and raising money to buy new books.

A variety of devices may be used to stimulate reading interest. Most of these are simple enough to be used in the classroom. The teacher can display book jackets on the bulletin board or have the students design the displays. Book jackets about dogs could be used to form the middle section of a dachshund with the front end and back end cut from construction paper. Book jackets may also be used to make mobiles having the jackets taped or glued back-to-back and suspended from coat hangers.

Book reviews written by students for the school paper disseminate students' recommendations for reading and publicize worthwhile new books. The class can publish its own paper using the duplicating machine if the school has one. One class wrote reviews of books for its paper, "The Bookworm News."

Book fairs have been successful in many schools. Students have a chance to use their creativity in presenting books to other students.

The artists in the class will have a chance to display their talents by making posters to advertise books. Others may wish to design and draw jackets for the books they have read, illustrating some feature of a book that will make others want to read it.

Interest can be perked up during a lag by giving the students a purpose for reading. A project in reading books by certain authors or books around definite topics could possibly provide the stimulation.

STUDENTS' REPORTING ON READING DONE

The formal book review has a place in any program where written expression is an integral part of the skill-development program, but it is by no means the only way of reporting on a book read. It is important for some students to acquire ability in writing a book review, particularly college-bound students, but it is not important for all.

If one of the major educational purposes is to encourage broad reading and to establish an attitude toward reading as a pleasurable leisure-time activity, the required writing of a formal review is often a deterrent to reading rather than an impetus. Students are often "turned off" from reading not by the reading itself but by what they must do after they have read.

There are many ways of evaluating the range and quality of a student's response to his reading if teachers will use their imagination. In choosing any devices for reporting on reading, a teacher should be guided by three criteria:

1. It should provide a quick means of keeping in touch with the amount and quality of the reading.
2. It should be interesting for the student to do.
3. It should serve as a motivating factor for the student doing the reading and for other students to read the same material.

Students should be allowed to choose the kind of reports they wish to make on a book most of the time. This is not to say that some specific kinds of reporting should not be demanded, but rather that the student be given some reasonable alternatives. The following are a few suggestions for reporting:

1. Report by locating the setting for the book on a map and telling briefly what influence the setting had on the story.
2. Write a paragraph characterizing the principal characters in the story.
3. Have the student keep a record of his reading by using the student's reading record form prepared by the National Council of Teachers of English (508 South Sixth Street, Champaign, Ill.).
4. Have the student prepare a commercial book "blurb" designed to motivate others to read the book.
5. Write a tabloid book review—a series of pictures which tells the story or an interesting happening in the story.
6. Cast a story for the movies with an explanation as to what actors and actresses should play the key roles and why they were selected for the characters.
7. Read to the class interesting excerpts designed to stimulate interest.
8. Have students prepare brief comments on cards to be filed and used by other students making book selections.
9. Report orally or in written form on one or more new things learned from the reading.
10. Write an episode from a book in news-story form.

Teachers are limited in the types of activities only by their own imagination and creativity. In the following section a teacher describes a project and gives examples of responses she got when she asked her students to pretend they were a character in a book writing to another character in the same book.

BOOK-REPORTING PROJECT

This project was carried out in a classroom of eighth-grade students. Not all wished to participate in this extra-credit work. First we talked about letter writing in general and there were groans when the pupils realized they would be expected to undertake more of a subject they had thought was well behind them for this semester.

I read a few letters from collections—Theodore Roosevelt's *Letters to His Children*, Sir George Grey's *Letters to Young Fly Fishermen*, *Letters of Mark Twain*, and Albert Schweitzer's *African Notebook*. Then we talked about what the writers were trying to say in their letters and what could be done through writing letters.

We agreed on certain areas: (1) exposition or argumentative, upholding an idea you feel very strongly about, (2) description, (3) narration, telling in a few paragraphs an event in which the person receiving your letter would be interested, (4) characterization, description of a person or animal you think your friend would like to know, (5) stepping into another's shoes—assuming the personality of a character from a book, you are to write to another character in the book, and (6) flights of fancy—no limitations.

After writing, each author read his own letter to the class. Some preferred not to tell what book they were using as a background but to have the class guess. Others told what book they had used and what they were trying to do. (One boy had to explain that although the person whom he was addressing in his letter had been dead since 1945 he was still writing as if he were still alive!) Many of the letters were hilarious and all agreed that this had given them a new slant on letter writing. One or two were going to use their letters as actual correspondence with friends.

Argumentative
Biographies of Moderns
by David Ewen

Portland Road
Brunswick, Maine
May 3, 1962

Mr. Bela Bartok*
c/o Boosey & Hawkes, Music Publishers
Lynbrook, New York

Sir,

You have betrayed me. I would like to tell you what has happened since my music teacher, Mr. Eves, gave me the volume of your music one short week ago—last Thursday, April 26 to be exact. Usually I do my practicing before the school bus comes while I'm fresh, as Mum says. But Friday I had to pack as we were leaving right after school to visit my sister in Camden, and since she doesn't have a piano, my music wasn't put out of my roll until Monday.

That morning I tried to get in an hour's practicing and opened the book and tackled what looked so simple—the composition you call "Thirds Against a Single Voice." It was, alas, "Thirds Against the Three McLeans"—that's my father, my mother and me. After two measures my father, who used to play the clarinet said, "For Pete's sake, son, look at the signature." I already had looked but looked again. But that didn't mean a thing. It said one flat but it just wasn't the usual key of F. I started to play again and my father left the room muttering and my mother came in saying something about my being awfully rusty and careless and I would just have to make up the practice I lost over the weekend.

That meant I couldn't play in the mixed doubles with Kristine in the badminton tourney, and boy, was Kris mad. I think she wanted a chance to wear our Bach and Beethoven sweatshirts we ordered through Mr. Eves. I left her trying to sign up Gerard to play and caught the school bus home.

I worked on my Hanon studies, the Chopin preludes and some exercises and was about to start on "Thirds" again when Dad came in and I

*Bartok died in 1945, as the students knew.

just knew it would give him indigestion to hear all that dissonance before supper. After he went out for the evening I tackled the "Thirds" in earnest. Gretchen, my dachshund, howled and my mother put her hands over her ears and said, "Mark, you can't be playing the right notes." And the more I played the more she protested.

Tuesday morning I overslept and just caught the bus. Mum said I couldn't stay for the ball game but would have to come and practice I was doing so poorly. When I squawked Dad said it was a waste of his money and Mr. Eves' time if I didn't practice and I'd better study that new piece and learn it right. Well, Tuesday night I set out determined to learn "Thirds." Do you know what I discovered? There are sharps where there should be flats and naturals in one hand and sharps in the other. In fact, Mr. Bartok, it is a musical mess. Usually I can fake and play by ear when I haven't practiced, which makes Mr. Eves mad because he says I've got to learn to sight-read.

Anyway, by today's lesson I still couldn't read all that crazy stuff, even the section marked Lento. My Lento was almost a complete stop as I couldn't fake a thing. I was, as the book says, undone. I should have known from what David Ewen says about you in your biography that you were the worst of the unmelodic fellows. Give me a tune I can fake anytime. I just never know what you plan to next. Modern music stinks.

Mr. Bartok, your picture will never appear on a sweatshirt like the three great "B's" because you can't or won't write the way they did . . . music a boy and his parents and his dog can understand.

Sir, I shall not play you in the June recital.

Sincerely,

Mark McLean

Narration
Adventures in Nature
by Edwin Way Teale

Cape Mugford, Labrador
April 24, 1962

Mr. Chet Honkly
Carrituck Sound
North Carolina

Dear Chet,

Can't imagine why you want to stay in North Carolina in all that heat. We arrived in Labrador a little later than usual, partly because of the ten-day delay in starting and partly because of the lack of tail winds until we hit Maine. The flight was regular but slow from North Carolina to the Jersey coast. Feeding grounds there were packed with the usual migrating crowds. We only stayed a couple of days and then had the usual exciting flight over New York City.

One of the duck hawks, who was on an earlier flight, was perched on the mooring mast of the Empire State Building as we came by. Those boys are mean the way they wait there to hurl themselves on the smaller birds who go through at night. Guess meanness must run in the Hawk family.

Was glad to see most of the smaller birds remembered to climb higher going over the city. It's always such a grand sight to see New York by night. All those lights make me glad I can travel at night instead of during the day.

After we hit the Sound I remembered that the bird watchers were probably below so I reminded Doug Headwards, who was leading our V, that we ought to make the best V possible for their benefit and do a little honking so they would be sure to see us silhouetted against the moon . . . one of their favorite subjects for photography, I am told.

We followed the coastline into Massachusetts but most of the marshes there were pretty dirty. We just couldn't wait to get to Merry-meeting Bay. There's always good feeding there and safe in spring when no hunters are around.

We were there about ten days waiting for the flock to come up from Portland. That sporty crowd with the bird bands always stops off in that horribly dirty Back Bay just to be caught and recorded by the Bird Club boys. The weather was foul . . . I could make a pun here, but in considera-tion of your fine sensitivities, I won't. It took the Portland group several days to get caught but they seem to think the delay was worth it. Their membership in the National Wild Bird Life Association seems to mean so much to some silly geese.

While we were waiting, romance blossomed on Merrymeeting Bay and many more paired off en route so we have been busy building nests since our arrival ten days ago. Such activity.

Forgot to tell you that in Maine that weasel, Edward R. Burrow, gave us a couple of bad nights trying to get at some of the older geese but we moved them out into the Bay and then kept a watch brigade going day and night.

There were the usual few who think Labrador is becoming too crowded with the hoi polloi and who left yesterday to go off up north to Hudson's Bay . . . they are the same group who talked about wintering in the Mississippi Valley next year instead of dear old Carrituck Sound.

Guess I'm too fond of old places and old friends to change. Speak-ing of old friends, when are you going to finish that special assignment and come north, Honkly, old boy?

Goodnight, Chet,

Beakly

William Weiner, Grade 8-1

Description
Living Free
by Joy Adamson

Rotterdam-Blydorp Zoo
Rotterdam, The Netherlands
May 5, 1960

Dear Elsa,

We have not heard from you for a long time. How are things in the bush country? Here in the zoo life is easy and never dull. We sometimes feel sorry for you and wish you might have things a little easier.

Our keeper brings us huge juicy steaks with no hide on it to tear at your intestines and we have the best of medical care if we are ever sick. We have a constant water hole filled by a man with a hose several times a day. Our manes are brushed and there isn't a flaw on our well-kept bodies—no tufts caught on thorn bushes, no scratches like Mother used to have.

People come and stand outside our cages and make stupid remarks, we have fun sometimes when "Big One" just ignores them and pretends to be asleep until they get real close and look as if they were going to poke us. The "Big One" jumps out of his sunny spot and roars and snarls at them. Everyone backs back and says how ferocious we are! And yet we have almost forgotten how to tear a goat apart since all our food is served to us.

Outside our cage this morning all along the walks we can see beautiful flowers called tulips and hyacinths. Over by the elephant house there are more flowers and a fountain. It is so pleasant here.

We hate to think of you in that wild jungle even with good friends like the Adamsons. Tell them you want to join us here. I am sure there is plenty of food for us all and there is plenty of room if you don't mind being a little crowded. Don't continue to live the hard way.

All our love,

Your brother, "Big One" and
Your sister, Lustica

Reservation #4
Kenya, Africa
June 15, 1960

Dear Brother and Sister,

Thank you for your consideration of my feelings expressed in your letter. So much has happened since you left. Of course you read all about it in the book Mrs. Adamson (I call her Joy) wrote about me, "Born Free." Didn't it make you just a little homesick for your old home?

I wish you could see your beautiful nephews and niece. Yes, I have three wonderful cubs who are nearly ten and a half months old. Since you are in the family, you won't mind if I boast a little about them.

When they were only six weeks and two days old they swam the big river where we used to find the zebra tracks. Gopa is very timid and I thought he would never take the plunge. But when he saw Jespah and Little Elsa safe on the other side he dove in, whining all the time more like a dog than a lion.

Jespah is my pride and joy. His coat is lighter than the others and he is much livelier. Yet he is most devoted to me. He is popular with all the new tribe. I expect great things from him. At fourteen weeks he had learned to bury surplus meat and now he is housebroken enough so I can take him fairly often for prolonged stays with the Adamsons in camp. His mane is just beginning to show and I think he is going to be very handsome. He is lying at my feet now, chewing at some sansevieria.

Gopa and his sister are very playful and romp like kittens, but Elsa met her first croc the other day and stood her ground in a very brave way. She is attractive . . . very feminine and grooms herself constantly.

Poor Gopa is a trial in many ways but he does try. I thought he would never learn to climb a tree. He excels in tail twitching, however and brought me some goat meat the other day, so he has his good points.

The Adamsons are very good to us. They always make sure there is plenty of fresh-killed game around when hunting is poor for us and I can always take the children to them to pick out the tsetse flies (they are awfully thick this year).

We love the life here . . . the nights under the stars, the interesting rocks to climb and hide among, and the attention of George and Joy Adamson. We have our fun, too, pretending to be very fierce and wild when some of the helpers are around. Some of the natives can look so scared so we love to tease them.

So you see there is no reason for my wanting to leave. I have three lovely children who love this wild life and we all love the excitement of hunting for our own food. Besides, who would keep the crocs in line if we left?

I look around now and see my three dears sleeping like kittens and I am content here in the sun chewing on the twig of sansevieria Jespah left. My, it tastes good! Have some?

All my love,

Your sister,

Elsa

Annette Mott
Grade 8-1

Stepping Into Another's Shoes
Johnny Tremain
by Esther Forbes

Silsbee's Cove, Mass.
April 29, 1775

My Dearest Cilla,

Doctor Warren knows of a courier who can get this through to you. Oh, Cill, my darling, so much has happened since I left you.

My heart is grieving because Rab, our own dear Rab, is dead. I cannot break it to you gently and I can scarcely believe it myself. I found Doctor Warren on Lexington Green this morning and he took me to Rab. Rab had been wounded in the first volley shot at Lexington. I knew when I saw him that it was very bad.

They had taken him to Buckman's Tavern and that is where we found him, in the back chamber of the second floor. Oh, Cill, he looked so white. First he asked about the battle and then about you and what had happened in Boston. Then his mind began to wander and he spoke about his boyhood days . . . the strangest and sometimes very humorous events. He seemed to want to relive his whole life in the few hours he thought he had left. But it was to be only minutes, Cill. I knew from the way he kept wiping blood away from his mouth.

He gave me his musket—the one with the good stock and the flint he had knapped. Then he told me to find his grandsire here at Silsbee's Cove. And then he died.

I did as he wished, coming here to Silsbee's Cove. I am in grandsire's kitchen now writing. No one is here. Grandsire's old musket is gone and I am sure he has gone off, as I must do, to take up arms. I know there will be fighting, lots of fighting. How many will die? Hundreds and hundreds, perhaps. But at least we know what we are fighting for . . . "so a man can stand up."

God keep you safe till I return, Cilla.

Your devoted servant,

John Lyte Tremain

Lyn Baird
Grade 8-1

CENSORSHIP OF BOOKS

Within the last few years there has been an increase in the pressures exerted on schools to restrict the access of students to certain books. In many communities successful attempts have been made in removing some modern writers from classrooms and libraries because of alleged pornography. A list of these authors reads like a "Who's Who" of distinguished authors: John Steinbeck, Thomas Mann, Ernest Hemingway, J. D. Salinger, Thomas Wolfe, John Hersey, Archibald MacLeish, and William Faulkner.

In some school systems the administration has defended the teachers and the right of the students to read the material, while in others they have succumbed to pressure and fired the "offending" teachers. Where the books and teachers have been removed, the result has been a climate hostile to free inquiry and an atmosphere of restriction and fear.

In reference to the Supreme Court case, *Adler* vs. *Board of Education* in 1952, Justice William O. Douglas made the following statement:

> Where suspicion fills the air and holds scholars in line for fear of their jobs, there can be no exercise of the free intellect. . . . A problem can no longer be pursued with impunity to its edges, fear stalks the classroom. The teacher is no longer a stimulant to adventurous thinking; she instead becomes a pipeline for safe and sound information. A deadening dogma takes the place of free inquiry. Instruction tends to become sterile; pursuit of knowledge is discouraged; discussion often leaves off where it should begin.

The right to read is basic to the society we live in. But to ensure this right the teacher must use it wisely. Care must be taken to select books that do not embarrass the students when discussed in open groups. It is important, however, for the teacher to feel he had the freedom to recommend books for individual students when the books have educational significance for that student. The teacher must also feel that he has the freedom to discuss any book discovered by the student himself whether or not the book has been recommended for reading.

Censorship of books tends to narrow the grasp of the ideals and culture of the student. It is because of censorship that many writers are not represented in our schools, or are represented by their poorer but "safer" works.

Counteracting Censorship

In order to counteract the censorship of books the National Council of Teachers of English has recommended that every school undertake the following program to protect the student.

1. The establishment of a committee of teachers to select books and to screen complaints.
2. A campaign to enlist the public in establishing a climate to support the freedom to read.

Each department within a school must discuss and establish a criteria and procedure for selecting books chosen. No one individual should select books for a department because no one is as well qualified to choose books for the classroom as the person who is prepared in the field. Every department needs to frame a clear statement of what is being taught and the standards for selection. If standards used for making selections differ for various groups of students, the differences should be early outlined.

It is often valuable to have the public well informed on what is being read in the schools. Every school should have a group of teachers organized to

1. Keep the community informed on book choice.
2. Enlist the support of certain groups within the community.
3. Consider any and all complaints against books.

Every public school should protect itself in regard to the materials being used for instruction. Leading members of certain selected groups from within the community can be asked to serve on the book-selection committees. This will be a valuable asset if difficulties should arise.

Defending the Books

Regardless of the care and precautions to avoid conflict, occasional objections to book selections will be made. Some of these be well intended but ill informed; others will be frankly hostile to any free inquiry, while others will fear that harm will come from reading a certain book.

If a complaint is made, the complainant should be asked to submit a formal statement to the book committee. The NCTE form for this purpose follows:

CITIZEN'S REQUEST FOR RECONSIDERATION OF A BOOK*

Author   Hardcover   Paperback

Title

Publisher (if known)

Request initiated by_____

Telephone _____ Address _____

City _____ Zone_____

Complainant represents

_____himself

*From "The Student's Right to Read," by the National Council of Teachers of English, 1962. Reprinted with permission of the publisher.

_____ (name organization)_____

_____(identify other group)_____

1. To what in the book do you object? (Please be specific; cite pages.)

_____

_____

2. What do you feel might be the result of reading this book?

_____

_____

3. For what age group would you recommend this book?

_____

4. Is there anything good about this book?

_____

_____

5. Did you read the entire book? _____ What parts?

_____

6. Are you aware of the judgment of this book by literary critics?

_____

7. What do you believe is the theme of this book?

_____

_____

8. What would you like your school to do about this book?

_____ do not assign it to my child

_____ withdraw it from all students as well as from my child

_____ send it back to the English department office for reevaluation

9. In its place, what book of equal literary quality would you recommend that
   would convey as valuable a picture and perspective of our civilization?

_____

                                  _____

                                  Signature of Complainant

Once this form is returned, the committee of teachers to review complaints should meet and reevaluate the selection. If the selection is judged to be
justifiably available to students the committee should not hesitate to back their
decision. Needless to say, this demands the support of strong and enlightened
administration.

Freedom to read is essential if students are to be truly educated. Every
effort must be made to resist the demands of those who would have us put
blinders on the minds of students.

SUMMARY

In our population, adults and adolescents read much less than they should,
especially in comparison to the amount of reading material readily available. A
significant reason for this lack of reading may be that too few schools provide
programs designed to develop the reading interests of teenagers. Although research in this area is far from complete and merely suggestive, secondary school
teachers should be aware of the research available on the interests of adolescents.

Teachers in the secondary school should attempt to discover the interests
of their individual students, possibly by administering an interest inventory or
another type of indicator, and then effectively utilize the results obtained. Race
and sex differences should be considered in planning the reading interest curriculum.

Interest ineading can be stimulated by providing students with a "reading
area," incorporating recreational reading into the general curriculum and em-
ploying stimulating and creative reading-interest activities.

Reports on reading done may take forms other than the common written
report, if only a teacher will use her imagination—or better, allow the students to
use _their_ imagations and choose their own methods of reporting.

Unnecessary censorship can be thwarted if teachers who are genuinely
concerned with the stimulation of adolescent reading interest will attempt to
establish a group within their ranks designed to select books and screen complaints to protect the students' right to read.

REFERENCES

Gunderson, Doris V. "Research in Reading Habits and Interests at the Junior High School Level," *Improvement of Reading Through Classroom Practice*, XI (1964), pp. 182-184.

Olson, Arthur V., and Carl L. Rosen. "A Comparison of Reading Interests of Two Populations of Ninth Grade Students," *Adolescence* (Winter 1966-67), pp. 321-326.

Shores, Harlan J. "Reading Interests and Informational Needs of High School Students," *Reading Teacher*, XVII (April 1964), pp. 536-544.

Soares, A. T. "Salient Elements of Recreational Reading of Junior High School Students," *Elementary English*, IV (December 1963), pp. 843-845.

Stewart, J. S. "Content and Readership of Teen Magazines," *Journalism Quarterly*, XLI (1964), pp. 580-583.

Thorndike, Robert L. *A Comparative Study of Children's Reading Interests Based on a Fictitious Annotated Titles Questionnaire*. New York: Bureau of Publications, Teachers College, Columbia University, 1941.

Vaughn, J. "Reading Interests of Eighth Grade Students," *Journal of Developmental Reading*, VI (1963), pp. 149-155.

Witty, Paul A. "Some Interests of High School Boys and Girls," *Improvement of Reading Through Classroom Practice*, IX (1964), pp. 186-187.

ADDITIONAL READINGS

Baker, E. H. "Realistic Tastes in Reading," *Instructor*, LXXVII (April 1968), pp. 34-35.

Calder, C. E., Jr. "Self-directed Reading Materials," *Reading Teacher*, XXI (December 1967), pp. 248-252.

Empacher, M. R., and K. W. Trickey. "Easy-to-Read Adult Books for Senior High School Students," *English Journal*, LVII (February 1968), pp. 193-195.

Frey, R. J. "Reading for a Reason," *Instructor*, LXXVII (June 1968), p. 57.

Hinze, R. H. "Who Switches Reading to Go?" *Claremont Reading Conference Yearbook*, XXXI (1967), pp. 135-140.

Jungeblut, Ann, and John H. Coleman. "Reading Content that Interests Seventh, Eighth and Ninth Grade Students," *Journal of Educational Research*, LVIII (May-June 1965), pp. 393-401.

Lowery, L. F., and W. Grafft. "Paperback Book and Reading Attitudes," *Reading Teacher,* XXI (April 1968), pp. 618-623.

Robinson, H. A. "Developing Lifetime Readers," *Journal of Reading*, XI (January 1968), pp. 261-267.

Stone, V. "Interest Stimulators," *Instructor*, LXXVII (March 1968), p. 99.

Thomas, E. L. "Books Are the Greatest," *Journal of Reading*, XII (November 1968), pp. 119-124.

Times Educational Supplement. "Bookworm Gets an Outboard Motor: School of Dynamic Reading, London," (Apr. 19, 1968), p. 311.

REQUIRED READINGS FROM BOOK OF READINGS

IX. Reading Interests

Interest in Recreational Reading of Junior High School Students— Anthony T. Soares and Ray H. Simpron.

A Comparison of Reading Interests of Two Populations of Ninth-Grade Students—Authur V. Olson and Carl L. Rosen.

Developing Reading Tastes in the Secondary School—Arthur W. Heilman.

Fostering Interest in Reading in Grades Nine Through Fourteen—Frances M. Beck.

The Promise of Paperbacks—David A. Sohn.

Obscenity, Censorship, and Youth—Frederic R. Hartz.

chapter 11

Adolescent Literature

Charles Billiard

In Chapter 10, research by Gunderson was cited indicating that American adolescents and adults are not wide and avid readers. Fries (1964) found that among many of our population the time spent reading books averages less than four minutes a day. Indeed, few English teachers have not heard students speak with intense feeling: "Books turn me off." "I hate books." "There ain't no good books in this school." "I'd rather listen to rock music and watch TV."

SOME BASIC FACTORS AFFECTING ADOLESCENTS AS READERS OF LITERATURE

Why are so many American adolescents and adults reluctant readers? For teachers who earnestly want their students to find in literature a lifelong source of pleasure, enlightenment, and understanding, the need to find answers to this question is urgent. Teachers who, with Burton (1970), view the ability to read literature in depth as a powerful liberating force freeing the individual from ignorance and conformity are searching for better approaches to this problem. Undoubtedly many forces working against the cultivation of literacy in our society cannot be directly affected by teachers. On the other hand, teacher decisions regarding the choice of literature, sequence of materials, teaching methods, and whether reading skills are to be taught in the literature program may have a profound influence on reading habits of individuals long after they have left the classroom.

Selecting Literature Appropriate for Study in the High School

One approach recommended for helping solve this problem is to select for teaching in high school those literary works offering the richest aesthetic experiences (Knapton and Evans, 1967). This approach is based on the proposition that the greatest value literature can offer to adolescents is aesthetic in nature. Since a fundamental characteristic distinguishing good and great literature from mediocre writing is its power to stir the imagination and emotions through the artistic organization of words, why not assure high school students the best possible exposure to literature by selecting works characterized by excellence of artistic structure? Thus the first priority in selecting literature for study in secondary schools, according to this view, is to seek those works having the highest potential for providing aesthetic experience. The nature of the human experience—its bearing on the background and immediate lives of the students— presented in the work would of necessity be of secondary importance to its verbal structure, the source of aesthetic experience in literature. The sequence of selections in the high school English curriculum suggested by Knapton and Evans would be based, in effect, on increasing complexity of literary organization.

Focusing attention on the literary quality of works to be studied and the transmission of the literary heritage, the Commission on English of the college Entrance Examination Board (1965) recommends that the selection of literature for use in secondary schools be based on the consensus of members of individual departments of English, such a consensus implying mainly a content of "American and English literature because this literature is what all English teachers are likely to know systematically and at first hand. Along with major and minor classics it will certainly include a selection of more recent books." The Commission further views the teaching of "literature of adolescence" as unjustified expediency: "The competent teacher can bridge the distances between good books and the immaturity of his students."

Murphy (1968), in a comprehensive view of the teaching of literature in high school, sees the function of a work of literature as providing (1) aesthetic experience which is to be found in the perception of order in the work, (2) cognitive development through broadening the reader's awareness of the complexity of human conditions, and (3) moral insight and sensibility—a fuller understanding of human behavior. To realize these functions, Murphy suggests that works selected should be (1) valid in terms of literary quality, (2) relevant to concerns of adolescence in the sense of theme, insight, experience, and basic issues of human conduct—not just in terms of topic or subject matter, (3) appropriate to the student's reading ability, and (4) suitable for the student's ability to maintain aesthetic distance—his ability to handle attitudes and values in the work in conflict with his own.

Recognizing Adolescent Interests and Problems

Viewing the adolescent as an individual to be met on his own grounds, Loban, Ryan, and Squire (1969) maintain that appreciation of literature is most likely to develop when the student has the opportunity to read many books relating directly to his life. Inherent in this view is the major responsibility of the teacher "to guide the selection of books and to help adolescents read literature as human experience." Significant experiences for adolescents will not necessarily be found in books that give literary experiences to adults. This approach to the selection of works does not exclude the classics from the reading program; rather it places first priority on finding books that relate to the reader's experience. Is there not a time in a boy's life when Stevenson's *Treasure Island* may be "right"? Missed, the reader cannot return years later and experience the high adventure he might have known with Jim and Long John Silver. As Carlsen (1967) has shown, disregarding the experience of adolescents and their stage of maturity in the selection of literary works for use in the classroom may permanently damage the adolescent's attitude toward reading and make certain works forever distasteful to him.

Perhaps a part of the answer to our dismal failure to develop reading tastes and literary appreciation and to cultivate in our students a love of reading that will endure throughout their lives is to be found in the selection of reading materials and the use of teaching techniques which encourage the self-involvement of our students. Research supports this view. Squire, in his study *The Responses of Adolescents While Reading Four Short Stories* (1964), found a high correlation between literary judgment and self-involvement:

> Readers who become strongly involved emotionally in a story tend, either while reading or more frequently at the end of reading a selection, to analyze the elements in the story which give rise to their involvement. Involved readers are more likely to make statements which might be coded as literary judgments than are readers who are not so involved. Thus, they tend to be superior readers in that they open themselves to a maximum of facets, accommodate imaginatively to the widest possible number of avenues to literary experience.

Thus if emotional involvement of adolescents tends to produce superior readers, it follows that one highly important criterion for the selection of literary works to be studied in secondary classrooms should be content which involves experiences significant to adolescents. A loving acquaintance with literature is not enough; the secondary English teacher needs a similar acquaintance with adolescents. Chapter 10 explores the interests and issues of genuine concern to adolescents and suggeste methods of discovering reading interests.

Matching Reading Abilities With the Verbal Complexities of Literature

Another cause of our failure to develop lifelong, discriminating readers of literature may be our inability or unwillingness to select reading materials within the range of the student's reading ability. As pointed out in Chapter 7, the choice of material may be poor because it is at a much lower level than the student is capable of reading and appreciating; on the other hand, the vocabulary, sentence structure, and literary use of language may make the work too difficult for the student. However, given the motivational drive that significant content can generate in the reader, he may often push beyond his reading level in search of meaning. Fader (1966) tells of a juvenile delinquent spending several months struggling through *The Scarlet Letter*, curious to learn how Hester won her *A*. Complicating even further the matching of the student's reading ability with appropriate selections is the difficulty of assessing the comprehension problems posed by the literary use of language. Reading formula are generally inadequate in measuring reading difficulty beyond the literal level of vocabulary and sentence structure. Thus the teacher must judge the complexity of linguistic organization of the material in such terms as its use of literary devices of imagery, symbolism, and satire; syntactic patterns involving ellipses and involutions; juxtaposition of scenes and characters.

Teaching Literary Skills of Appreciation

In addition to the selection of appropriate materials in terms of significant adolescent experiences and student's reading abilities, teaching students how to read literature may also be a prime factor in developing literate adolescents and adults. In *High School English Instruction Today*, Squire and Applegate (1968) found a distressing lack of attention given to the skills in reading literature. Only 16 of 112 English departments interviewed felt a major responsibility for teaching and skills of literary appreciation. Further, English teachers individually seemed unimpressed by the need to teach reading. Yet one may wonder how the student learns to grapple with the increasingly complex use of language in more highly organized imaginative writing. Somehow he must become aware of the multiple levels of meaning in literature: the literal, the allegorical, the symbolic. He must learn the clues to major and minor themes given through symbol, character development, action, point of view, and setting. He must learn the significance of mode and tone; the skills for reading various genres; the use of dialects to give insight into character; the use of words to create sound effects, imagery, and figures of speech. He must grow sensitive to the author's use of foils, to satire and irony. To deal effectively with these and other elements making up the complex verbal organization of a work of literature requires special reading skills—skills which the teacher cannot assume the student has acquired by the time he reaches high school or will acquire by some magic of self-instruction.

Our past failures to stimulate many of our students to travel in the realms of gold may indeed by the result of myopic vision. We may have been concentrating too intently on literature and barely seeing in our peripheral vision the adolescents in our classrooms. On the other hand, we may have been looking so intently at our students, meeting them where they are, that we have done little to help them move off the plateau and up the next hill. In sight of mountains, who does not want to climb? But climbing takes skills, and who would tackle the Matterhorn or Mount Everest without first practicing on smaller ranges?

To enlarge our vision then in order that we may help our students enjoy reading and ultimately become lifelong readers of literature—hopefully much of it of high quality—we need to be aware of the variety and changing patterns of adolescents interests, the wealth of literary materials ranging from adolescent literature to adult classics appropriate for high school students, and the reading abilities of our students and the skills they will need to read increasingly complex literary works.

READING INTERESTS, READING ABILITIES, AND VERBAL ORGANIZATION OF LITERATURE AS CONTINUA

Each of these elements—adolescent interests, literary reading skills, and organizational complexity of literary materials—may be thought of as continua. Adolescents tend to grow along the continuums of interests and reading skills at varying and uneven rates. And increasing literary quality may be conceived of as a continuum of increasing verbal complexity.

The Changing Spectrum of Adolescent Interests

As pointed out in Chapter 10, research has identified differences in reading interests among junior high school students on the basis of mental ability, sex, and ethnic identity. Carlsen (1967) has identified broad patterns of interests typical of early adolescence (ages 11-14), middle adolescence (ages 15-16), and late adolescence (ages 16-18). According to Carlsen's studies, during the early adolescent period youth are enthusiastic readers of stories about adventure, mystery, animals, sports, home and family, and supernatural happenings. The middle adolescent period is characterized by strong interests of boys in nonfiction accounts of adventure and war stories and of girls in historical and romantic novels. Both boys and girls during this period enjoy stories depicting adolescents two or three years older confronting problems and issues of everyday living. The late adolescent segment of the continuum is a transition period during which youths seek books concerned with personal values, social issues, and the outer limits of human experince. Teachers need to keep in mind that these are generalizations which will have many exceptions in individual readers. Further, any interests displayed by an adolescent should be considered as a kind of focal point that can be widened to include other interests. Undoubtedly, too much catering to present reading interests can be as damaging as too little concern for these interests. But above all, students should not be expected to jump from one end of the continuum to the other—from fairy tales and fantasy to adult classics.

Variations in the Literal and Imaginative Use of Language in Literature

Besides considering changing interest patterns in guiding the reading of adolescents, the teacher should be keenly aware of the ways in which literature varies in linguistic complexity, and consequently in reading difficulty. As pointed out in Chapter 7, each content field demands special reading skills. Furthermore, in reading literature the student must also take a different attitude toward words. He has to understand that the writer of literature is making words perform in unusual and extraordinary ways. He must push beyond literal meanings and develop skills for comprehending the imaginative use of language. In his famous essay, "The Literature of Knowledge and the Literature of Power," Thomas De Quincey (1848) long ago made an important distinction between literal and imaginative writing:

> There is, first, the literature of knowledge, and, secondly, the literature of power. The function of the first is to *teach*; the function of the second is to *move*: the first is a rudder; the second an oar or a sail. The first speaks to the mere discursive understanding; the second speaks ultimately, it may happen, to the higher understanding, or reason, but always through affections of pleasure and sympathy.

Thus De Quincey's distinction between the literal and imaginative would generally place newspapers, mathematics and physics textbooks, cookbooks and other "how to" books in the category of literature of knowledge, but the novel, short story, drama, and poetry would be in the realm of literature of power. Not that there is always a clear-cut dichotomy in the use of words in these two types of writing. For example, Humphrey's *Ways of the Weather* (1942) is a blend of imaginative and logical writing. Within the same paragraph, Humphrey presents a mathematical formula for determining the pitch of tree branches vibrating in the wind and speaks figuratively of the whistling of the white pine trees and the grumbling of the oaks.

Murphy (1968) presents a useful way to visualize the variations of verbal organization in literature by suggesting five patterns or clusters along an imaginary continuum, each cluster representing a higher degree of verbal organization along the continuum. The first two clusters identified by Murphy correspond approximately to De Quincey's literature of knowledge: cluster 1 is the typical everyday conversation or note to the milkman, having syntactic regularity, e.g., basic word order and morphemic form; cluster 2 includes factual reporting typically found in history textbooks and news stories—writing characterized by syntactical, chronological, and logical organization; cluster 3 encompasses biographies, essays and critical articles having a closely knit organization and using words frequently as images and symbols; cluster 4 clearly represents De Quincey's literature of power, including the short story, novel, drama, and poetry and involving a high level of organization in the use of words, e.g., image, symbol, balance, repetition, rhythm, and juxtaposition of characters, scene, and parallel plot lines; cluster 5, as defined by Murphy, would be made up largely of lyric and dramatic poetry, forms demanding ever greater reading skills because each word may be functioning in several ways at the same time—, to create rhythm, sound effects, imagery, connotation.

Another approach to literary organization frequently used in the planning of sequential teaching of literature is based on the structural differences of genres. One sequence differing from those usually found in high school literature anthologies is that recommended by Simmons (1966). Instead of starting with the short story, Simmons suggests a sequence beginning with the conventionally structured novel (chronological plot line with little or no flashbacks and the predominance of physical action), then moving into a study of the short story (condensation of ideas and events often requiring inference skills) and finally to the reading of poetry. On the other hand, Dunning (1968) views the short story as a form "congenial to young readers" and as posing fewer problems than other genres.

Actually, a great range of literary complexity can be found in both the short story and the novel. For example, the plot line of Richard Connell's short story "The Most Dangerous Game" is chronological, the conflict is physical, and the character motivation clear and uncomplicated—to kill and avoid being killed. On the other hand, even the frequently anthologized version of Faulkner's "The Bear" is complex: the boy matures in his repeated experiences with the bear; possible multiple meanings intrigue the adolescent as well as the adult reader; allusions and symbolic use of language require depth reading. Many examples of a similar variation in literary organization can be found in the novel. For example, Henry Felsen's novel *Street Rod* is chronologically straightforward and Rick's motivation uncomplicated; Edith Wharton's *Ethan Frome*, by contrast, requires much greater reading maturity: the adolescent reader must be sensitive to irony, aware of changing character motivation, and alert to the use of flashback.

Variations in Reading Abilities of Adolescents

The third continuum of profound importance to the secondary English teacher is the great range in reading abilities found among adolescents. Even in so-called homogeneous classes, the range in reading grade level is spectacular and tends to broaden when specific attention is given to the development of reading skills. With standardized test results for high school classes showing variations in literal reading abilities spanning the primary grade level to college level, one can expect the variations in abilities to read imaginative literature to be at least as great.

The task, then, of the high school English teacher in teaching literature is highly complex and difficult. It involves matching adolescent feelings and interests with an appropriate content of human experience in literature; it further requires the approximate matching of the student's literary skills of appreciation with the complexity of linguistic organization in literary works. When the teacher succeeds in this delicate art of human engineering, the student may indeed find joy in reading, grow in skills of literacy appreciation, and gain a deeper understanding of himself and his society.

SEQUENTIAL MODELS OF LITERATURE FOR EARLY, MIDDLE, AND LATE ADOLESCENCE

Many different sequential reading models or designs could be proposed, considering that there are a great number of excellent books for adolescents and that adolescent reading abilities and interests vary greatly. Here the purpose will be to suggest typical sequential models representative of discrete points on the continua of adolescent interests, reading abilities, and verbal conplexities for the short story, novel, and poetry and to suggest some appropriate teaching approaches. Underlying these models are widely accepted principles of learning: the need to individualize instruction, to involve and motivate the student, to establish an organizational pattern of learning discernible to the student. In effect, the need to individualize instruction has been emphasized repeatedly in this textbook in recognizing the range of reading abilities and interests found in high school English classes. And given the right book, the student is likely to become involved in reading as a meaningful and enjoyable experience; a successful encounter with a book may provide the energizing force, the motivation for the student to continue reading on his own. Also, careful planning by the teacher to enable the student to discern relationships among various literary selections—the recognition of key qualities and characteristics—may help the student to apply these generalizations in his independent reading. For example, the teacher may organize instruction in such a way as to aid the student in recognizing salient qualities of a literary genre, such as the short story, and thus increase the sensitivity of the student to these characteristics in other short stories; or the teacher may encourage the student to see the likenesses and differences in the structure of the short story and the novel. Awareness of relationships and patterns is recognized as a prime factor in learning (Loban, Ryan, and Squire, 1969).

THE SHORT STORY

Many teachers have found a unit on the short story a psychologically effective place to begin a sequence in literature for the school year, expecially if the short stories are carefully selected in terms of the reading abilities and interests of the students. As a beginning in the literature sequence, the short length of this genre is an attractive feature to many students, offering a quick plunge before the long swim required of a full-length novel. Furthermore, along with the use of such devices as the Olson Reading Interest Inventory (Chapter 10), the teacher has the opportunity to discover reading interests, as well as make some appraisal of reading abilities, in the short trial runs offered by the short story, whereas launching a unit on the novel involves a much greater commitment of class time. Then, if the novel proves to be inappropriate for the particular class, the teacher faces the unattractive alternatives of doggedly plowing ahead or unceremoniously dropping the unit in midstream.

As an illustration of short stories at significant points along the imaginary continua of adolescent interests and literary organization, consider the following selections: Will James' "Midnight," John MacDonald's "Hit and Run," and Ernest Hemingway's "In Another Country." In the order listed, these short stories represent increasing maturity of ideas and emotions and complexity of verbal organization.

Early Adolescence

Will James' "Midnight" (1967) appeals to the early adolescent's passion for animal stories. The animal-human relationship dominates the story. This relationship, characterized by loyalty and confidence between the cowboy and his horses, is superior to the human relationships in the story: " . . . I found as I covered the country, met different folks, and seen many towns, that the pin-eared pony under me (whichever one it was) was a powerful friend, powerful in confidence and strength. There was no suspicious question asked by him. . . . " Since the literal reading level of "Midnight" is approximately seventh-grade level (based on vocabulary and sentence structure), and the content is appropriate for the early adolescent period, many students in the late elementary and junior high classes can read this story with pleasure. But the teacher wanting to help lead students beyond the literal level will need to determine what reading skill or skills of literary appreciation can best be developed within the context of this story. To avoid killing the interest of students by too much analysis, the teacher should focus attention on one or two appreciation skills to be developed in a story.

Useful criteria for selecting skills to be emphasized in teaching a particular story are (1) the unique literary organization of the work, e.g., its structure may require the use of certain reading skills for adequate interpretation or lend itself especially well to the development of specific reading skills, and (2) the sequence of skills being developed, e.g., a skill taught earlier may need strengthening in a new literary context.

"Midnight" is a "Western" story told from the first-person point of view in the language of a cowboy. Essentially, the narrative is chronological, broken only by minor and easily followed flashbacks. Ironically, the two characters, the horse Midnight and the cowpuncher, are drawn together yet kept apart by the consistency of their natures. Although incidental teaching of the recognition of irony and theme are promising possibilities, the teaching of reading skills involved in making inferences about character could be profitably pursued in this story. Since the cowpuncher talks about himself, the student can be asked to compare the consistency of these direct statements with indirect evidence: the cowpuncher's actions and reactions, reactions of others toward him, statements of others about him. Thus the teacher should prepare questions that will require students to exercise the skill of drawing inferences from clues about character:

Inferring a person's feelings from his speech:

From the cowpuncher's statement " . . . even though some [horses] showed me fight and I treated 'em a little rough, there'd come a time when we'd have an understanding and we'd agree that we was both pretty good fellers after all," what is implied about his feeling toward mustangs?

Inferring something about a person's character from the reactions of other people:

From the reaction of the boys to the cowpuncher's decision to give up running mustangs, what is implied regarding his dependability and skill in rounding up mustangs: "The boys wasn't at all pleased when I told 'em I'd decided to leave."?

Inferring a person's motives and character from his statements and his actions:

The cowpuncher says he "always wanted to drift over that blue ridge ahead." What does this statement suggest about a basic drive in the man's character? How is this suggestion of motive confirmed later, especially in the cowboy's treatment of Midnight?

Inferring a person's character from his actions and reactions:

Does the cowpuncher's confession "For a second I feel like kicking myself for letting such a horse go" make him more or less convincing as a friend of horses?

Requiring the student to search the text for clues to support or enlarge his interpretation of a character is, in effect, demanding active thinking and developing his reading ability to draw inferences.

Middle Adolescence

The content of MacDonald's story "Hit and Run" (1968) is close to issues and emotions of youth in the middle adolescent years. This short story gives the reader a way of seeing and testing himself in misunderstandings with his parents. Gary, a couple of years older than the ninth- or tenth-grader who is about to get his driver's license, believes one of his parents has been involved in a hit-and-run accident which killed the mother of two small children. Likewise, the boy's father, for a time, believes his son was the killer. The content, then, makes the story appropriate for the middle adolescent years.

The literary organization of the story moves it along the continuum toward greater complexity than that found in "Midnight." Even though the characters are superficially sketched, there is clear-cut conflict between the father and his son Gary, as well as between the special investigator and both father and son. Further, the structure of the plot is complicated by a major flashback and numerous instances of foreshadowing. On the other hand, the language usage is primarily literal (approximately on the tenth-grade level), although the word choice is often vivid and concrete. Considering the literary structure of "Hit and Run," the teacher might well concentrate instruction on finding foreshadowing clues and tracing steps in the development of the story, especially noting the clues which signal flashback and the return to normal chronology.

Late Adolescence

For contemporary youth, late adolescence is perhaps even more of a period of questioning, probing, and searching for personal values and direction in life than it was for earlier generations. Ernest Hemingway's "In Another Country" (1927) is substantial fare for the late adolescent's reading diet, requiring a bit of "chewing and digesting." In today's war-torn world, an adolescent's search for "things he cannot lose" will find powerful expression in this short story set in Italy during World War I.

The linguistic structure of "In Another Country" places it well along the imaginary continuum into the spectrum of literary excellence. Characteristic of Hemingway's style, the phrasing is terse and consise. In this story, words count in more than one way, or on more than one level of meaning, often setting tone or carrying symbolic meaning. Thus the story lends itself to teaching reading skills useful in sensing the prevailing tone of a work and in discovering the symbolic meaning of words:

Sensing the prevailing tone:

> In the first two sentences of the story, what tone is suggested by the words *fall*, *cold*, and *dark*? In the last two sentences of the same paragraph, what phrases reinforce this tone? ("stiff and heavy and empty," "cold fall," "the wind came down from the mountains")

Relating the prevailing tone of the setting to the psychological state of the characters:

> Based on his actions and speech, find clues to the Major's feeling about his possible recovery. For instance, does the Major's winking give a clue to the tone of voice which he asks the doctor about his recovery and the implied answer to the Major's question, though unspoken at the moment?

>> He winked at me when the doctor examined his hand, which was between two leather straps that bounced up and down and flapped the stiff fingers, and said: "And will I play football, captain-doctor?"

> Now, expand the context for additional evidence. The doctor in an earlier paragraph assures the narrator that, despite a stiff leg, he will play football like a champion again. Keeping this immediate context in mind and the information that the Major had been the greatest fencer in Italy, what does the question "And will I play football, captain-doctor?" tell us about the

Major's confidence in regaining the use of his hand? Students can be encouraged to search for evidence showing how the state of mind of the Major and the tone of the setting complement and reinforce each other:

> Then he (the Major) looked down at the machine and jerked his little hand out from between the straps and slapped it hard against his thigh.

Discovering the symbolic meaning of words:

> The teacher might ask the students to consider whether there is any place on earth, any Shangri-La, where they could find peace. Could "another country" mean more than Italy in this story—a place where a man is not destroyed by war? In this story, what are the signs (symbols) of man's physical destruction by war?
>
> . . . the leg dropped straight from the knee to the ankle without a calf. . .
>
> Another boy. . . wore a black silk handkerchief across his face because he had no nose. . .

Practice under teacher's guidance in raising and answering these kinds of questions in class discussion should eventually enable students to ask the right kinds of questions as they read imaginative literature on their own.

Obviously these three short stories illustrate only three points along the continua of adolescent interests and literary organization. From the seventh grade through the senior high school many short stories would have to be read and discussed intensively in class and many others read independently to provide for the gradual development of literary skills and tastes of adolescents.

A Teaching Approach Combining the Three Continua

As a means of taking into account the third continuum, the great range of reading abilities found among adolescents, and at the same time fostering growth of reading interests and skills of literary appreciation, the "reading cyclotron" (Lazarus, 1964) provides a practical answer. This approach, expecially effective in introducing a unit on the novel, involves three levels of reading activity: (1) each individual reading books of his own choice, (2) small groups reading copies of the same book, (3) the entire class reading and discussing the same work. Lazarus visualizes this program in terms of three concentric circles. The outer circle represents the individualized reading program during which each student develops momentum by reading books of his own choosing on or near his reading level and in areas of personal interest. By observing the selections made by each student, the teacher is then able to form small groups of readers of similar interests: cliques of mystery addicts, sports fans, hot-rod enthusiasts, and mountain climbers. The reading momentum now generated is represented by the middle circle. These small groups read and discuss the same book and as a panel, often report their reactions to the entire class. The final phase of this program, represented by the inner circle, is a harnessing of the reading momentum generated in the personal and small-group reading phases. It involves the entire class in the reading and discussion of a single work carefully selected by the teacher. Especially at this level the teacher should be helping the students develop literary skills of appreciation and stimulating the refinement of literary tastes.

In practice, the teacher can launch this program by bringing to class an armful of paperback novels. From the stack of books spread out on the desk, the teacher selects certain ones, reading brief, exciting passages; discussing interesting characters or strange, distant settings in others; displaying attractive covers and raising questions about the probable content of the novels. Each student is invited to take a book for sampling. The teacher might well set a good example by also choosing one. One student might start with *Black Like Me*, then select *Go Tell It On the Mountain*, and eventually read *The Autobiography of Malcolm X*; another might choose *Seven Days in May*, then *Fail-Safe*, and eventually *On the Beach*. For small groups interested in war stories, copies of *The Bridges at Toko-Ri* might be appropriate for reading and discussion. Finally, the teacher and class might select such a book as *Hiroshima* to read and discuss in detail. Of course, such a program depends on a ready source of paperbacks.

THE NOVEL

For the television-trained adolescent, the novel in colorful paperback form is promising bait for "hooking" reluctant readers on literature. Accustomed to the direct impressions of life given by television, youngsters can find in the novel a palatable counterpart to television, for the scope and depth of the novel usually does succeed in conveying a strong impression of human experience. It is this quality of the novel that the high school English teacher often needs to capitalize upon before forcing her fledgings into the icy depths of the novel as a work of art. An occasional good bull session relating the novel to the lives of the students may save a potential nonreading adult.

To emphasize further the importance of viewing the adolescent's growth in literary appreciation as a gradual process, the following sequential models illustrate novels at various points along the imaginary continua of literary organization and adolescent interests. As with the short story, the reader will undoubtedly think of many other possible sequences and additional titles to fill in the sequences suggested. On any grade level, the study of the novel might well follow a unit on the short story. Generally, in comparison with the short story, the novel presents characters in more involved social relations, conflicts are more complex, character development is more complete, and the possibilities of character change greater; in addition, greater range in levels of meaning is often present.

The first of these models to be considered is composed of Jack Schafer's

Shane, Walter Van Tilbury Clark's *The Ox-Bow Incident*, and Nevil Shute's *On the Beach*. In the order given, these novels represent increasing maturity of content and literary organization.

Early Adolescence

On its most elemental level, *Shane* (1949) makes a strong appeal to interests typical of early adolescence. Shane lives a dangerous, adventurous life, riding out of a mysterious past and disappearing into an unknown future. Further, the novel is set in the past, the summer of 1889, and in a remote place in the Wyoming Territory. To satisfy the fascination of the early adolescent in the animal-human relationship, there is the devotion between Shane and his powerful steed.

The literary organization of *Shane* is relatively simple and its literal reading level approximately eighth-grade. The plot, though obviously characterized by considerable physical conflict of hand-to-hand combat and gun play, offers the teacher an opportunity to help students probe for psychological conflict. For instance, students saturated with viewing TV westerns might ponder the reason for Shane's not carrying a gun or infer something of Shane's character from his remark: "A gun is just a tool . . . as good—and as bad—as the man who carries it." There are no subplots, and the point of view is first person:

> I was a kid then, barely topping the buckboard of my father's old chuck-wagon . . . I cound see him plainly, though he was still several miles away.

But the point of view is actually more complex, for Bob is retelling the events in retrospect, giving the experiences of youth the perspective of greater maturity. Students might be asked to compare this use of the first-person point of view with its use in "Midnight" and to comment upon the advantages of being able to judge one's decisions and actions today from some vantage point in his future. For the more capable or older students, the thematic question of whether it is possible to break out of patterns of past behavior; whether an individual can throw off the weight of the accumulated past that tends to make each man what he is. And Shane wrestles with the moral issue of whether the use of physical force or gunplay is justified, under any circumstances, to protect weak persons from harm and defend property rights. Is the Christian ethic of turning the other cheek viable in Shane's world? These are questions of theme to be answered by a careful reading of the text.

Middle Adolescence

The Ox-Bow Incident (1943), another Western devoid of the sensationalism typical of many novels set in the West, concerns the lynching of three innocent men by a mob. Although physical violence is an obvious appeal of the book to teen-agers, the more subtle issues—the nature of man and his responsibilities in organized society, the degree of man's civilization, the meaning of justice and who should administer it—make this a book suitable for middle and late adolescence. The literary organization of *The Ox-Bow Incident* is more complex than that of *Shane* and its literal reading level approximately tenth-grade. The plot line, as in *Shane*, is chronological and the point of view first person, but the forward progression of the action is halted frequently by the vacillation of characters and the undisciplined nature of the mob. The swift forward movement of plot in *Shane*, with its clear cause-and-effect relationships, is missing in *The Ox-Bow Incident*. But the slowing of action allows for more interaction of characters, for more dialogue and discussion that lays bare the inner conflict of men taking justice into their own hands. And then after the climax—the lynching—there is time for characters to react and reflect upon their moral responsibilities. Thus the novel offers many possibilities for studying the interrelationships between character and action and for developing skills of inferring character from action and dialogue. Furthermore, the juxtaposing of scenes in the novel gives the teacher an opportunity to develop the students' sensitivity to the effects of this technique in heightening the prevailing mood or atmosphere. The peace and grandeur of the opening scene as Art and Gil ride off the ranges contrasts with the quarreling and ugliness they find in the town. Students may be asked to speculate on how this contrast in scenes foreshadows coming events and parallels the ironic discrepancy between the cowboys' anticipated tragic events awaiting them. Also, students may be asked to compare the effects of reinforcing a single tone in scene events, and characters in such a short story as Hemingway's "In Another Country" with the effects produced by the use of contrasting elements in this novel.

Late Adolescence

On the Beach (1957) fits the pattern of interests and problems of concern during the period of late adolescence. The creation of the atom bomb has given man a glimpse of apocalypse and has made doomsday more than a metaphor. High school juniors and seniors are ready to speculate on the implications of technological achievements that threaten the obliteration of humanity. The literary structure of this novel draws on all of the skills needed to comprehend the previous works and makes new demands on the literary reading skills of the students. The plot line of *On the Beach* is frequently complicated by subplots as the thoughts and feelings of the four major characters are followed during the last six months of their lives. The demands on the student to maintain aesthetic distance are considerable in such situations as the following: Dwight goes on talking about his family as though they are well and happy when he knows with certainty they are dead; the young mother continues talking about her little daughter's future and plants flowers which would bloom the following year; a young married couple must face the decision of giving their baby an injection that will take her life. Students should search for clues to character motivation and character growth in an attempt to understand why most of the people choose to live out their lives in normal ways, as though the inevitibility of doomsday were not a reality. This is a terrifying book that involves the adolescent in seeking answers to problems facing mankind; but reading and discussing it need not turn into bull sessions on current events. As Squire's *The Response of Adolescents While Reading Four Short Stories* has shown, students involved emotionally in a story tend to evaluate the literary elements which account for their involvement.

READING MODELS BUILT AROUND THEMES AND ISSUES

Another dimension can be introduced in the development of sequential models: a central issue or problem can be used as an organizing principle. The following model adds this dimension by focusing on the problems of the Negro in American society. This sequence includes Louisa Shotwell's *Roosevelt Grady*, Richard Wright's *Black Boy*, and *The Autobiography of Malcolm X*.

Roosevelt Grady (1963) which has a literal reading level of approximately grade 5, is the story of a ten-year old Negro boy who travels with his family from one migrant workers' camp to another. Roosevelt and an orphan boy Manowar devise a plan to assure the Grady family a permanent camp for the winter so that Roosevelt can attend school and his younger brother can have surgery performed on his deformed leg. This is a realistic portrait of the family life of migrant workers and of girls during early adolescence. The literary organization of the novel is uncomplicated; the plot line is chronological with a very limited number of characters to follow. The characters' motives are explicit and the literary function of the language largely confined to the creation of concrete images.

The autobiography *Black Boy* (1945) written on a literal reading level of approximately grade 7 concerns the bleak and isolated world of Richard Wright's early childhood in the South; the acute physical and spiritual hunger of his adolescent years, assuaged partly by his discovery of books; and his full entry into the world of knowledge and ideas through books and a growing awareness of his own integrity and dignity as a human being. This book appeals to both boys and girls of various ethnic origins in middle and late adolescence. For many adolescents it presents the kind of problems they are facing, especially the intense search for personal direction in their lives. For others, it is a book of deep social significance, picturing economic deprivation and racial inequalities. The literary organization of this book places it well along the continuum as imaginative, powerful literature. Juxtaposing of scenes is one of Wright's techniques: the beauty of a Southern landscape is contrasted to the violence of its racial atmosphere. A conscious awareness of the use of this technique will increase the reader's awareness of Wright's purpose and give a fuller comprehension of the autobiography. Wright exploits freely the literary use of language. His use of dialogue creates a dramatic realism. His use of images of whiteness suggests the world of white power; his images of fire represent the violence and destruction which erupt from oppression. Irony of situation is also present. Thus there are possibilities for the development of skills of literary appreciation in the intensive class study of this book.

Appropriate for mature high school readers, *The Autobiography of Malcolm X* is an amazing story of growth and realization of human potentialities, of growth from ignorance and hatred to militancy tempered with compassion. Although the literal reading level of this book is approximately ninth-grade, the range of human experiences presented and the stark realism of scenes described in language appropriate for the subject and speaker make it suitable for the late high school and adult years. The human and social insights to be gained in reading this autobiography commend it to all ethnic groups and social classes. In many high school classes a problem for both students and teachers may be the acceptance of the language as appropriate and useful for the speaker, the occasion, and the subject.

For middle and late adolescence, some paperbacks expecially suitable for small group and individual reading, concerning the Negro seeking intellectual and social liberation, are James Baldwin's *The Fire Next Time,* John Griffin's *Black Like Me*, Robert Lipsyte's *The Contender*, Bob Teague's *Letters to a Black Boy*, Dick Gregory's *The Shadow That Scares Me*, and Ann Fairbairn's *Five Smooth Stones*.

POETRY

Research has been previously cited showing that American adolescents and adults are not avid readers of literature. If one considers the special case of poetry, the evidence is even more discouraging. Poetry in America, having virtually no public support, simply does not sell. *Poetry* magazine, published for nearly sixty years, continues to operate with a yearly dificit. Aside from the powerful currents in American culture running against poetry and beyond the direct influence of the English teacher, the challenge in the classroom is largely one of motivating interest in poems and teaching the reading skills of a difficult genre. Poems of quality are usually highly organized literary structures, consiciously contrived, with language often functioning in several ways. To become sensitive to the organizational structure of a poem and the way words are working in it is a demanding task requiring the cultivating of special reading skills. But the development of these skills will be encouraged when there are immediate rewards to the reader in the context of the material being read—that is, in the discovery of meanings in the poem that are relevant to the student's life.

Some Reasons Why Students Dislike Poetry

By the time adolescents reach high school, (and often earlier), many of them are indifferent to or even hate poetry, despite the fact that children love to play with the sounds of words and respond to the beat of nursery rhymes and poetry in the early elementary years. Little empirical evidence is available to account for this change in attitude, but the personal testimony of concerned teachers and turned-off students gives insights into possible causes. Among frequently mentioned causes are the following: (1) many English teachers do not know how to teach the reading of poetry; (2) many English teachers do not read and enjoy poetry; (3) the study of the mechanics of poetry (metrical patterns, metaphor, simile, personification) is often made without considering how these devices contribute to the total meaning of a poem; (4) often poems selected for study are inappropriate in terms of length, content, and reading difficulty for particular classes; (5) an inordinate emphasis is often placed on matters not central to the experience of the poem, i.g., biographical data, the cultural and intellectual milieu in which the poem was written, historical development of the particular subgenre; (6) overemphasis on analysis or imposition on the class of the teacher's explication of the poem destroys the students' natural curiosity and satisfaction in discovering meaning through their own efforts; (7) an extensive unit on poetry, because of its intense nature, is usually too demanding and turns pleasure into drudgery; (8) teachers sometimes take a sentimental, gushy approach toward poetry.

Some Strategies for Motivating the Study of Poems

Certainly personal testimony points up the importance of carefully planned teaching strategies and the selection of poems suitable to the reading abilities of students and capable of engendering enthusiasm. One approach to poems which this writer has found successful is through popular songs and folk music. Such an approach can be an intrinsic part of the study of poetry. For instance, the teacher can bring to class and play Simon and Garfunkle's record "Sounds of Silence." Why did this record sell over a million copies? The students have ready answers. They like the sound, the rhythm, the beat of the music; they admire the performers. Someone may even say he likes the words! The alert teacher should have a copy of the words on a transparency to be projected at this moment in the discussion and ask questions such as the following: The music has a beat. Do the words of the song have a beat when read aloud? Do the beat of the words and the beat of the music work together? What pictures in the lyrics (poem) are especially vivid ("my words like silent raindrops fell," "people bowed and prayed to the neon god they made")? How are these images related to the title of the song? What is unusual or seemingly contradictory about this title? How can silence have sounds? Can you find other apparent contradictions in the song ("people talking without speaking," "people hearing without listening")? What feelings do the words give you? Do the words reinforce the mood of the music? The teacher must be careful not to push the questioning too far; and after the discussion is completed, he should play the song again, thus giving the students the experience of hearing the words and music put back together in the musicians' performance of the song.

By careful selection of popular songs, the teacher can illustrate specific literary devices in the lyrics; e.g., Paul Simon's "Sparrow" lends itself especially well to demonstrating the use of symbolism: the answers to the sparrow's question of who will care for it are symbolic of characteristics of human nature. The oak tree's unwillingness to shelter the sparrow symbolizes the indifference of the powerful to help the weak and unfortunate; the haughty refusal of the swan to speak a kind word in behalf of the sparrow suggests the vanity of human nature. Simon's "Bleeker Street" is useful in demonstrating the connotative power of concrete imagery to create tone, e.g., gloom and sadness: "Fog rolling in of the East River bank/ like a shroud it covers Bleeker Street"; "Voices leaking from a sad cafe ..." Leonard Bernstein demonstrates in his recording *What Is Jazz*? (Columbia CL 919) the close relationship between metrical patterns of poetry and rhythmic patterns of jazz. For instance, he shows that the blues is based on a classical poetic form—the rhymed couplet in iambic pentameter.

It is but a short step from the popular song to the folk ballad. In the folk song, sound, story, and imagery combine in delightful ways. Hearing these combinations in songs can often help students sense these elements in the printed words of the ballad. Such ballads as "John Henry," "Tom Dooley," "Jesse James," and "Frankie" are readily available on disk or tape recordings and are useful in making students aware of the basic elements of beat and imagery.

A multimedia presentation of poems is often effective in "hooking" reluctant readers on poetry. Although commercial multimedia presentations are available, there are real advantages in the teacher's preparing his own multimedia interpretation of poems. For one thing, the teacher investing valuable time in the preparation of multimedia interpretations of poems will weigh carefully the suitability of selections for particular classes and will not waste time on poems for which he has little particular enthusiasm. One method of creating such material is to take 35-mm color slides representing images in the poem and to tape-record appropriate background music along with a sensitive reading of the poem. In the presentation of the poem, the tape recording of words and music is synchronized with the projection of the slides. Jane Warren, imaginative junior high school teacher of DeKalb County, Georgia, armed with a 35-mm camera and tape recorder, produced exciting interpretations of poems for use in her classes. For example, she accompanies a sympathetic reading of James Tippett's "Sunning" (1966), a delightful poem about an old dog happily and lazily sleeping in the summer sun, with 35-mm pictures of the family dog in appropriately sleepy-eyed poses and the music of Gershwin's "Summer Time." The experience of May Swenson's "Southbound on the Freeway" is captured by accompanying the reading of the poem with background noises of traffic and the projection of 35-mm slides of traffic on an Atlanta expressway. Not having the vantage point of a tourist from Ceres or Pallas hovering over the expressway in a flying saucer, this teacher took pictures of the "metal and glass" creatures from an overpass. The combination of music, words, and color slides produces an exciting experience with poems for students who often say they hate poetry.

Another advantage of the teacher's learning how to create interpretations of poems is that he will then be able to help students produce their word-music-picture interpretations of poems. Such projects require students to select poems of genuine interest to them and to comprehend the poems before "producing" them in multimedia dimensions.

A simplified variation of this poem-visualization method is for the teacher to read a short poem of potentially high interest to the class, pass out copies of the poem for discussion, and then reread the poem. Next, the teacher invites the students to search through magazines and newspapers for pictures and cartoons which will illustrate a central image, event, a meaning, or the tone of the poem. Among the illustrations brought to class, the students are then asked to select the picture which best represents the poem. This discussion should involve the students in a close rereading of the poem in order to support their choice of pictures for posting with the poem on the bulletin board. Eventually, enough interest may be aroused so that students will bring to class favorite poems with accompanying pictures for posting in various places around the classroom.

Another approach often successful in increasing the interest of students in the poetic combinations of words, and eventually in reading poems enthusiastically, is the voluntary assignment to write a short poem or even a single line completing a poem. Present the assignment as a kind of game—a word puzzle to be solved for the fun of it, in much the same spirit Frost is believed to have written "Stopping by a Woods on a Snowy Evening." John Ciardi (1959) says that Frost, largely for the fun of it, "took on a hard rhyme-trick and made it work." (Frost set himself the task of creating a quadruple rhyme in the poem and finally resolved the puzzle by the highly effective repetition of the next to last line of the poem: "And miles to go before I sleep/ And miles to go before I sleep.") First, students might be given four lines of a limerick and invited to complete the fifth line. Bennet Cerf's *Out on a Limerick* (1960) is an excellent source of examples of this nonsense verse. A more challenging word puzzle for the students would be to write a complete limerick and then to try creating the punch line for a cinquain. Next, the students might be asked to induce the complete structure of the cinquain from a sample such as the following by Carolyn Smith:

> Whose woods
> These are I think
> I know. They are Purdue's.

> Yet ere we graduate, chop-chop.
> Blacktop.

From samples of the cinquain, the students discover that it is a highly structured verse form of five lines made up of iambic feet, the first line having one iamb, the second two, the third three, the fourth four, and the fifth one. They also discover that the first four lines present a situation and the last line a pungent comment, a punch line. Even though there is no rhyme, the rigid structure of the metrical pattern makes the cinquain a demanding form and a try at writing it may help give students an understanding of the way words are used in poetry. Another seemingly simple poetic form useful in developing students' awareness of the imaginative use of language in poetry is the hiaku. It provides a simple framework for students to follow in writing their poems and gives them insight into the use of concrete imagery in suggesting mood.

Selecting poems appropriate for the reading abilities of students and capable of appealing to adolescents' interests is of major importance. Not that the quality of a poem should be judged by its content, but rather that as a matter of teaching strategy for overcoming prejudices against poetry, the teacher, often with the help of the students, should choose poems that are close to the life experiences of the students.

As an example of poems at significant points along the imaginary continua of changing adolescent interests and increasing linguistic complexity, the following are suggested among a great number of possibilities: Eve Merriam's "Oz," Robert Frost's "Out,Out—," and Karl Shapiro's "Auto Wreck." Each of these poems is relatively short, deals with experiences and interests close to the lives of adolescents of various age groups, and lends itself well to concentrating on one or two reading skills needed to comprehend and enjoy poetry.

Early Adolescence

Eve Merriam's "Oz" (1966) appeals especially to the interests of early adolescents, but for that matter delights youngsters of all ages—seven to seventy. For one thing, there is the puzzle: What is this ounce that belongs to the cat family? For another, there is the play on the word *ounce,* punning on the double meaning of the word: "the ounce/ as one of the smallest amounts" and "This jungle ounce/ will jounce/ you out of your complacency." Also, there is the multiple rhyming of *ounce, jounce, trounce, flounce, bounce, pounce,* so pleasing to the ear. To experience the word music and the humor of the poem, the teacher should read the poem, then encourage the students to discover the multiple rhyming perhaps and consider the appropirateness of the concrete verbs *flounce, bounce, pounce.* Then the poem should be put back together again by another reading of it by the teacher or a student who can read it effectively. Development of sensitivity to sound effects and awareness of the play on word meanings is quite enough to emphasize in this poem.

Middle Adolescence

Robert Frost's "Out, Out–," (1963) appeals to middle adolescents as they begin to assume responsibilities, to have jobs, and start to philosophize on self and the importance of life. Students of this age see themselves often as quite alone in the world with no one to understand or sympathize with their problems. The poem incorporates all these aspects of this level of growth.

"Out, Out–" is an excellent poem for teaching foreshadowing. The title itself should be associated with *Macbeth,* and the teacher should quote the lines from the play if the class is unfamiliar with them or have them read by some student if the class has studied the play. Ask the question, why is "Out, Out–" used as the title? What do you think this poem might be about?

Having caught the interest of the class, the teacher should read the poem to the class. Since it is a narrative poem by structure, the whole story needs to be revealed in one reading. Most students identify in a personal and emotional manner with the outcome. They are even stunned at the comment, ". . . And they, since they/ Were not the one dead, turned to their affairs." The students are quick to philosophize on how true to life this poem is: a boy at an everyday job suddenly has an accident. No one except him realizes how serious it is or how it will affect his future life. And finally, after his death, no one seems to care much!

Foreshadowing is found, therefore, in the title as it alludes to Macbeth's lament. Foreshadowing is indicated many other times throughout the poem. For example, the teacher might ask, how had the work gone that day? ("And nothing happened: the day was all but done.") Query, is there anything in these words to indicate there was still time for trouble? What about ". . . nothing happened"? Does the fact that the uneventful is mentioned hint that something might occur?

Then the teacher should note a wish hinting that the workers should have stopped earlier: "Call it a day I wish they might have said/ To please the boy . . ." Do these lines suggest that something serious could develop?

Further, ask how the boy intuitively saw what was to happen to him and how his attitude changed as he recognized the crisis. ("The boy's first outcry was a rueful laugh. . . . Then the boy saw all–. . . He saw all spoiled.") Question what the students think the "all spoiled" alludes to: does it mean the boy will be crippled for life, or does it hint at worse consequences?

Finally, what do these terse words foreshadow: "No more to build on there." They suggest the youth's death, the loss of his dreams and ambitions, and explain the loss of interest of the other people as they "turned to their affairs."

Of course, there are other literary devices at work in this poem, such as onomatopoeia, imagery, and irony; but the teacher must be careful not to over-analyze the poem. Many students will want to talk about the attitude so common today: the indifference and callous reaction of people to suffering and death. They may wish to relate experience of their own as they talk over the matter-of-fact philosophy of the poem. Even though such discussions may lead the class for a short time away from a consideration of the poem as an artistic structure, the interest generated in the exchange of ideas may provide the motivation for reading more poems.

After the emphasis upon these particular literary devices, with the stress on foreshadowing, the teacher or a capable student should read "Out, Out—" again to give the students the total experience of the poem.

Late Adolescence

Karl Shapiro's "Auto Wreck" (1962) raises philosophical questions of broader scope and greater depth than does "Out, Out—." The death experience in Frost's poem is intensely personal and is directed inwardly as the reader vicariously experiences the agonizing realization of wasted, used-up youth and feels the indifference of the living toward the dead, whereas "Auto Wreck" probes beyond the immediate experience of death on the streets to the abstract and timeless questions of "Who shall die?" and "Why must they die without cause or logic?" Such deep questions of ultimate cause and human fate and destiny appeal generally to youth in their late adolescence.

The verbal complexity of "Auto Wreck" will require special emphasis on certain reading skills. Since it is a lyric poem without the strong narrative organization of "Out, Out—," the teacher may help students in their initial approach to the poem by having them note the overall organizational pattern of the three stanzas. The first stanza creates the image of an ambulance "with its terrible cargo". The second expresses the stunned emotional reaction of the bystanders, "We are deranged, walking among the cops . . . ," and the third presents a reflection on the meaning of the experience, "Already old, the question Who shall die?" Following this overview, the teacher should read the poem to the class. To help assure the students comprehension of this poem, the teacher will need to deal with its syntactical peculiarities. For example, in the first stanza the students will not grasp even the literal meaning until they find the subject and verbs virtually buried in the first seven lines: " . . . The ambulance . . . dips down and brakes speed . . . " The relationship of images suggesting life and death will need consideration: "And down the dark one ruby flare/Pulsing out red light like an artery"; "The stretchers are laid out, the mangled lifted/And stowed into the little hospital." The use of words in fresh and unusual ways is part of the artistry of this poem; thus full comprehension and appreciation of the poem will require specific study of these words in their context: "But this invites the occult mind,/ Cancels out physics with a sneer/ And spatters all that we know of denouement/ Across the expedient and wicked stones." In a sense *denouement*, usually used denotatively to identify a structural element of drama and fiction, applied to life itself in these lines? If necessary, ask the students to consider syntactic clues, particularly observing that *denouement* is the object of *splatters* and *this* (the accident) is the subject of the verb. Also, the teacher might ask students to consider the effect of pairing *expedient* and *wicked* as modifiers of *stones*. Which modifier is the more striking and ironic in the context of this poem? In what sense are the *stones* expedient? Wicked?

SUMMARY

Far too many American adolescents are reluctant readers and, as adults, do virtually no reading of imaginative literature. High school English teachers who seriously want their students to discover in literature a lifelong source of pleasure and enlightenment can improve the quality and amount of literature read by their students and the future citizens of our country. The teacher's decisions regarding the choice of literature to be made available, the sequence of literature to be studied in depth, the teaching methods and strategies employed to motivate and involve students in reading, and the literary skills of appreciation to be emphasized in specific works profoundly influence the reading habits of individuals long after they leave the classroom.

Fundamental factors which should be considered in making these decisions are (1) the changing patterns of adolescent interests, (2) the great range of verbal complexity in literary materials, and (3) the reading abilities of the students and literary skills of appreciation needed for the comprehension and enjoyment of specific works. Taking these factors into account, the English teacher is involved in the complex and difficult tasks of matching adolescents' feelings and interests with appropriate content of human experience in literature and in promoting the growth of reading skills by an approximate matching of students' literary skills of appreciation with the verbal complexity of literary works.

SELECTED BIBLIOGRAPHY OF ADOLESCENT LITERATURE

Early Adolescence

Annixter, Paul. *Swiftwater*. Houghton Mifflin, 1950. (pa)* The happy put poor Callaway family is depicted living in the backwoods with assorted forest creatures. Bucky's growth to manhood can be studied on two levels: that of an animal story or a highly symbolic story for more skilled readers.

Bishop, Curtis. *Rebound*. Bantam, 1961. (pa) The exciting story of high school varsity basketball and the ups and downs of its hero when consolidation affects his school and he is placed in keener competition to maintain varsity status.

Burnford, Shelia. *The Incredible Journey*. Franklin Watts, Inc., 1966. A heartwarming story of three animal friends, a Labrador retriever, a bull terrier, and a Siamese cat, who set out to find their way back home after being inadvertently lost by their human family.

*(pa) indicates book available in paperback edition.

DeAngeli, Marguerite. *The Door in the Wall*. Doubleday, 1969. A simple plot with some symbolism tells the story of a crippled English boy who matures from self-pity to courageous manhood as he tries to help save the kingdom at the time of the Crusades.

Dunning, Stephen. *Reflections on a Gift of Watermelon Pickle*. Scott, Foresman, 1967. An up-to-date collection of poetry dealing with our environment and its nature in such a way as to be enjoyed by sixth-graders as well as adults.

Felson, Henry. *Hot Rod*. Bantam, 1963. (pa) The hero creates a hot rod out of bits and pieces of other cars and through his adventures with the car grows from youthful irresponsibility to maturity.

Frank, Anne. *The Diary of Anne Frank*. Washington Square Press, 1952. (pa) The poignant and tragic autobiography of a thirteen-year-old girl and her family caught in Holland during the occupation by the Germans in 1942 - 44. The author tells of the fear and fortitude of eight of her family as they hide out from the Nazis.

Hilton, James. *Goodby Mr. Chips*. Houghton Mifflin, 1943. (pa) A lovable story of an English schoolmaster who through flashbacks tells the story of his life, revealing certain values which he admired and which he felt were becoming increasingly rare in the modern age.

L'Engle, Madeleine. *A Wrinkle in Time*. Ariel, 1962. A quality science fiction story telling of three teen-agers' attempts to rescue their friend who is imprisoned in time and space.

London, Jack. *White Fang*. Airmont, 1964. (pa) A naturalistic novel based on the thesis that an animal's life is controlled by its environment. A wolf, White Fang, learns to survive the threats of humans and finally gives undying loyalty to one man, Weldon Scott.

McKay, Robert. *Canary Red*. Meredith, 1968. After believing that she was an orphan, a teen-ager discovers that her father is returning to her from jail. The story of an adolescent's struggle to love, trust, and accept a man she has never known and help him adjust to a suspicious world unravels in this novel.

McSwigan, Marie. *Snow Treasure*. Scholastic Book Services, 1942. (pa) A true story of children in a Norwegian village who help save nine million dollars' worth of gold from the Nazi troops by pulling the camouflaged gold on their sleds to a hidden Norwegian freighter.

Saroyan, William. *The Human Comedy*. Dell, 1966. (pa) A story of the maturing of a young boy as he works as a telegraph delivery messenger seeing firsthand the reactions of other humans to the contents of the telegrams, happy and sad, that he delivers. The final touch is the telegram he has to deliver to his own parents telling of his older brother's death in the war.

Seton, Ernest T. *Biography of a Grizzly*. Grosset and Dunlap, 1958. (pa) A good nature study book telling of the life of a bear from his being left motherless by a hunter, through his becoming king of the forest, to his losing power to a younger grizzly.

Shotwell, Louisa. *Roosevelt Grady*. Grosset and Dunlap, 1964. (pa) A heartwarming story of a young Negro boy of a migrant family and his attempt to get an education in spite of his work in the fields and the frequent moves of the family.

Wells, H. G. *The Time Machine*. Airmont, 1964. (pa) A science fiction story developed through flashbacks telling of a fourth dimension in time. Excellent as an adventure story but challenges the better reader with some interesting scientific hypotheses.

White, E. B. *Charlotte's Web*. Dell, 1967. (pa) Humor and sarcasm give quality to this barnyard story of animals and insects struggling to outwit man in a battle of the survival of the fittest.

Wojciechowska, Maia. *Shadow of a Bull*. Atheneum, 1964. A major theme of self-discovery and loyalty to tradition grows out of the story of a bullfighter. Manolo's father is a bullfighter and Manolo stands in his shadow, expected by tradition to follow in the father's footsteps.

Middle Adolescence

Bonham, F. *Durango Street*. Scholastic Book Service, 1965. (pa) This story of a black youth's struggle to go straight under difficult circumstances develops the theme of conflict between self and environment.

Brontë, Emily. *Wuthering Heights*. Houghton Mifflin, 1965. (pa) A complicated story of love and revenge set in the eighteenth century moorland country of England.

Carson, John. *The Twenty-third Street Crusaders*. Ariel, 1958. A thrilling action story, full of suspense, about problem kids growing up in an adverse environment. Exciting, often funny, and always realistic, yet easy for students with limited reading skills.

Costain, Thomas B. *Below the Salt*. Doubleday, 1957. Historical fiction telling of the period of English history when knighthood was in flower and tyrants like King John ruled. The significance of the Magna Charta is stressed in an unusual story of a youth living in the present who is given the power to look back in time.

Du Maurier, Daphne. *Rebecca*. Pocket Books, 1968 (pa) A dead woman's presence is felt throughout the book as her character develops through the living characters of the novel. Rebecca, the dead wife, dominates a new marriage, blighting its chance of success.

Forbes, Esther. *Johnny Tremain*. Dell, 1969. (pa) An exciting, realistic story of a handicapped fourteen-year-old boy in Revolutionary America who becomes a productive citizen through determination and courage. An historically accurate account, including the Boston Tea Party and Paul Revere's Ride.

Hemingway, Ernest. *The Old Man and the Sea*. Scribner, 1960. (pa) This story can be read as a simple story of adventure of an old fisherman or it can be treated as an allegory of man against the universe. It is easy to read but the deeper meanings of life and man's inner self require advanced reading skills.

Hersey, John. *Hiroshima*. Bantam, 1966 (pa) A vivid, no-holds-barred report of the dropping of the H-bomb in 1945 on the Japanese city of Hiroshima; questions whether or not war is justifiable under any circumstances.

Hinton, S. E. *The Outsiders*. Dell, 1968. (pa) A novel about the slums of New York City and the teen-age gangs that thrive there, warring against each other and against society itself. The story develops the idea that teen-agers have to understand themselves before they can live with the rest of the world.

Kaufman, Bel. *Up the Down Staircase*. Avon, 1964. (pa) A satire of the life of a school teacher mixed up in today's administrative red tape in a metropolitan high school as she tries to find time to teach in spite of all the reports and paperwork required of her.

Killilea, Marie. *Karen*. Noble, 1967. (pa) The story of a child handicapped with cerebral palsy and her parents who are determined not to put her in an institution but to care for her themselves.

McCullers, Carson. *The Members of the Wedding*. Houghton Mifflin, 1946. (pa) A twelve-year-old girl struggles to find the "we of me" . . . to identify with something lovely. She has no one to help her but a six-year-old playmate and an old mammy. The primary conflict is psychological and requires the perception of a more mature reader.

Michener, James. *The Bridges of Toko-Ri*. Bantam, 1963. (pa) This Korean War story tells of American pilots who fight and die in little known places in a war nobody understands and wants. Some knowledge of history of the times is needed to follow the plot of the book.

Orwell, George. *Animal Farm*. Harcourt Brace Jovanovich, 1946. (pa) An amusing political allegory requiring an understanding of satire and allegory. The domesticated animals of a farm force the owner to leave so they can set up a Utopia for themselves.

Portis, Charles. *True Grit*. New American Library, 1969. (pa) Fourteen-year-old Mattie Ross, in true Wild West fashion, is out to find the man who shot her father. She teams up with a ruthless Federal marshal and together they have some remarkable adventures proving they have "true grit."

Richter, Conrad. *The Light in the Forest*. Knopf, 1953. (pa) A story of a white boy captured by Indians and raised as one of them. Under a treaty with white men, he is sent back to live with his white parents, but he finds life in "civilization" intolerable. The theme of the corruption that civilization brings to man is woven throughout this novel.

Rawlings, Marjorie. *The Yearling*. Scribner, 1966. (pa) A story of a boy and his pet deer set in the primitive wilds of Florida develops a theme of youth facing up to realities.

Speery, Armstrong. *Call it Courage*. Macmillan, 1940. A novel about Polynesians telling the story of a maturing youth who is fearful of the sea—the mainstay of life of his village. Taunted by the villagers, he finally runs away, takes to his canoe and ends up shipwrecked on a deserted island.

Steinbeck, John. *Of Mice and Men*. Viking, 1963. (pa) A story of two itinerant workers, tilling the soil but never reaping a personal harvest from their labors, develops the theme of man being his brother's keeper.

Steinbeck, John. *The Pearl*. Viking, 1965. (pa) A story from folklore, on the surface very simple of structure with an exciting plot line, tells of a struggle against forces of evil as a man tries to better the material status of his family.

Steinbeck, John. *The Red Pony*. Viking, 1965. (pa) This novel deals with the love of a boy for a pony and takes the young boy through all the experiences of birth, life, and death.

Late Adolescence

Abrahams, William. *Prize Short Stories 1969—O. Henry Awards*. Doubleday, 1969. These short stories reflect the attitudes of our changing times and require sophisticated literary reading skills.

Anouilh, Jean. *Becket*. Coward, 1960. (pa) Historical drama of the struggle of two boyhood friends, King Henry II and Thomas Becket. The former is devoted to life and the latter is devoted to God.

Baldwin, James. *Another Country*. Dell, 1960. (pa) In a powerful story of a young Negro and his white friend in the Harlem slums, the problems of racial strife, drug abuse, and crime are all dealt with. The plot is complex and the characters are carefully drawn and become real people to the reader.

Baldwin, James. *Go Tell It on the Mountain*. Dell, 1965. (pa) The setting is Harlem and involves a family in quest of sainthood, although they are encompassed by sin. This novel is complex requiring a command of literary skills of appreciation.

Bevington, Helen. *Charley Smith's Girl*. Simon and Schuster, 1965. An autobiographical account of a young girl growing up, made more complex by the divorce of her parents and their lack of understanding of her problems.

Bradbury, Ray. *The Martian Chronicles*. Doubleday, 1958. (pa) Written in the style of a chronicle, this book tells about earthmen's arrival on Mars, the contamination they cause, and the problems of communication with Martians.

Brontë, Charlotte. *Jane Eyre*. Houghton Mifflin, 1965. (pa) A love story set in England, this novel requires a mature reader to understand its difficult vocabulary, symbolism, and dramatic sequences. Jane, a governess in love with the master of the mansion, discovers on her wedding day that he is already married.

Caldwell, Taylor. *Dialogues With the Devil*. Faucett, 1968. (pa) A book philosophizing on what makes Heaven and Hell as told through conversations between the archangel Michael and Lucifer. It has excellent literary quality but requires the ability to make idealized and abstract concepts applicable to daily life and experience.

Conrad, Joseph. *Heart of Darkness*. New American Library, 1950. (pa) A complicated ploy involving a story within a story and use of difficult, symbolic language. The narrator, Marlowe, tells a tale of a white man in the heart of the jungle who loses all civilized culture.

Conrad, Joseph. *The Secret Sharer*. New American Library, 1950. (pa) A sea story in the short novel form telling of one man's friendship for another who had committed murder. It is slow-moving and difficult to comprehend because of its symbolism, allegory, and vocabulary of sea terms.

Crane, Stephen. *The Red Badge of Courage*. Houghton Mifflin, 1964. (pa) In a theme of finding freedom and courage through defeat, a story is told of a youth who turns coward and flees in the height of battle. Then remorseful, he returns to his companions in the lines of the battlefront.

De Saint-Exupery, Antoine. *The Little Prince*. Harcourt Brace Jovanovich, 1968. (pa) A tale of a pilot forced down in the Sahara Desert and his struggle to repair the airplane before his water supply is exhausted. The Little Prince is a young child who appears from another planet and tells tales of stars peopled with creatures whose lives are empty and barren.

Faulkner, William. *The Unvanquished*. Random House, 1965. (pa) Civil War time in a fictitous county in the South over a period of eight years is the setting for this novel written in typical Faulkner style of long sentences and difficult chronology. The narrative tells of two twelve-year-old boys and the grandmother of one in a battle of wits with Yankee troops invading their home. For students able to cope with Faulkner, it is a good beginning.

Gibson, William. *The Miracle Worker*. Knopf, 1957. (pa) The story of Helen Keller and her devoted teacher Annie Sullivan. The general theme is that love, patience, and discipline make a giant task manageable. An understanding of symbolism is needed to fully appreciate this story.

Golding, William. *Lord of the Flies*. Putnam, 1959. (pa) Some English schoolboys crash-land on an uninhabited island as they escape a nuclear war. As they struggle for survival, they lose most of the veneer of civilization. The novel deals with the conflict among the boys between the forces of reason and sanity and evil impulses deep within the human soul.

Greene, Graham. *The Power and the Glory*. Viking, 1958. (pa) A new government in Mexico is persecuting religious leaders. As the story begins, all priests have either renounced their faith or been killed, except one. The priest involved escapes and lives as a secular man until his conscience will not let him stray longer from his profession, even though it brings death.

Griffin, John Howard. *Black Like Me*. Houghton Mifflin, 1961. (pa) A white reporter colors his skin black with the help of a doctor and moves to live among the blacks to see what it is really like to be Negroid. When he returns to white society, he finds his associates unwilling to accept him and he is literally a man without a race. A stinging indictment of our thoughtless, needless inhumanity to one another.

Haley, Alex (ed.). *The Autobiography of Malcolm X*. Grove Press, 1966. (pa) Concerned with black pride, militancy, self-awareness, and hope for racial harmony, this powerful autobiography tells of an obscure, unknown Negro's evolution into a powerful, articulate leader of the black revolution.

Hansberry, Lorraine. *A Raisin in the Sun*. New American Library, 1961. (pa) Named the best American play for 1958 - 59 and winner of the New York Drama Critics Circle Award, this play, set in a dingy tenement in Chicago's Southside, involves the members of a black family in their attempts to fulfill their dreams with a $10,000 insurance check. Emotionally charged dialogue lays bare issues of assimilation, black pride, and black-white relationships. Scenes can be easily adapted for class presentation.

Hardy, Thomas. *Jude the Obscure*. Houghton Mifflin, 1965. (pa) Set in nineteenth-century England, this novel depicts the conflict of a man who wants to study at the university but is thwarted by his own poverty, lack of education, sex drives, and the mores of his time. The reader needs to understand the differences in customs of the nineteenth and twentieth centuries and be sensitive to the use of irony and symbolism.

Hemingway, Ernest. *The Sun Also Rises.* Scribner, 1926. (pa) A tragic novel for mature students of life in Paris and Spain after World War I. James Barnes of the "lost generation" lives with others of his kind in a disillusioned life. The hero who cannot love physically loves better emotionally than all the other characters.

Heyerdahl, Thor. *Kon-Tiki.* Rand McNally, 1950. (pa) A true adventure in which the author and his six-man crew on a voyage in a native style handmade craft try to prove that the inhabitants of Polynesia originated in Peru.

Hilton, James. *Lost Horizon.* Morrow, 1933. (pa) A haunting and timeless story about a Shangri-La, a utopia high in Tibet where aging does not occur. The vocabulary is challenging as are the English dialect and the long paragraphs.

Hoffmann, Peggy. *Shift to High!* Westminster, 1965. The story of three adolescents who build a car out of bits and pieces of junked automobiles and the adventurous trip they make in the car, affectionately called Crate the Great.

Ibsen, Henrik. *A Doll's House.* Washington Square Press, 1968. (pa) A play for the mature reader sensitive to satire and symbolism. Here is an early example of social drama in which a woman seeks intellectual and personal equality with her husband.

Knowles, John. *A Separate Peace.* Macmillan, 1960. (pa) Man's constant inner struggles and his attempts to make peace with them are depicted in this story of two college friends. In their relationship the thin line between love and hate is often crossed and friendship turns into jealousy and rivalry.

Lewis, Sinclair. *Arrowsmith.* New American Press, 1961. (pa) Transition to adult life is the story line of Martin Arrowsmith as he experiences the complacencies and insufficiencies of American life. Although the novel is social criticism of twentieth-century American life, particularly focusing on the medical profession, in a broader sense, the book stimulates soul-searching and questioning of ethics and adult values.

McCullers, Carson. *The Heart is a Lonely Hunter.* Houghton Mifflin, 1940 (pa) In a small Southern town various characters are drawn together by a bond of loneliness and unfullfilled ambitions. Mr. Singer is a deaf mute who is a friend to many yet unable to communicate his problems to those who tell him of their troubles. Mature readers will enjoy the imagery and symbolism.

Miller, Arthur. *The Crucible.* Viking, 1964. (pa) A thought-provoking, realistic play set in the days of Salem during the witch hunts, giving insights into "witch hunting" today, especially in politics.

Orwell, George. *1984.* Harcourt Brace Jovanovich, 1949. (pa) A science-fiction type dealing with the future when no one has freedom. Double-think is the language—"War is peace, freedom is slavery" are typical examples of the twisted use of language. This is an engrossing novel of the Inner-Party's power over all men's actions and thoughts, even love!

Potok, Chaim. *The Chosen*. Fawcett Publications, 1967. Jewish tradition and heritage is revealed in this story of two Jewish boys and their fathers in Brooklyn, one a very stern Rabbi and the other a college professor. This novel concerns the pain of growing up and the bonds between father and son that have to be broken with maturity.

Potok, Chaim. *The Promise*. Knopf, 1969. In a sequel to *The Chosen*, the two friends pursue their future careers, Reuven as a rabbinical student and Danny as a student in clinical psychology.

Remarque, Erich Maria. *All Quiet on the Western Front*. Fawcett World Library, 1969. (pa) The horrors of World War I are told by a young German officer in this psychological study of the gradual stripping away of the hopes and dreams of life until men become hard, suspicious, pitiless and vicious.

Stuart, Jesse. *Daughter of the Legend*. McGraw-Hill, 1965. A moving story involving racial segregation in Virginia. A young lumberjack marries a Melungeon girl from the Tennessee hills. The Melungeons are a mixed race living isolated lives, and the lumberjack determines to tear down the walls shutting them away from the outside world.

Stuart, Jesse. *Taps for Private Tussie*. World Publishing, 1969 (originally pub. 1943). A satire on abuses of government relief, this novel tells of relatives who suddenly show up to claim part of the insurance money Grandpa gets. It is a humorous story, full of dialect and the satire is always close to the truth.

Thomas, Dylan. *The Beach of Falesa*. Stein and Day, 1963. (pa) A screenplay in "reading form" based on Robert Louis Stevenson's short story of the same name. The literary quality is excellent and the reader needs to be able to sense foreshadowing and appreciate detailed actions and skillfully drawn characters. This is an island story about a trader and the native girl he marries in strange rites in the jungle. Evil surrounds them as well as voodoo and suspicion. Thomas wrote many such scripts for BBC during World War II.

Turgenev, Ivan. *Fathers and Sons*. Macmillan, 1962. (pa) The generation gap is dealt with in this novel set in Russia. The major characters, an aristocrat and a peasant, provide insight into the political conflict in Russia just before the liberation of the serfs. This is a novel for the mature reader who is interested in political issues and history.

Wilder, Thornton. *The Bridge of San Luis Rey*. Washington Square Press, 1939. (pa) The collapse of an ancient bridge in Peru costs the lives of five people. Searching for an ultimate answer to the cause of the accident, a friar delves into the lives of the five victims.

REFERENCES

Burton, Dwight L. *Literature Study in the High Schools*. New York: Holt, Rinehart and Winston, Inc., 1970, pp. 5 - 13.

Carlsen, G. Robert. *Books and the Teen-age Reader*. New York: Harper & Row, Publishers, 1967, pp. 22 - 23, 120 - 129.

Ciardi, John. *How Does a Poem Mean*. Boston: Houghton Mifflin Company, 1959, pp. 674 - 675.

Clark, Walter Van Tillburg. *The Ox-Bow Incident*. New York: New American Library of World Literature, Inc., 1943.

College Entrance Examination Board Commission on English. *Freedom and Discipline in English: Report of the Commission on English*. New York: College Entrance Examination Board, 1965, pp. 42 - 50.

De Quincey, Thomas. "Literature of Knowledge and Literature of Power," in George B. Woods (ed.), *English Poetry and Prose of the Romantic Movement*, Glenview, Ill.: Scott, Foresman and Company, 1929, pp. 1101 - 1103.

Dunning, Stephen. *Teaching Literature to Adolescents: Short Stories*. Glenview, Ill.: Scott, Foresman and Company, 1968, pp. 1 - 3.

Foder, Daniel N., and Elton B. McNiel. *Hooked on Books: Program and Proof*. New York: G. P. Putnam's Sons, 1960, pp. 65 - 67.

Fries, Charles C. *Linguistics and Reading*. New York: Holt, Rinehart and Winston, Inc., 1964, p. 41.

Frost, Robert. "Out, Out—" in Edmund Fuller and B. J. Kinnick (eds.), *Adventures in American Literature*. New York: Harcourt Brace Jovanovich, Inc., 1963, p. 255.

Hemingway, Ernest. "In Another Country," in Robert Freier, Arnold Lazarus, and Herbert Potell (eds.), *Adventures in Modern Literature*. New York: Harcourt Brace Jovanovich, Inc., 1962, pp. 46 - 50.

Humphreys, William J. *Ways of the Weather*. New York: The Ronald Press Company, 1942, pp. 6 - 7.

James, Will. "Midnight," in Soloman Schlakmann (ed.), *Stories to Remember*. New York: The Macmillan Company, 1967, pp. 138 - 161.

Knapton, James, and Bertrand Evans. *Teaching a Literature-Centered English Program*. New York: Random House, Inc., 1967, pp. 6 - 8.

Lazarus, Arnold. "An Anti-Cyclotron of Reading," *Journal of Developmental Reading* (Winter 1964), pp. 141 - 142.

Loban, Walter, Margaret Ryan, and James R. Squire. *Teaching Language and Literature*. New York: Harcourt Brace Jovanovich, Inc., 1969, pp. 436 - 440.

McDonald, John D. "Hit and Run," in Elizabeth Scheld (ed.), *Designs in Fiction*. New York: The Macmillan Company, 1968, pp. 29 - 42.

Murphy, Geraldine. *The Study of Literature in High School*. Waltham, Mass.: Blaisdell Publishing Company, 1968, pp. 16 - 21, 21 - 29, 38 - 43.

Schaefer, Jack. *Shane*. New York: Bantam Books, Inc., 1949.

Shapiro, Karl. "Auto Wreck," in Robert Freer, Arnold Lazarus, and Herbert Potell (eds.), *Adventure in Modern Literature*. New York: Harcourt Brace Jovanovich, Inc., 1962, p. 403.

Shotwell, Louisa R. *Roosevelt Grady*. New York: Grosset and Dunlap, Inc., 1963.

Shute, Nevil. *On the Beach*. New York: Bantam Books, Inc., 1957.

Simmons, John S. "The Reading of Literature: Poetry as an Example," in Arthur V. Olson and Wilbur S. Ames (eds.), *Teaching Reading Skills in Secondary Schools: Readings*. Scranton, Pa: International Textbook Company, 1969, pp. 260 - 262.

Sivenson, May. "Southbound on the Freeway," in Stephen Dunning, Edward Lueders, and Hugh Smith (eds.), *Reflections on a Gift of Watermelon Pickle*. Glenview, Ill.: Scott, Foresman and Company, 1966, p. 82.

Squire, James R., and Roger K. Applebee. *High School English Instruction Today*. New York: Appleton-Century-Crofts, 1968, pp. 152 - 156.

Tippett, James. "Sunning," in Stephen Dunning, Edward Lueders, and Hugh Smith (eds.), *Reflections on a Gift of Watermelon Pickle*. Glenview, Ill.: Scott, Foresman and Company, 1966, p. 86.

Wright, Richard. *Black Boy*. New York: Harper & Row, Publishers, 1945.

X, Malcolm. *The Autobiography of Malcolm X*. New York: Grove Press, 1964.

REQUIRED READINGS FROM BOOK OF READINGS

VIII. Developing Reading Skills in the Content Areas
Attitude of High School Content Area Teachers Toward the Teaching of Reading—Arthur V. Olson.
Reading: In and Out of the English Curriculum—Margaret J. Early.
The Reading of Fiction—Edward J. Gordon.
The Reading of Literature: Poetry as an Example—John S. Simmons.

chapter 12

The Reading Needs of
Special Groups

In many secondary schools adjustments have to be made in the reading program to provide for the special needs of certain students. The range of ability in academic achievement as well as the unique character of the secondary school program necessitates a number of changes. Although the majority of students need developmental instructional programs, secondary schools also contain slow learners, handicapped readers, gifted students, school dropouts and college-bound students.

THE HANDICAPPED READER

Any student who has not learned to read well usually dislikes reading and will do anything to avoid it. By the time most such poor readers have reached junior high school they have given up trying. The period in school when the reading skills should have been learned has passed. Failure has piled upon failure until there is no desire to try again. Because of this pattern of failure the problem of teaching reading to the handicapped reader at the secondary school level is a much more difficult task than that faced by teachers in the elementary grades.

Another factor that contributes to the frustration of such students and their teachers is the number of years the student has practiced poor habits in his reading, as well as the number of incorrect and incomplete concepts formed. It may be necessary for the student to put as much time and effort into *unlearning* as he would into learning.

For the purpose of the secondary school, a handicapped reader can best be defined as a student with average or above-average intellectual ability who is reading two or more years below the average reading level of the grade in which he is placed. For example, Jim is a sophomore in high school with a tested IQ of 118 and is performing at a seventh-grade reading level. He obviously has the ability but for some reason(s) is unable to use it effectively. Bob, in the same grade, has an IQ of 80 and is reading as well as the average student entering the seventh grade. According to the definition, Bob is not a handicapped reader, as

216

he is working up to his ability. As for Jim, once his difficulties are evaluated and a program planned, there should be fairly rapid and substantial growth.

Causes of Poor Reading

The conditions that lead to difficulty in reading are many and varied. It is seldom that one factor can be pinpointed as the cause of failure. They are usually found in combinations of infinite variety. It is vitally important that the teacher understand this multiple causation of the problem if real help is to be given.

Some of the possible factors which could cause reading problems are
1. Poor teaching of reading skills in the elementary and secondary school.
2. Interrupted education due to moving or sickness so that the sequential instruction of the reading skills was constantly interrupted.
3. Home and school environment that has not stimulated interest or developed the need to learn.
4. Emotional and personality problems that are preventing the development of the reading skills.
5. Physical problems such as visual difficulties, hearing difficulties or neurological impairments.

Some of the students handicapped in reading will be unable to be helped by the regular subject-matter teacher. Some will need not only the help of reading specialists but medical attention and psychological help as well.

The handicapped reader at the secondary school level is usually a very unhappy person. Because of his age group he has a great need to be on a par with his peers. He wants to be like them and to compete with them, but each year he faces more difficulty and more educational failure. In order to compensate for this need, he may engage in activities where educational ability is not a factor. He may daydream or he may take the course of destructive action in protest. His behavior is then symptomatic of a need for social acceptance.

Helping the Handicapped Reader

The factor of primary importance in the development of a program for the handicapped reader is the need for success. The student must feel that he is making progress as well as doing something worthwhile. He must believe that what he is doing is not "beneath his dignity." Success is of utmost importance, but there can be no success unless the student accepts the materials given him as worthy of his age group.

The materials, directions and assignments must all fit his abilities and needs; yet at the same time the differences must not isolate him from the rest of the group. If materials are given to the student that parallel the topic discussed in class he can be drawn into the group and have a real feeling of participation. He can interact with others in reading experiences even though the content was not from the same book. Every content-area teacher has two tasks: (1) to discover that kinds and levels of materials the students can read successfully, and (2) to develop into learning experiences the different materials that contribute to the common educational goals of the whole class.

For the handicapped reader the content material should be presented in as many visual and auditory ways as possible. It is through these avenues, rather than through reading, that he will begin to develop the skills and understanding needed for reading and writing.

Materials. If teachers are to work effectively with the handicapped reader, there must be plenty of carefully selected reading material available. The poor reader can become a good reader only through reading. He must have material at his disposal. Handicapped readers will certainly remain handicapped readers unless they are provided with practice in the skills.

If progress is to be made, the materials used for directed reading activities should be at the students' reading level. The materials used for independent reading, without the aid of the teacher, should be a year or more below the instructional level.

In some cases, if the interest is high a student can read independently at a higher level. This is possible if the student has a solid background of vocabulary and concepts in the area in which he is reading. Some handicapped male students often find it possible to read a book on cars or mechanics, that would be incomprehensible if there were no interest and background.

Reading materials should be used in a way that expands rather than limits the opportunities for reading. Books should be ordered at three or four levels of difficulty rather than in class-size lots of 35 or, even worse, 135. Since any test results will show that not all the students are performing at the same level, it is uneconomical to buy materials that cannot be used, to say nothing of the educational implications.

Multiple texts, rather than a single text, can be used for directed reading activities for some students and for independent reading by others. Materials can be shared and exchanged by teachers to meet the needs of the groups as well as subject matter being presented. Worn-out textbooks often contain materials suitable for certain parts of the program. These can be cut out and used as supplementary resources. Sometimes these are an advantage because they are less bulky than a regular textbook and thus have an appeal to the poor reader. Bulky or "thick" books are frightening to the book-shy student.

Sometimes workbooks are a valuable source for practice in particular skills. An effective way to make use of this kind of material for more than one student is to cut out the desired pages, encase them in a clear plastic folder, and have the student write on the plastic with a grease pencil or crayon. The plastic can be wiped off and used over and over again as the need arises. The pages can also be placed in a file and sorted according to skill and difficulty to offer ready exercises to meet particular needs.

Using the Materials. Materials themselves do not ensure a good program.

The teacher is the key to success or failure, and what is done or not done will have direct bearing upon the education of students. Some of the things a teacher can do are

1. Show an interest in the student's progress and encourage him.
2. Try to stimulate independent reading by discovering the students' interests, making material available for them and varying the kinds of materials.
3. Help the student to understand the reasons for doing specific exercises. He will do a better job when he understands what his problems are and how the teacher is going to help him.
4. Give the student instruction in the skills in which he is weak and then provide practice in the skills.
5. Use workbooks for specific instructional jobs and not for "busy work."
6. Encourage students to keep independent visual records of their own progress.
7. Make assignments to fit the needs and abilities of the individual students, or groups of students, but not the same assignment to everyone who happens to be in the same room.
8. Remember that skill in teaching reading does not come overnight, but the student who needs help now won't be better next year unless teachers do something.

THE SLOW LEARNER

A slow learner is a student who has a limited amount of ability. Verbal ability is of greater significance in determining a student's ability than a nonverbal score because success in school is largely based upon verbal ability. On the verbal section of an IQ test, the slow-learning student would probably score between 60 to 90. Using this criteria, about 10 percent of the secondary school population could be classified as slow learners.

Slow-learning students are generally slightly inferior physically and have more minor illnesses than brighter students. They usually dislike school, are frequently absent, and drop out of school at the first opportunity. Those who do stay and eventually graduate despite their limited ability usually have reinforcement and encouragement from the home whereas the dropout does not have that support.

The slow learner who is reading up to his capacity—and this is rare—will not profit greatly from any effort to give him special help in his reading. If for example he is in the tenth grade, but reading at seventh-grade level (his capacity level), no amount of added instruction would produce permanent increase. For the slow learner working to his ability level, the best results will be produced if the teacher helps the student to increase his breadth of interest rather than teaching more complex skills.

It is unusual to find the slow-learning student working up to his capacity level. By the time he reaches the secondary school, failure has become so much a part of his everyday experiences that he accepts it as a fact of life. Little or no provision is made for most of the slow learners in public schools. Even in schools where the students are grouped homogeneously, it is not unusual to find all of the students in any given course reading from the same textbook. What is even more amazing than this inexcusable practice is that the teacher is often unaware of what to do to correct the situation.

Principles Essential in Teaching Slow Learners

The slow learner should develop at the rate that is best for his capabilities to learn. Slow learners usually need a great deal of readiness activities because of their inability to relate past experience to an understanding of a new concept. Part of the understanding will develop from a chance to verbalize new concepts. By learning to talk better, to express themselves using the new vocabulary of the content they are about to learn, they will gain a depth of understanding essential for reading.

Slow learners should have practice and systematic instruction in the reading skills. They require more practice in the word-recognition skills and vocabulary development for new learning material than the average or above-average reader. Continuous help must be given to these students in using dictionaries and the other instructional tools available in the classroom.

Usually, slow learners dislike reading because of their failures to comprehend what they read and their lack of word knowledge. These students should work for accuracy and complete mastery in the basic skills so that they can enjoy reading. They will usually derive pleasure from simple routine exercises and feel a sense of achievement when they have mastered the material. Because the teaching of these students necessitates a great deal of practice and repetition, the teacher must progress at a slower rate and cannot expect them to achieve at the same level as more able students.

For the slow learner the statement "A picture is worth a thousand words" is most applicable. Films, filmstrips, demonstrations, and experiments should be used frequently to reinforce the concepts being developed. The low ability of these students demands that more use be made of concrete methods of teaching than is needed by the more able students.

Frequently in the secondary school the slow learner finds that the book assigned for his grade or content area is not appropriate for his reading level. In many cases this happens because the teacher is unaware of the material available for the student who reads at a lower level than the rest of the class. The Follett Publishing Company, the J. B. Lippincott Company, and Science Research Associates all publish materials that can be used with slow learners.

THE GIFTED STUDENT

It is often stated that the more able readers in secondary schools are those who receive the least amount of the instructional time and are more retarded in their reading than any other one group. In most cases, they are retarded not because they are reading below grade level, but because they are reading so far below their capacity level. To a large extent, gifted students are underachievers.

The more able student usually likes to work independently because of his ability to work faster and his breadth of interests. He has good comprehension of abstract materials and a constantly inquiring attitude.

It is of vital importance that the able learner be given reading experiences that will keep his interests alive. Reading from a single textbook is more likely to stifle interest than to stimulate it. The student should be given material to read in other reference materials and encouraged to investigate related areas. Superior students respond to different and creative assignments that inspire them to go beyond the routine reading expected of the majority of the class members. However, any reading assignment given should be a substitute for the general assignment, not an addition to it.

Superior students very often have the insight needed to help themselves gain proficiency in reading, but they can be saved the unnecessary trial-and-error approach by having appropriate instruction when needed. They can quickly acquire more flexibility in their reading rate as well as the more creative aspects of reading if given instruction. In order to provide for effective instruction, the following principles should be considered.

1. Give them the instruction they need.

2. Don't waste their time by asking them to do things that have no value or are so far below their ability level that they can be done without thinking.

3. Enrich their curriculum by providing them with materials in which they have an interest.

4. Give them a chance to discuss with each other varying points of view on a topic or on evaluations of what they have read.

5. Let them have the freedom to select some of their own reading materials. Book lists rigidly imposed by a teacher may be detrimental to the brighter student.

THE SCHOOL DROPOUT

The school dropout is usually poor in academic achievement. However, he is no less academically talented than students with similar ability who finish their schooling. The difference seems to be in their motivation and in the support they get from the family group. The problem then is not how to encourage them to stay in school but rather how to provide proper motivation and support from the school.

If a student drops out because the academic requirements are unrealistic for him, encouraging him to return to school is dishonest unless the school is willing to provide him with a program different from that encountered the first time around.

The truth of the matter may be that most schools really don't want the dropout to return to school. Such students are usually highly verbal in their criticism of the school and often question some of the tight regulations imposed by school officials. Teachers also look upon the returned dropout as a potential troublemaker. The one-time dropout quite often returns because he realizes what the demands of living are going to be for him. He has little patience with the reading required by some teachers for the purpose of "becoming acquainted with good literature." He would rather read material with "some guts in it" that has meaning to him and his life. This type of material can also be good literature.

If a program is to encourage the dropout to return to school, it must offer the hope of success. In order to ensure this success the program must first provide for the instructional level of the returning student, and second it must give him something worthwhile and useful. The former dropout may have a much better insight than the teachers as to what his educational needs are. His ideas cannot be dismissed by simply saying he is immature. Merely by coming back to school he has shown a level of maturity that might not be matched by some of his teachers. It is not a matter of the returned dropout being given another chance; he is giving the school another chance. By committing himself to returning to school he opens himself to a great deal of personal psychological injury. The school, on the other hand, is open to no danger at all. In most cases the school doesn't even make a commitment.

The same principles that apply to the handicapped reader also apply to the school dropout with one important exception. In organizing a program the maturity level of the former dropout should be carefully considered.

THE COLLEGE-BOUND STUDENT

College-bound students more than any other group are likely to profit greatly from instruction in reading. They have the ability and the interest to make lasting and substantial gains. The demands that will be made upon them in college are likely to exceed those made by the high school, and they have to be prepared.

In order to develop the advanced skills necessary for academic success, several areas of skills require developing. These are

1. Greater depth in understanding of some of the complex comprehension skills in different types of reading materials.
2. More versatility in applying study skills to the different types of reading required.

3. Emphasis on using context skills to understand the meaning of unknown words and to increase the speaking vocabulary for more effective communication.

4. Developing note-taking skills while listening to materials that are organized in a variety of ways.

5. Adjusting the rate of reading to various reading purposes.

In one situation, where the authors were teaching a college-bound group, approximately 30 words per week were selected from the individual student's list to be used as a class study list. The words and their meanings, plus contextual usage, were mimeographed and given to the students. In addition, the words were written on 3 × 5-inch file cards, with meanings on the back for use in small group work. Another effective method involved the tape recorder. The words were recorded, leaving space for the student to supply the meaning and contextual use of the word. After the student had completed this task he would hear the correct meaning and usage on tape, to reinforce or reject his answer. By using multiple headphone connections a number of students could use the recorder at the same time and yet work independently.

Another general area that the students needed help in was note taking. This was begun by relating it to textbook study and then expanding it into listening. Short lectures, or excerpts from lectures, were recorded and the students asked to follow the material, taking notes as best they could. Then the most effective ways of listening and note taking with the particular material were discussed. While the students were taking notes, the teachers also took notes on an overhead projector and then compared theirs with those of the students. Films were also used for note taking, covering a variety of subject areas.

One of the distinct advantages of providing reading instruction for the college-bound student is the progress that can be made. It develops in the student a great deal of independence and reliance on his ability to perform.

SUMMARY

A secondary school is generally not composed of a homogeneous population of students, and therefore there will always be certain groups that must be taken into account when planning a reading program. Each of these groups has certain needs, most of which can be provided for within the boundaries of the general curriculum.

Handicapped readers are students of average to above average intelligence who are reading two or more years below grade level. There are numerous and varied causes for poor reading among this group of students, and the resultant problems they face at the adolescent level are compounded because of their need for peer approval. Once a handicapped reader's difficulties are evaluated and a program planned, there should be fairly rapid and substantial growth.

Slow learners are students with below average IQs who are generally working below grade level by the time they reach high school. These students must be worked with slowly; they require substantial reinforcement of reading skills covered.

Gifted students are generally underachievers because they are not reading at their potential level. This is often because they are neglected in the general curriculum plan and are therefore not stimulated. These students should be given creative assignments, in lieu of the general assignment, which would encourage them to go beyond general expectancies.

School Dropouts are generally not less academically talented than those who graduate, but are poor achievers because the demands of school seem unrealistic to them. These students generally receive no encouragement at home, and the school must provide them with motivation.

College-Bound Students, more than any other group, are likely to profit from reading instruction. They have the ability and interest to make lasting and substantial gains and they need to be prepared for their higher education. Vocabulary development and note-taking skills should be emphasized with this group.

ADDITIONAL READINGS

Benson, Josephine T. "Teaching Reading to the Culturally Different Child," *Progress and Promise in Reading Instruction.* Pittsburgh, Pennsylvania: A Report of the Twenty-Second Annual Conference and Course on Reading, 1966, pp. 140–151.

Carlton, Leslie, and Robert H. Moore. "Culturally Disadvantaged Children Can Be Helped," *NEA Journal* (September 1966).

Goldberg, Miriam. "Methods and Materials for Educationally Disadvantaged Youth," *Education for the Disadvantaged.* New York: Holt, Rinehart and Winston, Inc., 1967.

Kantrowitz, V. "Bibliotheraphy with Retarded Readers," *Journal of Reading,* XI (December 1967), pp. 205–212.

Olsen, Edward G. "Teacher Education for the Deprived: A New Pattern," *School and Society* (Apr. 1, 1967).

Price, Mark (ed.). "Schools Intensify Reading Program in Poverty Areas," *Staff Bulletin, the Public Schools of New York City.* New York: Board of Education of the City of New York, Vol. 6, No. 4 (November 1967), pp. 1, 10.

Smith, Mildred B. "Reading for the Culturally Disadvantaged," *Educational Leadership,* XXII (March 1965), pp. 398–403.

REQUIRED READINGS FROM BOOK OF READINGS

X. The Teaching of Reading to Special Groups
     Our Disadvantaged Older Children—Dominic Thomas.
     A Reading Program for School Dropouts—Lillie Pope.

Salvaging Failures Through Improved Reading: Reading in Vocational
Classes—Robert L. Harris.

High School Reading for the Severely Retarded Reader—Nancy O'Neill
Vick.

Index